The Prehistoric Archaeology of the A477 St Clears to Red Roses Road Improvement Scheme 2012

Cotswold Archaeology Monograph No. 12

Published by Cotswold Archaeology with the aid of funds by the Welsh Government
Copyright © Authors and Cotswold Archaeology 2019
Building 11, Kemble Enterprise Park, Cirencester, Gloucestershire GL7 6BQ

ISBN 978-0-9934545-5-4

British Library Cataloguing in Publication Data
A catalogue record of this book is available from the British Library

Mapping in figures 1.1, 1.2, 2.1–2.4, 2.6, 2.7, 2.9, 2.10, 2.13–2.16, 2.19, 2.21, 2.37, 2.38 is reproduced from the Ordnance Survey on behalf of the controller of Her Majesty's Stationery Office, © Crown Copyright and database rights 2019 Ordnance Survey 0100031673.

Hawlfraint y Goron a hawliau cronfa ddata (2019) OS (0100031673)

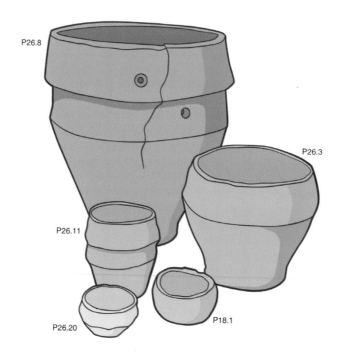

Front cover (clockwise from bottom left): P26.20 Accessory vessel; P26.11 (Small) Tripartite Collared Urn; P26.8 Tripartite Collared Urn; P26.3 Bipartite carinated Urn; P18.1 Accessory vessel

Back cover: Accessory vessel from the Bronze Age cremation cemetery; Aerial view during road construction looking south-west towards Vaynor Farm. Image by Aled Llyweln; Misty Sunrise: The A477 looking north-east towards Castle Motte. Image by Simon West

Cover design by Aleksandra Osinska, Cotswold Archaeology
Produced by 4word Ltd Page & Print Production, Bristol

The Prehistoric Archaeology of the A477 St Clears to Red Roses Road Improvement Scheme 2012

by Alistair Barber, Alan Hardy and Andrew Mudd

with contributions from

Evan Chapman, Andy Clarke, Sharon Clough, Sarah Cobain, Elaine Dunbar, Frances Healy, Jana Horák, Rob Ixer, E.R. McSloy, Phil Stastney, Jacky Sommerville, Elizabeth A. Walker and Nick Watson

edited by
Mary Alexander

Cotswold Archaeology Monograph No. 12

CONTENTS

List of Figures

List of Tables

Acknowledgements

The work was instructed by Ramboll and funded by the Welsh Government. Particular thanks go to Andy Buckley, Managing Director, AB Heritage for his close involvement in the project and his support throughout, together with Emily McVean, Emma Green and Roy Emberton of Ramboll. The fieldwork proceeded smoothly and in a safe environment thanks to the co-operation and support of the principal site contractors SRB Civil Engineering, for whom our principal contacts were John Duggan (Project Manager), Michael Gallagher (Deputy Project Manager) and Stephen Salvin (Construction Manager). Our appreciation also goes to Jim Hunter of Hyder Consulting (now Arcadis), for monitoring and advice during fieldwork. Professors Tim Darvill and Geoffrey Wainwright visited the cemetery site and offered comment and advice.

The fieldwork was managed for Cotswold Archaeology (CA) by Cliff Bateman and Richard Young. The excavation was directed by Alistair Barber, and thanks are owed to all the excavation team, but in particular project supervisors Greg Crees, Charlotte Haines, Matt Nichol, Tom Weavil and Jamie Wright. Sarah Cobain and Jonny Geber, both of CA, visited the site to advise on environmental and cremation deposit sampling. The post-excavation programme was managed by Nicola Powell and Mary Alexander.

Alistair Barber of Cotswold Archaeology undertook the site analysis and reporting, which was carried through into the publication stage by Alan Hardy, formerly of Cotswold Archaeology, now freelance. Individual authors are acknowledged in the report. Their work was built upon a foundation of finds and soils processing and quantification undertaken by CA staff. Conservation of the Bronze Age urns was undertaken by University of Cardiff Conservation Services. X-rays and metalwork cleaning were undertaken by Karen Barker Antiquities Conservation Service. Pieta Greaves at Birmingham Museums Conservation undertook the XRF on the awl. Radiocarbon dating was provided by Scottish Universities Environmental Research Centre (SUERC), East Kilbride, Scotland. John Coundon undertook the thin-section preparation on behalf of Rob Ixer. The geoarchaeological project was managed for ARCA by Dr Keith Wilkinson. The expertise and advice of Frances Healy was vital in determining the value of Bayesian analysis for relative dating of the site sequence. The report figures and finds illustration were undertaken by Dan Bashford, Rosanna Price and Aleksandra Osinska of Cotswold Archaeology. Copy edits were undertaken by Rachel Tyson. The volume was edited by Mary Alexander.

Summary

This volume is concerned with the archaeological discoveries along the 9.5km route of the A477 St Clears to Red Roses Road Improvement Scheme, Carmarthenshire. Archaeological excavation and recording was undertaken in accordance with a mitigation strategy devised following an extensive programme of preliminary desk-based and field-based investigation. Archaeological remains spanning early prehistoric to the recent past were recorded at many locations along the route. The most numerous discoveries related to prehistoric activity, in which ritual and funerary evidence were significant elements.

This volume reports on the prehistoric discoveries in detail, and provides a summary of the later evidence. Mesolithic worked flint scatters were found at two locations near Llanddowror on the flood plain of the River Taf (Sites 25 and 35). At Site 25 there were numerous pits and some hearths dated by Early Neolithic pottery, and a large assemblage of Neolithic worked flint, together interpreted as evidence for settlement or seasonal occupation. Neolithic occupation was also found at Sites 30, 35 and 37. At Site 37 on the high ground 3km to the east of Red Roses were two major concentrations of features including pits and the postholes of a possible structure, all dated to the Early Neolithic by pottery and radiocarbon dating. Contemporary pits were found at the adjacent Site 30. Structures from this period are rare, and what makes Site 37 more significant is the supporting evidence for domestic use and perhaps for the deliberate selection of a range of material for deposition in pits.

Bronze Age activity was found at eleven sites: Sites 12, 13, 18, 19, 25, 26, 32, 35, 36, 37 and 44. Dating came from characteristic pottery styles, augmented by a series of radiocarbon dates. The earliest dates for this period came from the Late Neolithic/Early Bronze Age 'Beaker' settlements at Sites 25 and 37. At the west end of the road corridor near Red Roses, at Site 32, a burnt mound associated with two troughs was radiocarbon dated to the Early Bronze Age.

The most notable discoveries from the Bronze Age were cremation burials and associated features at Sites 18 and 26. The entirety of a possible barrow was revealed, as well as much surrounding activity, including cremation burials close to the barrow and an adjacent feature used for burials and possibly for cremation pyres. With a total of 62 deposits of human bone, of which 38 were probably burials, the site provided an opportunity to study the varied nature of burial practices at this time and provided comparisons with published data of this date. Bayesian modelling of the radiocarbon dates suggested a sequence of funerary activity beginning with possibly female primary burials, over which a barrow mound was raised, then followed by mixed burials on the periphery. Analysis revealed that even the most 'complete' cremations do not contain an entire individual, even where the deposit survived intact. Radiocarbon dating suggests that burials in the area surrounding the barrow were contemporary with the duration of activity at the barrow and 'pyre', which is likely to have taken place over a span of some 200 years.

The discussion examines the features in terms of other processes and rituals that may not have always included the act of cremation. Understanding and interpreting the ritual aspect of the landscape here has been enhanced by the proximity of excavations undertaken in 2006 in connection with the Milford Haven pipeline. Here, the presence of a Neolithic Class II henge and Bronze Age burials indicate that the cremations from the A477 St Clears to Red Roses Road Improvement Scheme form part of a wider landscape of ritual activity, possibly with other barrows forming the focus for similar groupings.

Spreading west for over 2km from the focus of cremation activity was a dispersed distribution of pits and occasional postholes. Many pits contained concentrations of charcoal and burnt stone; some contained Early to Middle Bronze Age pottery. Similar features were found in excavations approximately 500m east of the cremation area, where a Middle Bronze Age radiocarbon date was obtained from a pit. Post-dating the cremation cemetery was a stone-lined pit or trough from Site 18, radiocarbon dated to the Middle Bronze, which probably represents the remains of a crop-drying oven. If the dating is robust, it stands as a unique example of this type of structure from mainland Britain. This report contributes to an understanding of how the landscape in south-west Carmarthenshire was used in prehistory, and how later ritual and funerary activity articulated with earlier prehistoric monuments.

The report includes a summary of the later findings, the most significant of which are the medieval dating of the earthwork remains of the Scheduled Monument at Dolgarn (Site 17) and the remains of a farmstead at Site 31 near the west end of the road scheme.

Crynodeb

Mae'r gyfrol hon yn ymdrin â'r darganfyddiadau archaeolegol ar hyd llwybr 9.5km y Cynllun i Wella Ffordd yr A477 rhwng Sanclêr a Ffordd Rhos-goch, Sir Gaerfyrddin. Ymgymerwyd â chloddio a chofnodi archaeolegol yn unol â strategaeth liniaru a luniwyd yn dilyn rhaglen helaeth o ymchwil ragarweiniol wrth y ddesg ac yn y maes. Cofnodwyd gweddillion archaeolegol yn ymestyn o'r cynhanesyddol i'r gorffennol diweddar mewn llawer o leoliadau ar hyd y llwybr. Roedd y darganfyddiadau mwyaf niferus yn gysylltiedig â gweithgarwch cynhanesyddol lle'r oedd tystiolaeth ddefodol ac angladdol yn elfennau o bwys.

Mae'r gyfrol hon yn adrodd yn fanwl am y darganfyddiadau cynhanesyddol gan ddarparu crynodeb o'r dystiolaeth ddiweddarach. Cafwyd hyd i wasgariadau fflint Mesolithig wedi'u trin mewn dau leoliad ger Llanddowror ar orlifdir afon Taf (Safleoedd 25 a 35). Yn Safle 25 roedd pydewau niferus a rhai aelwydydd a ddyddiwyd drwy grochenwaith Neolithig Cynnar a chasgliad mawr o fflint Neolithig wedi'i drin a ddehonglwyd gyda'i gilydd fel tystiolaeth o anheddu tymhorol. Canfuwyd tystiolaeth o anheddu Neolithig hefyd yn Safleoedd 30, 35 a 37. Yn Safle 37, ar y tir uchel 3km i'r dwyrain o Ros-goch roedd dau grynodiad pwysig o nodweddion gan gynnwys pydewau neu dyllau pyst adeiladwaith posibl i gyd wedi'u dyddio i'r Neolithig Cynnar drwy grochenwaith a dyddio radiocarbon. Cafwyd hyd i bydewau o'r un cyfnod yn Safle 30 cyfagos. Mae adeiladweithiau o'r cyfnod hwn yn brin a'r hyn sy'n rhoi mwy o arwyddocâd i Safle 37 yw'r dystiolaeth ategol o ddefnydd domestig ac efallai ddetholiad bwriadol o ddeunydd amrywiol i'w roi yn y pydewau.

Darganfuwyd gweithgarwch o'r Oes Efydd mewn deg safle – Safleoedd 12, 13, 18, 19, 25, 26, 32, 35, 36 a 37. Dyddiwyd y gweithgarwch yma ar sail arddulliau crochenwaith nodweddiadol a ategwyd gan gyfres o ddyddiadau radiocarbon. Deilliai'r dyddiadau cynharaf ar gyfer y cyfnod hwn o aneddiadau 'Biceri' yr Oes Neolithig Ddiweddar/ Efydd Gynnar yn Safleoedd 25 a 37. Ym mhen gorllewinol coridor y ffordd ger Rhos-goch yn Safle 32, dyddiwyd twmpath llosg cysylltiedig â dau gafn â radiocarbon i'r Oes Efydd Gynnar.

Y darganfyddiadau mwyaf nodedig o'r Oes Efydd oedd corfflosgiadau a nodweddion cysylltiedig yn Safleoedd 18 a 26. Datgelwyd crug posibl yn ei gyfanrwydd yn ogystal â llawer o weithgarwch cyffiniol gan gynnwys corfflosgiadau yn agos i'r crug a nodwedd gyfagos a ddefnyddid ar gyfer claddu ac o bosibl goelcerthi corfflosgi. Gyda chyfanswm o 62 o ddyddodion esgyrn dynol, 38 ohonynt fwy na thebyg yn gladdedigaethau, cynigiodd y safle gyfle i astudio natur amrywiol yr arferion claddu ar yr adeg yma ynghyd â chymariaethau â data cyhoeddedig o'r dyddiad hwn. Drwy ddefnyddio dulliau modelu Bayesaidd i ddehongli'r dyddiadau radiocarbon, awgrymwyd cyfres o weithgarwch angladdol a gychwynnodd gyda chladdedigaethau benywaidd o bosib gyda thwmpath crug yn cael ei godi drostynt a ddilynwyd wedyn gan gladdedigaethau cymysgryw ar yr ymylon. Datgelodd dadansoddi nad yw hyd yn oed y corfflosgiadau mwyaf 'cyflawn' yn cynnwys unigolyn cyfan, hyd yn oed lle mae'r dyddodyn wedi goroesi yn ei grynswth. Awgryma dyddio radiocarbon fod claddedigaethau o amgylch y crug yn gyfoes â pharhad y gweithgarwch ger y crug a'r 'goelcerth' sy'n debygol o fod wedi digwydd dros gyfnod o ryw 200 mlynedd.

Mae'r drafodaeth yn ystyried y nodweddion o ran prosesau a defodau eraill sydd efallai heb gynnwys y weithred o gorfflosgi bob amser. Mae deall a dehongli'r agwedd ddefodol ar y dirwedd yma wedi'u helaethu gan agosrwydd y cloddfeydd a wnaethpwyd ym 2006 mewn cysylltiad â phiblinell Aberdaugleddau. Fan hyn, mae presenoldeb hengor Neolithig Dosbarth II a chladdfeydd o'r Oes Efydd yn dangos bod y corfflosgiadau o'r Cynllun i Wella Ffordd yr A477 rhwng Sanclêr a Rhos-goch yn ffurfio rhan o dirwedd ehangach lle cafwyd gweithgarwch defodol, gyda chrugiau eraill o bosib yn ganolbwynt ar gyfer grwpio tebyg.

Yn ymledu i'r gorllewin am dros 2km o ganolbwynt y gweithgarwch corfflosgi roedd dosbarthiad gwasgaredig o bydewau ac ambell dwll postyn. Roedd llawer o'r pydewau'n cynnwys crynodiadau o siarcol a cherrig llosg; roedd rhai'n cynnwys crochenwaith o'r Oes Efydd Gynnar drwodd i'r Oes Efydd Ganol. Canfuwyd nodweddion tebyg mewn cloddfeydd tua 500m i'r dwyrain o'r ardal gorfflosgi, lle cafwyd dyddiad radiocarbon o'r Oes Efydd Ganol o bydew. Yn ôl-ddyddio'r fynwent gorfflosgi, yn Safle 18, roedd pydew neu gafn wedi'i leinio â cherrig ac wedi'i ddyddio drwy radiocarbon i'r Efydd Ganol – gweddillion popty i sychu cnydau fwy na thebyg. Os yw'r dyddio'n gadarn, dyma enghraifft unigryw o'r math yma o adeiladwaith o dir mawr Prydain. Mae'r adroddiad hwn yn cyfrannu i ddealltwriaeth o sut y defnyddid y dirwedd yn ne-orllewin Sir Gaerfyrddin yn y cyfnod cynhanesyddol a'r ffordd y bu gweithgarwch defodol ac angladdol diweddarach yn gysylltiedig â chofebion cynhanesyddol cynharach.

Mae'r adroddiad yn cynnwys crynodeb o'r darganfyddiadau diweddarach – y rhai mwyaf arwyddocaol yn eu plith yw dyddio i'r Canol Oesoedd weddillion gwrthglawdd y Gofeb Restredig yn Nôl Garn (Safle 17) a gweddillion fferm yn Safle 31 ger pen gorllewinol y Cynllun Ffordd.

Chapter 1
Introduction

Between January and September 2012, Cotswold Archaeology (CA) carried out a staged programme of archaeological recording along the route of the proposed A477 St Clears to Red Roses Road Improvement Scheme, Carmarthenshire (between NGR: 21957 21142 to 22675 21552; Fig. 1.1). The works were undertaken at the request of Andy Buckley (AB Heritage Limited), Project Archaeologist for Ramboll, on behalf of the Welsh Government and in accordance with the *A477 St Clears to Red Roses Road Improvement Archaeology Design* (Ramboll 2012) which outlined the archaeological investigation and mitigation strategy for the project. The document was approved by the Welsh Government's Archaeological Advisor, Jim Hunter of Hyder Consulting (now Arcadis).

The programme of archaeological recording was designed to mitigate the impact of the scheme on the environment, and followed on from preliminary archaeological works which included a site walkover, initial geophysical survey (ArchaeoPhysica 2010a; 2010b; 2010c) and baseline assessment undertaken as part of an Environmental Impact Assessment (EIA). The results of these preliminary works were set out within the Cultural Heritage section, chapter 6 of the *Environmental Statement and Reference Design (ES)* (Ramboll 2011). Subsequent works undertaken in advance of road construction included further geophysical survey (Stratascan 2012), archaeological trial trenching (CA 2012a–d), a metal-detecting survey by Archaeological Surveys Ltd, geoarchaeological boreholes (ARCA 2012a; 2012b; 2014) and test pits, a review of available LiDAR (Light Detection and Ranging) imagery, historic building recording, watching-brief works, and strip, map and sample excavation.

1.1 Location, topography and geology

The road corridor is approximately 9.5km in length and follows a broadly north-east/south-west alignment across what was agricultural land, predominantly pasture, between Red Roses and St Clears (Fig. 1.1). The south-western end of the scheme joins with the existing A477 south-west of Coldwell Farm near Red Roses at approximately 145m AOD (Above Ordnance Datum). The road corridor then rises steeply to the north-east to cross the existing B4314 Red Roses to Tavernspite road at approximately 170m AOD and then rises more gently to the north-east to Brandy Hill at 200m AOD. The ground level then drops away to approximately 105m AOD to an access road to two properties, Cnwce and Penlan, before rising again to a plateau to the north-east of Cnwce at 110m AOD. The road corridor then descends gradually to an access road to Vaynor Farm at 70m AOD before rising to a plateau south-west of Pentrehowell Farm at 110m AOD. The route then descends gradually to cross the Llanddowror to Tavernspite road before dropping steeply to the River Taf valley north-east of Llanddowror. The route then runs north-eastwards across the floodplain, at approximately 5m AOD, before rising gently to rejoin the existing A477 carriageway, at approximately 10m AOD, immediately south-east of Pont Newydd bridge at St Clears.

The solid geology of the south-western half of the road corridor, from immediately south-west of Red Roses through to an access road to the property named Cildywyll, is mapped as Milford Haven Group Argillaceous Rocks and Subordinate Sandstone and Conglomerate, Lower Old Red Sandstone and Conglomerate of the Devonian and Silurian periods, Slade and Redhill Formation Argillaceous Rocks, and Sandstone and Robeston Wathen Limestone and Sholeshook Limestone of the Ordovician period. The solid geology of the north-eastern part of the road corridor, from north-east of Cildywyll through to St Clears, is mapped as Mydrim Shales Mudstone Formation and Didymograptus Bifidus Beds of the Ordovician period. Although superficial geological deposits are not mapped across most of the road corridor, Quaternary alluvium, comprising sand, silts,

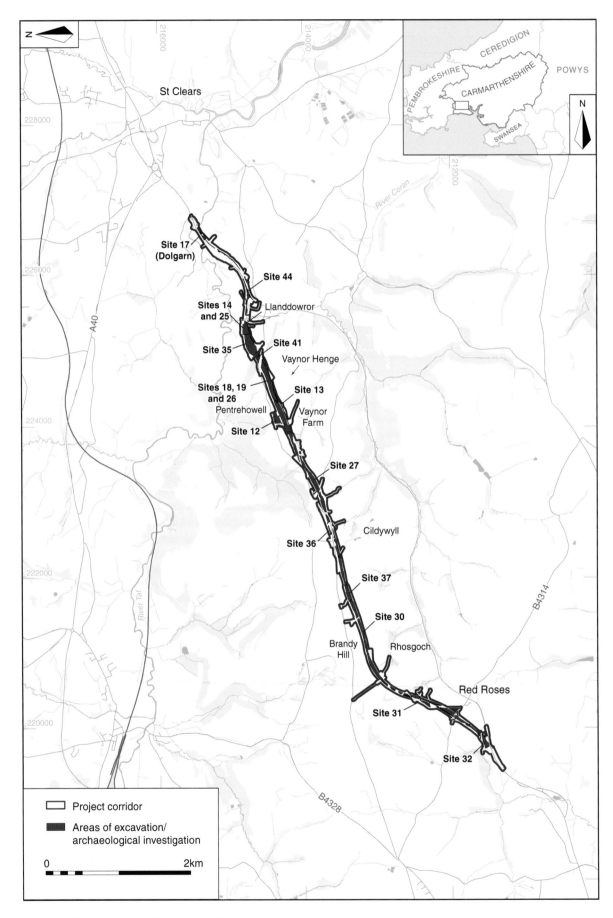

Fig. 1.1   Location plan. Scale 1:50,000

Table 1.1   Preliminary works along the route of the A477

Type of archaeological recording	Date	Reference
Site walkover	April 2010	Ramboll 2011
Geophysical survey – magnetometer	August 2010	ArchaeoPhysica 2010a, 2010b, 2010c
Baseline assessment as part of Environmental Impact Assessment	2010	Ramboll 2011
Geophysical survey – gradiometry	Feb 2012	Stratascan 2012
Trial trenching	Jan–Feb, March–April, June–August 2012	CA 2012 a–d
Metal-detecting survey – southern part of Dolgarn SM	2012	Archaeological Surveys Ltd
Geoarchaeological boreholes	June 2010	ARCA 2012a, 2012b, 2012c, 2014
Geoarchaeological test pits	June–Jul 2012	Wilkinson 2012
LiDAR	2012	Dolgarn SM
Historic building recording	April 2010, March 2012	Pont Newydd, animal sheds
Controlled Watching Brief (CWB)	Feb–Aug 2012	CA Post-excavation assessment report 2014a
General Watching Brief (GWB)	Feb–Aug 2012	"
Strip, map and sample	Feb–Aug 2012	"

clays and gravels, and Till are recorded within the River Taf floodplain (BGS 2013). The natural substrate encountered throughout the scheme included shaley mud and silt stone, sandstone, limestone, alluvial clays and gravels.

1.2 Preliminary work

A staged approach was adopted for the archaeological investigation, the first stage being to assess the archaeological potential of the (then) proposed road corridor. Chapter 6 'Cultural Heritage' of the *A477 St Clears to Red Roses Road Improvement Environmental Statement and Reference Design* (Ramboll 2011) reviewed the known cultural heritage for a 400m-wide corridor based upon the centreline of the proposed road, and included field reconnaissance of the centre line of the road and its immediate vicinity by the AB Heritage team.

Geophysical survey (magnetometer) was undertaken on a ridge above Vaynor Farm, Llanddowror, on land adjacent to Castell Motte, Llanddowror, and on land encompassing the southernmost part of Dolgarn Scheduled Monument near Bishopscourt Farm, St Clears (a total of five fields). This was followed by evaluation at three sites where the survey revealed geophysical anomalies, potentially representing archaeological features. A gradiometry survey was conducted across a further seven areas within the redevelopment scheme, and a metal-detecting survey was also undertaken by Archaeological Surveys across the southern part of Dolgarn Scheduled Monument, south of the existing A477, ahead of evaluation and excavation works. Other work included historic building recording, a review

of available LiDAR imagery and test-pitting (Fig. 1.2, Table 1.1).

These preliminary investigations were used to inform the *A477 St Clears to Red Roses Road Improvement Archaeology Design* (Ramboll 2012) which outlined the archaeological investigation and mitigation strategy for the project. In this, a number of sites were identified as requiring archaeological strip, map and sample excavation. In addition, those sites with geophysical anomalies untested by trial trenching were examined by means of controlled watching briefs (CWB; involving the archaeologically controlled removal of topsoil and subsoil, followed by excavation and recording of any archaeological features encountered). Further excavations were undertaken where archaeological features were encountered during the course of a scheme-wide general watching brief (GWB). The results of all of these evaluations, excavations and watching briefs within the road corridor form the subject of this report.

An initial stage of post-excavation work undertaken by Cotswold Archaeology between February and April 2013 included quantification of the site archive, initial processing of the finds and the conservation of the cremation urns and associated vessels. The work did not include the processing of human remains found in the investigations.

It was apparent at this stage that the results of the fieldwork programme included findings of archaeological significance that were of sufficient archaeological importance to warrant publication. The importance of the findings was enhanced by their proximity to the significant prehistoric evidence investigated during the construction of the Milford Haven to Aberdulais

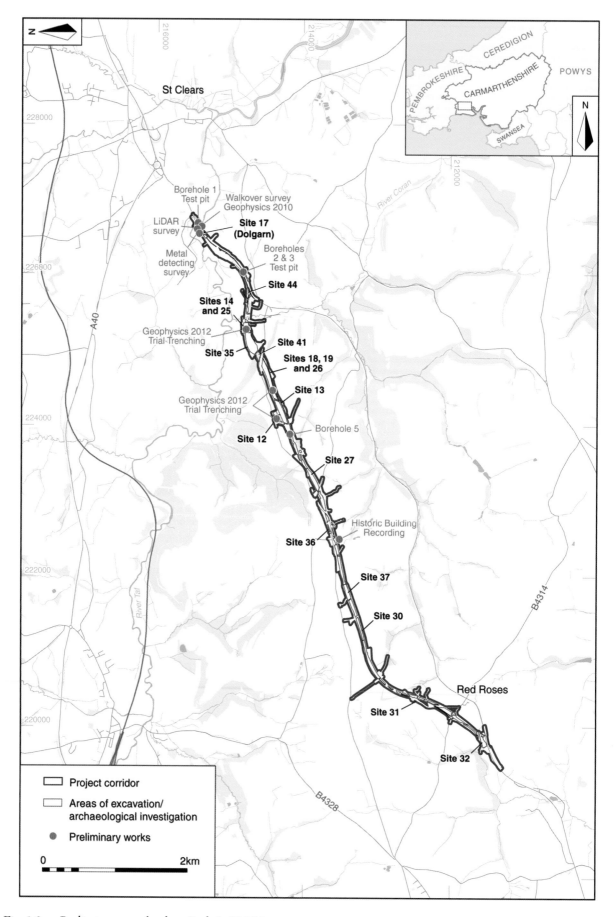

Fig. 1.2   Preliminary works plan. Scale 1:50,000

pipeline which ran south of the road corridor for some of its length (Barber and Pannett 2006; Walker forthcoming). A programme of post-excavation work was devised appropriate to the significance of the archaeological discoveries (Ramboll 2013). The prevailing aim of the published output was to allow all significant aspects of the results to be fully explored, and to reach the widest possible audience. The work was undertaken in accordance with the agreed Post-Excavation Project Design (CA 2013). This proposed full assessment of the results, after which a programme of further work and publication would be agreed and implemented. This report of the prehistoric archaeology of the A477 road improvement scheme represents the major component of the programme of further work outlined in the Post-Excavation Assessment and Updated Project Design (CA 2014a).

1.3 Archaeological background

The information detailed within the Chapter 6 'Cultural Heritage' of the *A477 St Clears to Red Roses Improvement Environmental Statement and Reference Design* (Ramboll 2011) is summarised here, together with additional research.

Prehistoric (*c.* 500,000 BC to AD 43)

Evidence for Palaeolithic activity is limited, and there is a bias towards cave sites in Wales, which probably reflects the ease of the identification of these types of sites (David 2007, 5). Amongst these the nearest to the road scheme is Hoyles Mouth Cave, near Tenby Pembrokeshire, a Late Devensian site and there is a possible Middle Devensian date from charcoal from an artefact layer in Coygan Cave, Camarthenshire approximately 8km to the south-east of the road scheme (ibid.). A handaxe recovered in the 1980s has been recorded to the west of the project (DAT: PRN[1] 14417).

Mesolithic evidence clusters around the coast particularly to the south and east in Wales. There is limited evidence in the immediate area of the sites, although excavations at Coygan Camp, Dyfed recovered a collection of Mesolithic flint implements (Wainwright 1967).

The Neolithic is well attested within west Wales, particularly ritual and funerary monuments such as chambered tombs, stone circles and long barrows. Close to the project were two handaxe findspots (DAT: PRN 3883 and 11105) and a cairnfield within Kiffig Deer Park (DAT: PRN 29504). Approximately 350m south of the road scheme, during archaeological investigation of the route of the Milford Haven to Aberdulais gas pipeline in 2006 (Barber and Pannett 2006) a Class II Neolithic henge was found to the north-east of

Fig. 1.3   Class II Neolithic henge, Vaynor Farm, from the west. 2m scales

Vaynor Farm (NGR: 224700 214170) (Fig. 1.3). The same pipeline project also revealed Early Neolithic pit clusters (Pannett 2012) at three sites in the Towy valley.

The Bronze Age in south-west Wales is characterised by round barrows and standing stones; their siting favours the uplands and prominent positions. Other evidence of Bronze Age activity, including burnt mounds, rarely leave upstanding remains, and discovery relies on below ground investigation and chance finds. Monuments are relatively evenly spread around the landscape suggesting a populated and popular area (Cook 2003). Within 2km north and south of the road are recorded: nine standing stones (DAT: PRN 5060, 8046, 3904, 11166, 11165, 11167, 11749, 11752, 11164), three cairnfields (DAT: PRN 13371, 13370, 29504), two clearance cairns (DAT: PRN 13373, 13372), one burnt mound (DAT: PRN 106792), and four round barrows (DAT: PRN 11753, 11162, 3867, 13061). Despite their abundance very few barrows have been fully excavated. Parc Maen (to the north-west of the road scheme in Pembrokeshire) is one of the few to be investigated, but due to the soil conditions no bone survived (Marshall and Murphy 1991).

---

1   DAT: PRN refers to Dyfed Archaeological Trust (Historic Environment Record): Primary Record Numbers

Close to the road corridor is Parc Garn Round Barrow, near Brandy Hill (DAT: PRN 11162), and Llain Y College Standing Stone, near St Clears (DAT: PRN 3904), respectively approximately 100m and 160m north of the road scheme (Barber and Pannett 2006). In addition, a burnt mound recorded west of Vaynor Farm (at NGR: 224010 214000), and a cremation cemetery 80m east of Vaynor Henge (NGR: 224700 214170) are also of Bronze Age date (Barber and Pannett 2006).

Further Bronze Age activity was identified on the route of the Milford Haven to Aberdulais gas pipeline in 2006 (Barber and Pannett 2006) including a ditch and Early to Middle Bronze Age pits at Mylett Farm near Laugharne (approximately 6km to the south at NGR: 22718 21443).

An urn burial, of possible Bronze Age or Roman date, was recorded from within the enclosure of Dolgarn Scheduled Monument near St Clears, when the turnpike road cut through the mound, although the precise location and dating of this find remains uncertain (NMRW: NPRN[2] 304173).

An Iron Age origin has been conjectured for the Scheduled Monument of Dolgarn, a moated earthwork (CM252) and Pen Coed Camp (2km to the south, also known as Castell Pen-y-Coed), and also for Llanddowror churchyard and Llanddowror Castell, whose rectangular forms have previously been seen as representing an Iron Age 'paired site' with two adjacent enclosures, one of which may have become a kin burial ground and the other a defensive platform (Ramboll 2011). No other sites of Iron Age date have been identified within 2km of the road scheme.

Romano-British (AD 43 to AD 410)

A Roman fort at Carmarthen (approximately 13km east of St Clears) was established during the late AD 70s and the subsequent Roman town (*Moridunum*) was thought to be the *civitas* capital of the *Demetae*. By the early 3rd century AD the town was of sufficient importance as a naval station to be mentioned in the Antonine Itinerary (Margary 1973). *Moridunum* was connected with several major Roman roads (Margary 1973), of which one has been identified as running west of Carmarthen and lies between 1–2km north of the road scheme at the St Clears end. This would have influenced settlement patterns in the wider environs and, although there is a paucity of evidence for Roman settlement within Carmarthenshire, there is evidence to suggest Roman occupation at Dolgarth, St Clears (NMRW: NPRN 301190) and the Dolgarn Scheduled Monument is also thought to have been occupied during the Romano-British period, although limited investigation of the monument in the course of this project did not confirm this. Romano-British

activity within the vicinity is firmly attested on the site of the Neolithic henge north-east of Vaynor Farm, where the final fill of the henge ditch, containing 1st to 3rd-century AD pottery was cut by a pit containing cremated animal bone and Roman pottery, and also by a four-post structure (Barber and Pannett 2006).

Early medieval (AD 410 to 1066)

During the early medieval period the lands formerly under control of the *Demetae* tribe became incorporated into the Kingdom of *Voteporix*. The 'Llan' element of the name of Llanddowror which lies 200m to the south of the road scheme corridor is suggested to have originally meant 'enclosure', although it is more popularly believed to refer to an early monastic foundation and could reflect the foundation of a church in Llanddowror during the Early medieval period. An inscribed standing stone of this date, originally recorded as a pair when surveyed in 1897, approximately 50m west of Llanddowror churchyard, is believed to be a remnant grave marker suggesting that the graveyard may have extended beyond its current location. No settlement evidence for an associated community in this area, around the 10th century, has yet been identified (Ramboll 2011).

Medieval (AD 1066 to 1539)

West Wales became subjected to English overlordship from the 12th century onwards, with tensions and division erupting periodically over the following centuries. Castle Motte, Llanddowror, has been considered to be a medieval defensive earthwork, and Dyfed HER also notes the suggestion that Dolgarn Scheduled Monument (CM252) may also have been used as a moated site during this period (DAT: PRN 3884). A large stone motte and bailey castle in St Clears, approximately 1km east of the road scheme is known to have been destroyed in 1215–16 (NMRW: NPRN 105023).

Post-medieval and modern (AD 1540 to present)

Extensive evidence of post-medieval and modern settlement activity, together with associated infrastructure, industrial and agricultural works, is recorded within the vicinity. Extant post-medieval settlement remains include Coldwell farmstead and four demolished cottages/farmsteads including Rhosgoch Fach Cottage, immediately adjacent to the road scheme corridor; Hungry Gate Cottage within the road corridor; Brandy Hill, immediately adjacent to the road corridor; and a cottage and pond recorded on the Llanddowror parish tithe map of 1845, within the road corridor (Ramboll 2011).

Evidence suggests a reduction in population and settlement size occurred prior to and during the initial part of the post-medieval period, leading to a nucleated medieval settlement pattern changing to a dispersed

---

2   NMRW: NPRN refers to the National Monument Record of Wales: National Primary Reference Number

pattern of farmsteads during the post-medieval period, associated with enclosure of common land for sheep farming, which was perceived as more profitable than cultivation for corn. Management of the River Taf floodplain drainage appears to have intensified during the post-medieval period. Cultural heritage sites dating to this period include bridges and fords, including Pont Newydd, quarry activity, milestones and evidence of 20th-century agricultural activity including former animal sheds (Ramboll 2011).

1.4 Methodology

Fieldwork

Intervention numbers, running from 1 through to 45, were allocated during the course of the project to specific office and field-based project tasks undertaken by CA. Field-based tasks included field evaluations, strip, map and sample/excavations, watching briefs, photographic and GPS surveys, historic building recording and geoarchaeological boreholes and test pits, and encompassed Interventions 9 to 45 (Interventions 1–8 applied to other aspects of the project work, such as management and health and safety). Each field-based intervention covered either one or more land parcels, and in some cases several different interventions occurred within the same area (for example evaluation followed by an excavation and/or watching brief at the same site). For the purposes of reporting the series of field-based Intervention numbers have been rationalised into a number of designated Sites. In cases where several field-based project tasks occurred within the same area, a single Site Number has been chosen to represent the area in this report (Table 1.2).

All machining during the course of the evaluations, excavations and controlled watching briefs (CWB) was undertaken with a mechanical excavator equipped with a toothless grading bucket, under constant archaeological supervision until the top of archaeological deposits or natural substrate was encountered. Archaeological features thus exposed were hand-excavated to the bottom of archaeological stratigraphy. Most machining undertaken during general watching briefs (GWB) was with a toothless grading bucket, but to levels determined by the contractor.

All features were planned and recorded in accordance with *CA Technical Manual 1: Excavation Recording Manual* (CA 1996). Deposits were assessed for their environmental potential, then sampled and processed appropriately in accordance with *CA Technical Manual 2: The taking of samples for palaeoenvironmental and palaeoeconomic analysis from archaeological sites* (CA 2003). All artefacts recovered from the excavation were retained in accordance with *CA Technical Manual 3: Treatment of finds immediately after excavation* (CA 1995).

Post-excavation work

Post-excavation work was undertaken following English Heritage standard guidance within Management of Archaeological Projects 2 (EH 1991), and MoRPHE (EH 2006) which recommends that projects are assessed for their potential to achieve the project aims following the completion of the fieldwork phase. Features were assigned to Periods based on a stratigraphic sequence established through single context excavation. These Periods were then dated, largely on the basis of the artefactual record and radiocarbon determinations, but in some instances features were assigned to a Period from their morphology and their location relative to other better stratified or dated deposits.

Radiocarbon dating was undertaken in order to confirm the dates of features along the route of the St Clears to Red Roses Road scheme (Table 2.1). The samples were analysed during January/February 2014, July, September and December 2015 at Scottish Universities Environmental Research Centre (SUERC), Rankine Avenue, Scottish Enterprise Technology Park, East Kilbride, Glasgow, G75 0QF, Scotland.

The samples were successfully dated using the AMS method. The uncalibrated dates are conventional radiocarbon ages. The radiocarbon ages were calibrated by SUERC using the University of Oxford Radiocarbon Accelerator Unit calibration program OxCal 4.1.7 (Bronk Ramsey 2009a) using the IntCal13 curve (Reimer *et al.* 2013).

A *Post-Excavation Assessment and Updated Project Design* (CA 2014a) was produced for the site, which summarised the potential of the archaeological data, established updated aims and objectives for the project, and concluded that the results of the project should be published to an appropriate level. It was determined that the most significant aspects of the project which centre on the prehistoric discoveries were to be published in a monograph format (this volume).

1.5 Aims and structure of the report

This report presents the results of the post-excavation analysis of the excavated data, and a synthesis of the available evidence for the prehistoric archaeology of the A477 road development corridor. The results of this synthesis are interpreted and discussed according to their significance within a local, regional and national framework. The archaeological remains which relate to later periods (Roman, medieval and post-medieval) are briefly summarised; these findings will be the dealt with in more detail in a separate report published in *Archaeology in Wales*.

The report follows a traditional format; this introductory chapter is followed by an interpretation of the sequence of excavated features discussed by Period in Chapter 2. Chapter 3 comprises the cremation burial

Table 1.2   The archaeological sites: concordance to interventions and summary findings

Site	Centre point Grid Reference: Easting/ Northing	Incorporates part/ all of fieldwork Interventions:	Summary findings	Figures
12	224068/ 214396	11, 12	Bronze Age: pit with Early to Middle Bronze Age pottery, pit with undiagnostic pottery. Pits dated by their similarities to the dated features.	1.1, 2.13
13	22385/ 214360	13	Bronze Age: scattered pits and postholes of probable Bronze Age date, but no obvious structures.	1.1, 2.14
17	226550/ 215424	10, 16, 20, 24	Prehistoric: undiagnostic worked flint in a medieval feature.	1.1, 2.38
			Later activity: medieval dating evidence for Dolgarn Scheduled Monument.	
18	224486/ 214458	18, 13, 19, 26	Prehistoric: undiagnostic worked flint in a Bronze Age feature.	1.1, 2.14–2.17, 2.21
			Bronze Age: scattered pits and postholes of probable Bronze Age date, but no obvious structures. Area of cremations, some with urns. Possible crop-dryer. Possible hearths. Environmental evidence from samples. Radiocarbon dating.	
			Later activity: a single Roman pit, medieval and later boundary ditches.	
19	224486/ 214458	19	Bronze Age: pits dated by their similarities to dated features in Site 26 to the north.	1.1, 2.21
			Later activity: post-medieval boundary ditches.	
25	225279/ 214790	14, 25	Prehistoric: large amount of undiagnostic worked flint from the interface between the overburden and the subsoil and as unstratified finds.	1.1, 2.1, 2.5, 2.6, 2.8
			Mesolithic/Early Neolithic: a number of Mesolithic and Mesolithic or early Neolithic worked flints from the interface between the overburden and the subsoil.	
			Neolithic: two clusters of activity including pits, postholes, tree-throws and two possible hearths. Some Early Neolithic flint and pottery. Radiocarbon dating.	
			Late Beaker/Early Bronze Age: cluster of pits and a posthole. Late Beaker/Early Bronze Age pottery. Environmental evidence from samples. Radiocarbon dating.	
26	224486/, 214458	18, 26	Prehistoric: undiagnostic redeposited flint.	1.1, 2.21– 2.36
			Mesolithic: one redeposited flint in a later feature.	
			Bronze Age: funerary site with barrow and pyre hollow, cremations, some with urns and accessory vessels. A number of scattered pits. Environmental evidence from samples. Geoarchaeological evidence. Radiocarbon dating.	
			Later activity: post-medieval boundary ditches.	
27	223190/ 213870	27	Later activity: Roman enclosure ditch dated by radiocarbon, late medieval pit, undated pits, postholes and field boundaries.	1.1, 1.2
30	221291/ 213227	30	Neolithic: cluster of pits dated by similarities to Neolithic activity to the east and Neolithic stone axe fragment.	1.1, 2.4, 2.5
31	220411/ 212532	31	Later activity: late medieval foundation trenches and enclosure ditches of farmstead.	1.1, 1.2

Site	Centre point Grid Reference: Easting/ Northing	Incorporates part/ all of fieldwork Interventions:	Summary findings	Figures
32	219796/ 211542	32	Bronze Age: burnt mound and troughs.	1.1, 2.9–2.11
35	225093/ 214751	35	Prehistoric: undiagnostic worked flint from the overburden and the subsoil.	1.1, 2.2, 2.18, 2.19
			Mesolithic/Early Neolithic: Mesolithic and Mesolithic or early Neolithic worked flints from the overburden and the subsoil. Pit of possible Neolithic date.	
36	222637/ 213693	36	Bronze Age: cluster of pits dated by similarities to other Bronze Age activity.	1.1, 2.12
37	221789/ 213406	37	Neolithic: two clusters of activity one comprising pits, the second includes a possible posthole structure and surface. Scattered pits and postholes. Possible structured deposition of flint, pottery and environmental remains: some whole pots represented. Radiocarbon dating.	1.1, 2.3, 2.5, 2.7, 2.8
			Bronze Age: small number of pits with pottery. Environmental evidence.	
41	224940/ 214620	41	Undated: earthwork enclosure and hollow-way.	1.1, 1.2
44	225393/ 214801	44	Bronze Age: worked timber. Environmental evidence. Radiocarbon dating.	1.1, 2.20

catalogue. Chapter 4 presents summaries of the analysis undertaken on the artefacts, and Chapter 5 presents summaries of the analysis of the zoological and environmental evidence. Chapter 6 draws together all the evidence from the preceding chapters in a period-based discussion and places the evidence in its wider context.

For the purposes of reporting, the series of intervention numbers allocated during the course of the site work to specific field-based project tasks have been allocated a Site Number (Table 1.2).

1.6 Overview of the results

This volume represents the culmination of a process of archaeological planning, survey, evaluation and excavation undertaken in advance of the A477 road improvements between Red Roses and St Clears. Linear schemes such as the A477 road improvements can provide excellent opportunities for archaeologists to examine transects across landscapes, and the 9.5km length of this scheme revealed significant evidence of human activity dating from the Mesolithic through to the medieval period. The majority of this activity derives from the Neolithic and Bronze Age periods, and it is the significance of those findings that is the focus of this volume. The factors that affect the outcome of archaeological investigations on linear developments such as road and pipeline replacement are well-known. Much of the preliminary work for a major development such as the A477 is directed towards reducing the impact of the development on the archaeological and historical

environment, and where possible, any known archaeological sites are avoided. The evidence is curtailed by the narrow width of the development, limiting our abilities to map the form and extent of the zones of archaeological activity that the development passes through. Moreover these schemes often pass across undeveloped and sometimes remote tracts of land where little previous investigation has taken place, and it is harder under these circumstances to envisage how the activity encountered sits within the past landscapes. Although many of these factors certainly apply to the A477 road scheme, a great deal has been gained from the analysis of our discoveries along the corridor of road development, as this report amply demonstrates.

In placing our discoveries in the context of the surrounding landscape the scheme has greatly benefited from the recent archaeological investigations during the construction of the Milford Haven to Aberdulais gas pipeline replacement, a stretch of which bisects the A477. In 2006 these pipeline works uncovered evidence for a prehistoric landscape of some significance, including the Class II Neolithic henge lying some 225m to the south of the A477 redevelopment at Vaynor Farm. Our knowledge of the presence of this earthwork, which remained visible in the landscape throughout the later prehistoric period has greatly enriched the interpretation and understanding of the archaeological remains along this stretch of the A477 development corridor. The work undertaken here will make a significant contribution to our understanding of the prehistory of the area and to a number of research themes that are prominent in the regional research agenda.

Amongst the most notable archaeological evidence discovered during the road scheme development were the Mesolithic activity at Site 25, Neolithic activity at Site 37, the burnt mound at Site 32, the Bronze Age cremation cemetery at Sites 18 and 26, and the possible Bronze Age corn dryer at Site 18. The discoveries that post-date the prehistoric period are not the focus of this report, but the investigation at Dolgarn (Site 17) is included here in summary form as its outcome was important in establishing with some certainty that the scheduled monument is medieval.

The evidence for Mesolithic activity was at its most numerous at Site 25, and it was only at this location that anything more than the most transient presence could be inferred. Chapter 6 discusses the evidence for human use of this location as a reflection of the location's relative accessibility and the range of habitats that could be exploited from this location. The contribution that the Mesolithic evidence from the road scheme can make to regional research for this period is limited, although Site 25 can be added to a body of evidence for inland locations; however the type or frequency of the use of this site cannot be determined from the available data. Early Neolithic evidence is also present here, and hints at continuity, with the later activity linked by charcoal evidence to land clearance in the immediate area. A more substantial Neolithic presence was identified at Site 37, where the crest of a hill was the location for settlement, and includes evidence for a structure. Structural evidence from this period is rare and what makes Site 37 more significant is that there is supporting evidence for domestic use. Chapter 6 discusses the evidence here in relation to other examples of Neolithic structures, and whether the example at Site 37 conforms to any regional traits. The site is also notable for the nature of the fills of the pits and postholes which suggest the deliberate placement of material. Another notable aspect of the prehistoric remains from the road scheme, is an apparent lack of activity that can be ascribed to the Middle or Late Neolithic periods. Chapter 6 discusses this absence in terms of shifting patterns of settlement, but also makes the interesting proposition that the henge at Vaynor may have influenced patterns of activity in the area, creating a tradition for ceremony rather than settlement that persisted into later periods.

As discussed above, linear schemes such as the A477 often clip the edge of areas of archaeological activity and hinder our ability to interpret their function or meaning. It was fortuitous therefore that the road corridor revealed the entirety of a Bronze Age barrow at Site 26, as well as much of the surrounding activity, which included cremation burial and pyre sites. With a total of 62 deposits of human bone, of which 38 are deemed to be intentional, the site provided an opportunity to study the varied and variable nature of burial practices at this time and compare this data with contemporary published data.

The site has benefited from the in-depth analysis of the second stage of the post-excavation programme, from which a different and more robust interpretation of the funerary monuments has emerged. Bayesian modelling of the radiocarbon dates has enabled events to be modelled with a greater precision than would otherwise have been possible, and has also allowed a subtle chronological modelling of the activity within the barrow area in relation to the adjacent pyre hollow, and surrounding features. The discussion in Chapter 6 brings our attention to more recent approaches to interpreting these remains which moves away from an emphasis on the typology of monuments to an understanding of all the features as the physical remains of aspects of ritual performances taking place on the site that may not have always included the act of cremation. The discussion examines the features in terms of other processes and rituals that may have taken place; in this regard it is a telling fact that even the most 'complete' of the cremations do not contain a complete individual, even where the deposit has survived intact.

From the presence of Bronze Age burials excavated on the Milford Haven pipeline in 2006 we can deduce that the cremations at Sites 18 and 26 form part of a much wider landscape of ritual activity, possibly with other barrows forming the focus for similar groupings.

An unforeseen outcome of a second stage of radiocarbon dates undertaken following the assessment phase was the number of features that returned a medieval date. Many of the undated features had been assigned to the prehistoric period based on similarities in fills and form, and by their proximity to dated prehistoric remains. In the light of this additional information the undated features were rigorously re-examined, and a small number were reassigned to an undated category to avoid misinformation. However it was determined that the initial interpretation of the majority of these features was valid and the overall impression of a landscape more heavily utilised in the prehistoric, rather than the later periods remains.

1.7 Location of the archive

The archive and artefacts from the project are currently held by CA at their offices in Kemble. Subject to the agreement of the legal landowners the site archive (including artefacts) will be deposited with Carmarthenshire Museum under accession number CAASG 2012:0143.

Chapter 2
Excavation Results

2.1 Site chronology

The definition of periods within the archaeological sequence rested on a chronological basis provided by dating evidence provided by pottery, flint and a small number of other broadly dateable artefacts. This was augmented by a suite of radiocarbon dating and supported by detailed analysis of the stratigraphic sequence, and of the form, character and spatial relationships of deposits and cut features. The periods as defined below cover the broad date ranges represented by the archaeological discoveries; for some areas of the project a more refined dating was achieved, and where this is the case the details are discussed within the text.

Period 1 Mesolithic *c.* 10,000 BC–4000 BC
Period 2 Early Neolithic *c.* 4000 BC–3000 BC
Period 3 Bronze Age *c.* 2400 BC–700 BC
Period 4 Romano-British 2nd to 4th century, early medieval–medieval 5th to 16th- century AD
Period 5 post-medieval 16th to 19th century

This report discusses the archaeology of the prehistoric Periods 1–3 in detail and summarises the findings from the later Periods 4 and 5. A fuller report on these findings will be published in the journal *Archaeology in Wales* (Hart and Alexander forthcoming). There was no archaeological evidence for activity in the Iron Age.

Radiocarbon dates have all been calibrated (see Chapter 1.4 for details) and they are all expressed at 95.4% probability, unless specified.

2.2 Period 1 Mesolithic

Only one feature can be securely dated to the Mesolithic date: a posthole from Site 25. The remaining evidence was restricted to scatters of Mesolithic flakes and microblades, most of which were found on the interface between the overburden and the natural deposits, and some from unstratified deposits. Flint occurred at all levels, from the top of the ridge to the floodplain.

Sites 25 (Fig. 2.1), 26, and 35 (Fig. 2.4) yielded worked flint that can be ascribed a Mesolithic date on the basis of typology. The location of the individual flints was recorded on Sites 25 and 35, as noted on the relevant area figures (Figs 2.1 and 2.4), but no clear pattern was discernible at either location. One microlith was found on Site 26 along with a number of other less diagnostic pieces. All were residual within later contexts. Site 25, on the floodplain of the River Taf produced the highest concentration of flints of which 15 Mesolithic bladelets and microliths were retrieved from the interface between the ploughsoil and underlying natural substrate; five came from unstratified contexts (Fig. 2.1). The charcoal-rich fill (250118) of a probable posthole (250117), measuring 0.4m long, 0.3m wide and 0.16m deep, yielded a radiocarbon date of 5762–5648 cal BC (SUERC-61260), suggesting a late Mesolithic date for the activity at Site 25.

However, it should be noted that flint evidence that could be categorised as 'Mesolithic' invariably occurred where there was also Early Neolithic activity. This does raise issues as to the distinction between these two periods. At Site 25, where Early Neolithic activity is indicated from a number of diagnostic flints as well as Early Neolithic pottery, a continuity of use is implied.

Beyond Site 25 the only supportive scientific dating came from a hazelnut shell recovered from shallow ditch 180502 on Site 18 (Fig. 2.16), yielding a Mesolithic radiocarbon date of 8537–8302 cal BC (SUERC-50315), but this must be considered a residual item as the ditch is of medieval date by virtue of artefactual evidence from its fill, and an additional radiocarbon date from the associated ditch 180487 (Fig. 2.21) which supported the medieval attribution. The hazelnut shell may have come from a Mesolithic feature cut by the ditch which had then become incorporated into the fill.

Table 2.1   Radiocarbon dating results and calibrations by site

Feature	Lab No.	Material	δ ¹³C	Radiocarbon Age	95.4% probability	68.2% probability
Site 17						
Context 170019 Ditch 170024	SUERC-50312	Carbonised seed – Bromes (*Bromus*)	−26.9‰	843 ± 29 yr BP	1059–1063 cal AD (0.6%) 1154–1263 cal AD (94.8%)	1165–1223 cal AD (62.8%)
Site 18						
Context 180058 Pit 180059	SUERC-50313	Charcoal – Oak – (*Quercus*) twig	−26.2‰	1616 ± 29 yr BP	387–537 cal AD (95.4%)	396–432 cal AD (36.4%) 490–531 cal AD (31.8%)
Context 180526 Slab-edged feature 180304	SUERC-50314	Charcoal – Alder/hazel (*Alnus glutinosa/ Corylus avellana*)	−24.3‰	3194 ± 29 yr BP	1513–1414 cal BC (95.4%)	1497–1439 cal BC (68.2%)
Context 180514 Ditch 180502	SUERC-50315	Carbonised seed – Hazelnut shell (*Corylus avellana*)	−25.0‰	9199 ± 31 yr BP	8537–8511 cal BC (5.9%) 8486–8302 cal BC (89.5%)	8451–8327 cal BC (68.2%)
Context 180081 Pit 180082	SUERC-61250	Charcoal – Alder/hazel (*Alnus glutinosa/ Corylus avellana*)	−26.2‰	1072 ± 30 yr BP	895–929 cal AD (22.2%) 940–1020 cal AD (73.2%)	904–917 cal AD (11.4%) 967–1016 cal AD (56.8%)
Context 180133 Hearth 180134	SUERC-61223	Carbonised grain – Barley (*Hordeum vulgare*)	−25.5‰	735 ± 29 yr BP	1224–1295 cal AD (95.4%)	1261–1295 cal AD (68.2%)
Context 180324 Pit 180323	SUERC-61251	Charcoal – Alder/hazel (*Alnus glutinosa/ Corylus avellana*) (twig)	−25.4‰	841 ± 30 yr BP	1059–1064 cal AD (0.6%) 1154–1264 cal AD (94.8%)	1165–1224 cal AD (68.2%)
Context 180434 Hearth 180435	SUERC-61252	Charcoal – Oak – (*Quercus*) twig	−29.3‰	896 ± 30 yr BP	1039–1214 cal AD (95.4%)	1047–1068 cal AD (30.6%) 1122–1139 cal AD (10.1%) 1149–1189 cal AD (27.5%)
Context 180491 Ditch 180487	SUERC-61253	Charcoal – Hazel (*Corylus avellana*)	−24.6‰	844 ± 30 yr BP	1058–1075 cal AD (2.5%) 1154–1262 cal AD (92.9%)	1164–1223 cal AD (68.2%)
Context 180529 Hearth 180485	SUERC-61254	Charcoal – Hawthorn/rowan/ crab apple (*Crataegus monogyna/Sorbus/ Malus sylvestris*)	−27.9‰	756 ± 30 yr BP	1220–1285 cal AD (95.4%)	1249–1281 cal AD (68.2%)
Context 180173 Cremation 180172	SUERC-61255	Cremated human bone	−24.0‰	3534 ± 30 yr BP	1948–1766 cal BC (95.4%)	1922–1874 cal BC (35.6%) 1844–1815 cal BC (19.0%) 1800–1779 cal BC (13.7%)
Site 19						
Context 190030 Pit 190027	SUERC-50316	Carbonised grain – Oat (*Avena*)	−25.4‰	893 ± 29 yr BP	1041–1108 cal AD (38.4%) 1116–1216 cal AD (57.0%)	1049–1085 cal AD (27.9%) 1124–1137 cal AD (7.8%) 1150–1190 cal AD (30.6%) 1199–1203 cal AD (1.9%)

Feature	Lab No.	Material	δ¹³C	Radiocarbon Age	95.4% probability	68.2% probability
Context 190021 Pit 190022	SUERC-61256	Carbonised grain – Oat (*Avena*)	–25.8‰	839 ± 30 yr BP	1154–1265 cal AD (95.4%)	1167–1225 cal AD (62.5%) 1235–1242 cal AD (5.7%)
Site 25						
Context 250065 Pit 250063	SUERC-50317	Carbonised seed – Hazelnut shell (*Corylus avellana*)	–25.6‰	3836 ± 29 yr BP	2456–2418 cal BC (6.7%) 2408–2375 cal BC (7.8%) 2368–2201 cal BC (80.9%)	2341–2272 cal BC (38.3%) 2258–2208 cal BC (29.9%)
Context 250118 Posthole 250117	SUERC-61260	Charcoal – Hazel (*Corylus avellana*)	–27.7‰	6830 ± 29 yr BP	5762–5648 cal BC (95.4%)	5734–5674 cal BC (68.2%)
Context 250132 Pit 250131	SUERC-61261	Charcoal – Willow/poplar (*Salix/Populus*)	–25.7‰	1135 ± 30 yr BP	777–792 cal AD (4.3%) 803–844 cal AD (8.0%) 857–986 cal AD (83.0%)	885–969 cal AD (68.2%)
Context 250062 Pit 250061	SUERC-61262	Charcoal – Hazel (*Corylus avellana*)	–26.0‰	3534 ± 30 yr BP	1948–1766 cal BC (95.4%)	1922–1874 cal BC (35.6%) 1844–1815 cal BC (19.0%) 1800–1779 cal BC (13.7%)
Site 26						
Context 260446 Cremation 260439	SUERC-50367	Cremated human bone	–23.9‰	3580 ± 25 yr BP	2022–1991 cal BC (8.9%) 1984–1882 cal BC (86.5%)	1956–1891 cal BC (68.2%)
Context 260409 Cremation 260407	SUERC-50368	Cremated human bone	–26.1‰	3537 ± 27 yr BP	1946–1771 cal BC (95.4%)	1923–1876 cal BC (41.6%) 1842–1820 cal BC (15.7%) 1797–1781 cal BC (10.9%)
Context 260337 Cremation 260339	SUERC-61272	Cremated human bone	–25.7‰	3390 ± 30 yr BP	1751–1619 cal BC (95.4%)	1737–1715 cal BC (19.5%) 1696–1643 cal BC (48.7%)
Context 260320 Cremation 260323	SUERC-61273	Cremated human bone	–25.2‰	3414 ± 30 yr BP	1869–1846 cal BC (3.8%) 1775–1628 cal BC (91.6%)	1749–1682 cal BC (62.4%) 1675–1666 cal BC (5.8%)
Context 260238 Cremation 260239	SUERC-61274	Cremated human bone	–21.2‰	3530 ± 30 yr BP	1943–1763 cal BC (95.4%)	1917–1872 cal BC (30.9%) 1845–1813 cal BC (21.4%) 1802–1777 cal BC (16.0%)
Context 260640 Cremation 260021	SUERC-61275	Cremated human bone	–26.9‰	3363 ± 30 yr BP	1744–1708 cal BC (12.2%) 1701–1607 cal BC (79.7%) 1585–1560 cal BC (3.5%)	1689–1623 cal BC (68.2%)
Context 260614 Cremation 260035	SUERC-61276	Cremated human bone	–23.0‰	3555 ± 30 yr BP	2011–2000 cal BC (1.7%) 1978–1868 cal BC (72.6%) 1848–1774 cal BC (21.1%)	1949–1879 cal BC (64.0%) 1838–1829 cal BC (4.2%)
Context 260345 Cremation 260342	SUERC-61118	Cremated human bone	–24.1‰	3571 ± 27 yr BP	2022–1992 cal BC (6.2%) 1984–1877 cal BC (85.0%) 1841–1822 cal BC (2.7%) 1795–1782 cal BC (1.5%)	1951–1887 cal BC (68.2%)
Context 260004 Cremation 260254	SUERC-61119	Cremated human bone	–23.2‰	3479 ± 29 yr BP	1887–1738 cal BC (91.0%) 1714–1697 cal BC (4.4%)	1877–1841 cal BC (26.9%) 1821–1796 cal BC (18.4%) 1782–1751 cal BC (22.9%)
Context 260420 Cremation 260424	SUERC-61120	Cremated human bone	–24.3‰	3563 ± 29 yr BP	2017–1995 cal BC (3.8%) 1981–1871 cal BC (79.5%) 1846–1812 cal BC (7.2%) 1803–1777 cal BC (4.9%)	1952–1882 cal BC (68.2%)

Feature	Lab No.	Material	δ¹³C	Radiocarbon Age	95.4% probability	68.2% probability
Context 260510 Cremation 260474	SUERC-61121	Cremated human bone	−24.9‰	3538 ± 27 yr BP	1948–1771 cal BC (95.4%)	1925–1876 cal BC (42.8%) 1842–1820 cal BC (15.0%) 1797–1781 cal BC (10.4%)
Context 260213 Cremation 260210	SUERC-61122	Cremated human bone	−23.1‰	3567 ± 29 yr BP	2020–1993 cal BC (5.3%) 1982–1874 cal BC (81.6%) 1844–1816 cal BC (5.2%) 1799–1779 cal BC (3.3%)	1952–1884 cal BC (68.2%)
Context 260030 Cremation 260029	SUERC-61282	Charred material – Indeterminate fruit flesh	−23.8‰	3403 ± 30 yr BP	1771–1623 cal BC (95.4%)	1743–1662 cal BC (68.2%)
Context 260490 Cremation 260489	SUERC-61281	Charcoal – Hazel (*Corylus avellana*)	−28.5‰	3450 ± 30 yr BP	1880–1688 cal BC (95.4%)	1871–1845 cal BC (15.2%) 1811–1804 cal BC (3.6%) 1776–1733 cal BC (31.8%) 1719–1694 cal BC (17.5%)
Context 260553 Pit 260561	SUERC-61280	Charcoal – Hazel (*Corylus avellana*)	−26.0‰	3522 ± 30 yr BP	1930–1755 cal BC (95.4%)	1897–1869 cal BC (19.6%) 1846–1775 cal BC (48.6%)
Site 27						
Context 270127 Enclosure ditch 270128	SUERC-50318	Carbonised seed – Cherry sp (*Prunus*)	−24.0‰	1775 ± 27 yr BP	141–197 cal AD (10.4%) 209–338 cal AD (85.0%)	230–260 cal AD (28.6%) 279–326 cal AD (39.6%)
Site 31						
Context 310005 Enclosure 310004	SUERC-62791	Carbonised grain – Oat (*Avena*)	−25.0‰ assumed	896 ± 34 yr BP	1039–1215 cal AD (95.4%)	1047–1090 cal AD (29.0%) 1122–1139 cal AD (10.1%) 1148–1191 cal AD (26.7%) 1199–1204 cal AD (2.4%)
Site 32						
Context 320016 Trough 320015	SUERC-50322	Charcoal – Hazel (*Corylus avellana*)	−23.9‰	3294 ± 29 yr BP	1634–1503 cal BC (95.4%)	1613–1595 cal BC (16.1%) 1589–1532 cal BC (52.1%)
Context 320009 Trough 320008	SUERC-61264	Charcoal – Hazel (*Corylus avellana*)	−25.7‰	3436 ± 30 yr BP	1878–1839 cal BC (13.3%) 1827–1794 cal BC (7.1%) 1784–1661 cal BC (75.0%)	1860–1854 cal BC (3.0%) 1771–1689 cal BC (65.2%)
Site 35						
Context 350034 Pit 350033	SUERC-61265	Charcoal – Hazel (*Corylus avellana*)	−25.9‰	3204 ± 30 yr BP	1525–1419 cal BC (95.4%)	1500–1443 cal BC (68.2%)
Site 37						
Context 370155 Pit 370153	SUERC-61266	Carbonised seed – Hazel (*Corylus avellana*)	−25.1‰	4915 ± 30 yr BP	3765–3722 cal BC (12.3%) 3716–3466 cal BC (83.1%)	3704–3656 cal BC (68.2%)
Context 370035 Pit 370037	SUERC-61270	Carbonised seed – Hazel (*Corylus avellana*)	−24.7‰	4930 ± 30 yr BP	3771–3651 cal BC (95.4%)	3712–3656 cal BC (68.2%)
Context 370021 Pit 370019	SUERC-61271	Carbonised seed – Hazel (*Corylus avellana*)	−25.5‰	4838 ± 30 yr BP	3696–3628 cal BC (62.1%) 3585–3531 cal BC (33.3%)	3656–3632 cal BC (48.6%) 3557–3539 cal BC (19.6%)

Feature	Lab No.	Material	δ¹³C	Radiocarbon Age	95.4% probability	68.2% probability
Site 44						
Context 440004	SUERC-64559	Waterlogged wood – Oak (*Quercus*) – heartwood	−26.4‰	3609 ± 29 yr BP	2034–1890 cal BC (95.4%)	2021–1993 cal BC (21.8%) 1983–1890 cal BC (46.4%)

2.3 Period 2 Early Neolithic

The evidence for Early Neolithic activity and settlement comprised archaeological features – pits and ditches – and artefactual evidence in the form of pottery, and flint with associated evidence of animal bone and environmental remains. The distribution of the evidence along the scheme was similar to that of the Mesolithic period, encompassing both the upland west–east ridge and the floodplain of the River Taf. Early Neolithic evidence was found at Sites 25, 30 and 37. In addition, a scatter of Mesolithic/Neolithic flint at Site 35 is a possible indication of further activity of this period.

Site 25 (Fig. 2.1)

Site 25 was located on an area of floodplain of the River Taf immediately north of the extant earthwork of Castell Motte, Llanddowror.

Several groups of discrete features were identified across the site, on the floodplain itself and cut into the shale bedrock outcrop exposed in the southern part of the site. Very few of the features yielded dateable evidence, therefore the groupings have been based on spatial relationships and fill characteristics, along with the varying disposition of worked flint recovered from the interface between the ploughsoil and the natural substrate. However, it is considered very likely that several of the slighter, more irregular features, represent tree throws or have other natural origins.

In the south-east corner of the site was a curving ring gully (250028) with a fill similar to the pits to the west. If this feature represents a structure it would fit more comfortably with a Bronze Age date, but as no dating evidence was recovered from the gully its derivation remains uncertain.

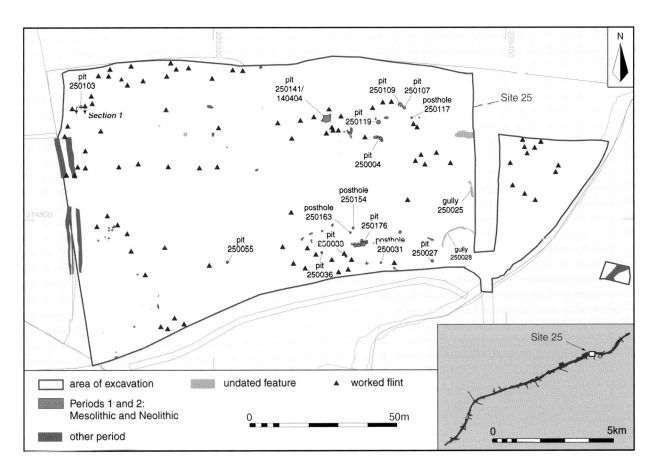

Fig. 2.1   Site 25 Mesolithic and Neolithic: Periods 1 and 2. Scale 1:1250

Some 10m to the north, an irregular linear feature (250025) was plotted measuring approximately 3.5m long by 0.12m deep. No finds were recovered from this feature, and its anthropogenic origin is doubtful. A scatter of worked flints was recovered from the topsoil/subsoil interface some 20m to the east of the feature, although no discrete features were identified.

To the west of the ring gully was a group of nine pits extending over an area of approximately 45m by 18m. The pit dimensions varied from 2.12m to 0.63m long and 1.5m by 0.3m wide by up to 0.26m deep. Their fills were similar, being a greyish brown silty clay, but only one feature (250176) produced finds (from fill 250177), namely six sherds of Early Neolithic pottery, including one decorated example (Chapter 4.2). Three possible postholes (250031, 250154 and 250163) were also identified in this area. A total of 13 worked flints were also recovered from the area. A total of 12 other discrete features with irregular shapes characteristic of tree throws suggest that there may have been a grove of trees here.

Four small pits (250027, 250033, 250036 and 250055) of comparable size and profile, were also located near this area and were distinguished from those of the pit cluster by their relatively charcoal-rich fills. None produced finds, although burnt stones were noted in the fill (250056) of pit 250055.

In the north-central part of the site was an area containing two shallow hearths or fire pits (250004 and 250107). Neither of the features produced dateable finds, although both fire pits contained burnt stones within their fills, along with charcoal. Both 250004 and 250107 were surrounded by a scatter of small pits and probable tree throws. Of these, tree throw/pit 250141/140404 was the only feature with dating evidence in the form of a complete blade and blade fragment, the latter on Greensand chert (Chapter 4.1). Analysis of charcoal from this area of the site shows that a wide variety of wood including oak, alder, hazel and alder/hazel, hawthorn/rowan/crab apple, cherry and willow/poplar was exploited (Chapter 5.3). The area also yielded 21 worked flints from the subsoil/natural interface.

In the north-west corner of the site, a total of 40 flints were recovered. While a number of probable natural features were scattered here, a small pit (250103) (Fig. 2.5, Section 1), was identified, whose single charcoal-rich fill (250104) produced a total of 27 sherds of Early Neolithic pottery, along with one flint core rejuvenation flake of Early Neolithic date and three fragments of burnt sandstone. Taken together this evidence could be indicative of a settlement, or seasonal occupation.

Site 37 (Fig. 2.2)

Situated on a fairly level plateau south of the Llanddowror to Tavernspite road at *c.* 190–200m AOD, the site revealed two major concentrations of archaeological features, both in the western half of the

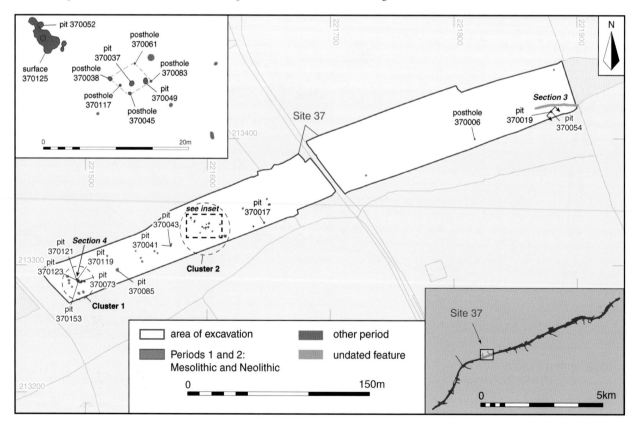

Fig. 2.2   Site 37 Mesolithic and Neolithic: Periods 1 and 2. Scale 1:3000

site. Fourteen of the pits in the most westerly concentration of features produced a large assemblage of Early Neolithic pottery (Cluster 1). The pottery was generally highly fragmented such that vessel profiles were indeterminate in most cases. Most are probably open bowls, although some carinated bowls may also be present. This area of activity appears to have extended west into the adjacent Site 30 where a cluster of probably contemporary pits were revealed (see below).

In the centre of the site was a second cluster of features (Cluster 2). Five postholes (370038, 370045, 370083, 370061 and 370117), typically 0.2m–0.3m in diameter and 0.2m deep possibly define the footprint of a rectangular structure. Three sherds of early Neolithic pottery were recovered from posthole 370083, and a single sherd recovered from each of two pits within this footprint (370049 and 370037). Pit 370049 also contained a Neolithic polished stone axehead fragment (Chapter 4.5). A radiocarbon date of 3771–3651 cal BC (SUERC-61270) was also obtained from the fill of pit 370037, which contained a varied assortment of charcoal, principally oak with some alder and hazel twigs (Chapter 5.3).

Approximately 7m north-west of the possible structure, the remnant of a possible working surface or floor (370125) was identified, comprising a compact layer of fine brown-grey silty clay, levelling up a possible natural hollow, and measuring up to 0.13m deep and covering an area of approximately 7m long and 3m wide, and arguably on a similar alignment (north-west/south-east) as the possible structure. A single Early Neolithic sherd was recovered from the deposit, and a further 11 sherds were recovered from pit 370052 which cut this feature.

The first concentration of features lay approximately 100m to the south-west (Cluster 1). It comprised 14 pits, averaging 0.25m deep, with varying concentrations of charcoal in their silty clay fills, and one in particular (370119) with a significant assemblage of Early Neolithic pottery sherds, all from the same vessel. The pit was adjacent to an undated pit 370121 containing large stones (Fig. 2.5, Section 4). Two other nearby pits (370123 and 370153) produced pottery, with sherds of decorated pottery from all three. A radiocarbon date of 3765–3466 cal BC (SUERC-61266) was obtained from charcoal in pit 370153 suggesting the two foci of activity were broadly contemporary.

The plant remains from both of these focal points of activity represented a variety of fruits, including crab apple, and cherry, along with emmer/spelt wheat and barley.

Between the two 'busy' areas occasional discrete features were identified, some anthropogenic, some likely of natural origin. Several contained charcoal-rich fills, and significant proportions of hazelnut shell fragments. Neolithic pottery was recovered from pits 370041, 370043 and 370085. To the east of the structural evidence 14 sherds of Neolithic pottery were found in

pit 370017. In the far north-east corner of the site, some 300m from the central focus, two isolated but nearly conjoined pits were identified. Pit 370019 measured 0.85m in diameter and 0.2m deep, with a flattish base and a lower fill (370021) of an ashy silt with a high charcoal content and a total of 83 Early Neolithic sherds (representing a whole vessel, the remainder derived from at least 10 different vessels) (Fig. 2.5, Section 3). A leaf-shaped arrowhead with a broken tip (Chapter 4.1), along with flint scraper and 13 other flint flakes and chips were recovered from the same fill (Chapter 4.5). The fill was also rich in emmer wheat and other indeterminate grain fragments. This evidence clearly indicates a domestic focus. A radiocarbon date of 3696–3531 cal BC (SUERC-61271) was also obtained from charcoal in this fill, indicating broad contemporaneity with the activity to the south-west. Almost touching pit 370019 was pit 370054, of similar dimensions, with a similar dark grey charcoal-rich lower fill. A total of 47 Early Neolithic sherds come from this feature, again representing a whole vessel, and fragments of others. These pit assemblages are suggestive of structured deposition. A single sherd of Neolithic pottery and a Neolithic polished stone axehead fragment (Chapter 4.5) were recovered from 370006, an isolated posthole some 70m to the west of these pits.

Site 30 (Fig. 2.3)

Five further sub-circular pits (300002, 300005, 300018, 300021 and 300025) averaging 0.22m deep and 0.8m in diameter were identified at the eastern end of Site 30 immediately to the west of the south-western cluster of pits on Site 37. All contained charcoal-flecked clay silt fills and one (300018, Fig. 2.5, Section 2) yielded part of a Neolithic stone axe (Chapter 4.5).

Site 35 (Fig. 2.4)

Four shallow discrete features were identified at the eastern end of the site. The sterility of their silty clay fills and lack of regular form suggest they are of natural origin, possibly tree throws. To the west of this cluster, a concentration of flints was recovered from the subsoil/natural interface. A few were diagnostically Mesolithic/Neolithic, but only a single possibly associated feature was identified, a small pit (350017), which was undated.

2.4 Period 3 Bronze Age: burnt mound and other sites

Evidence of activity thought to date to the Bronze Age has been found at Sites 12, 13, 18, 19, 25, 32, 35, 36, 37 and 44. Dating was derived from characteristic pottery styles and augmented by a series of radiocarbon dates. Many features remain undated, but have been included in this Period on the basis of their similarities and in some cases to their proximity to the dated features. At three sites (25, 37 and 44) radiocarbon dating and a

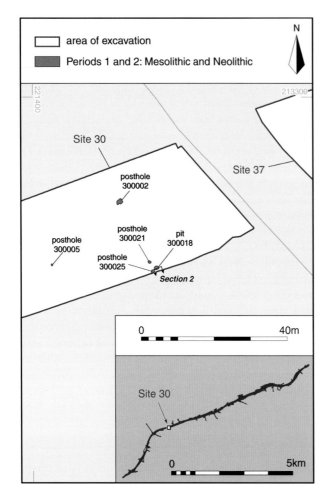

Fig. 2.3   Site 30 Mesolithic and Neolithic: Periods 1 and 2. Scale 1:1000

small corpus of pottery indicated a period of activity dated to the transitional period between the Neolithic and Early Bronze Age periods commonly referred to as the Beaker period (*c.* 2600 BC–1800 BC). At Sites 32 and 44 radiocarbon dating suggests the remains fall within the period known as the Early Bronze Age (*c.* 2400 BC–1500 BC). Activity at Sites 12, 13, 18, 19, 35 and 36 has been assigned a broad Bronze Age date. Sites 18 and 35 each included a feature that could be dated by radiocarbon determinations to within the Middle Bronze Age period (1500 BC–1100 BC) but these dates are not thought to be necessarily indicative of the remaining features at these sites, given the dispersed distribution of the features. These Sites are discussed in geographical order from west to east. The Bronze Age cremation cemetery area (Site 26) is dealt with in Chapter 2.5.

Late Neolithic/Beaker–Early Bronze Age

Site 25 (Fig. 2.6)

A close grouping of eight features – perhaps the remains of a domestic settlement – was identified at the western end of this site, comprising seven pits and a single posthole. Several of the pits were flat-bottomed and undercut (Fig. 2.8, Section 5), suggesting a possible original use for storage, although no pit contained any evidence of a lining. Most contained charcoal and burnt stone inclusions within a yellowish brown silty clay fill, along with charred plant remains, and in four pits (250073, 250079, 250091 and 250093) this was accompanied by Beaker/ Early Bronze Age pottery. The fine grog-tempered fabric

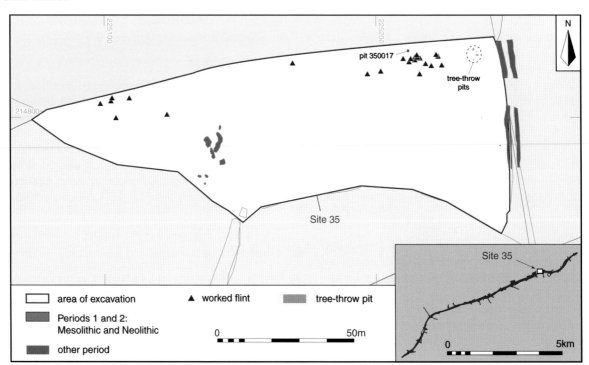

Fig. 2.4   Site 35 Mesolithic and Neolithic: Periods 1 and 2. Scale 1:1250

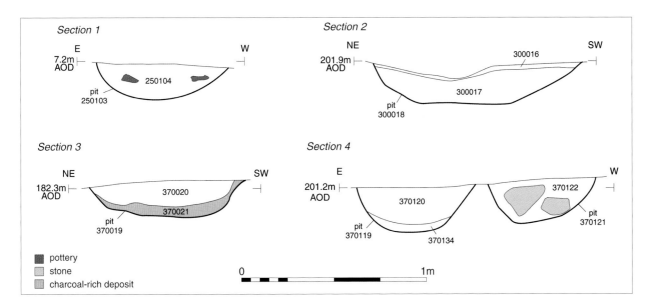

Fig. 2.5   Sites 25, 30 and 37 pit sections Neolithic: Period 2. Scale 1:20

of the pottery is typical of an Early Bronze Age period assemblage, although this date could not be assigned with absolute certainty due to the small size and poor condition of the sherds (Chapter 4.2). A large quantity of charred hazelnut shells, together with a large quantity of barley and indeterminate cereal grains, a smaller amount of emmer/spelt wheat grains, charcoal and a long, thin,

rectangular whetstone (Chapter 4.5, Cat. No. 1) were found in pit 250063. Samples taken from pits 250073 and 250093 both contained moderately abundant hazelnut shells and a small number of barley and indeterminate cereal grains (Chapter 5.3).

Supporting the artefact-based dating, a carbonised hazelnut shell from pit 250063 (fill 250065) produced

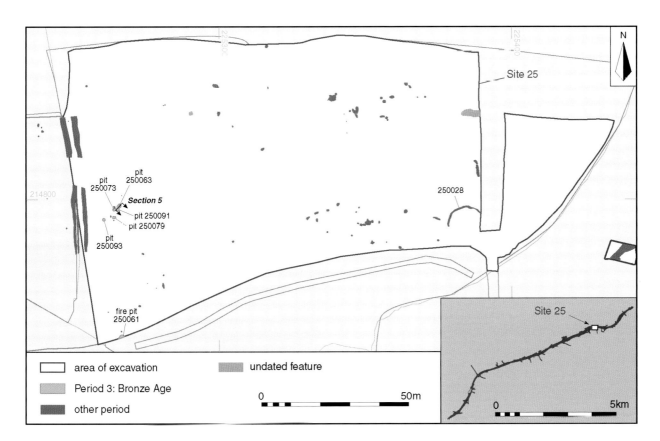

Fig. 2.6   Site 25 Bronze Age: Period 3. Scale 1:1250

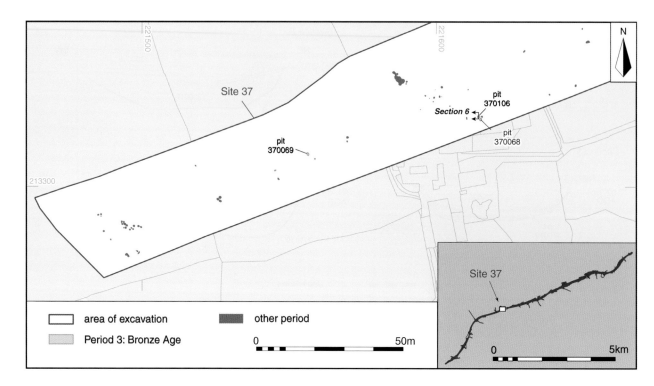

Fig. 2.7   Site 37 Bronze Age: Period 3. Scale 1:1250

an Early Bronze Age date of 2456–2201 cal BC (SUERC-50317).

A possible fire pit (250061) partially exposed at the southern edge of the site, some 40m from the above-mentioned features, produced an appreciably later radiocarbon date of 1948–1766 cal BC (SUERC-61262), indicating a later phase of activity – more contemporary with the Early Bronze Age burial activity described elsewhere.

Over 100m to the east of this activity was a curving gully (250028), including, at its western end, a terminus. The average depth of the gully was 0.12m; its average width was 0.55m. It is possible that the gully may have originally defined a circle of approximately 12m diameter, with an open western entrance, representing a structure or monument. Its fill of greyish brown silty clay was similar to that of the cluster of Neolithic pits that lay on its western side, and on that basis it has been discussed as a possible contemporary feature (Chapter 2.3 above). However structural evidence of this kind is more likely to be of Bronze Age date, but there is no dating evidence to support either interpretation. Interpretation is further discussed in Chapter 6.

Site 37 (Fig. 2.7)
Three pits were identified, two close together, on the southern edge of the site. Pit 370106, measuring 0.75m

Fig. 2.8   (Right) above: Sites 25 and 37 pit sections Bronze Age (Beaker period): Period 3. Scale 1:20. Right below: Site 37 pit 370106. 0.4m scale.

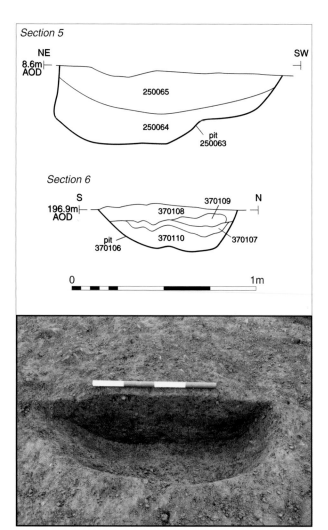

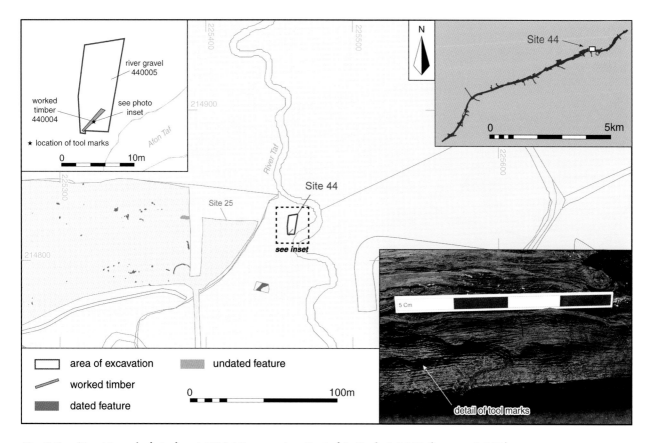

Fig. 2.9   Site 44 worked timber 440004 Bronze Age: Period 3. Scale 1:2500 (inset at 1:500)

long, 0.56m wide and 0.24m deep displayed a sequence of fills (Fig. 2.8, Section 6). Samples from the earliest two contained large amounts of carbonised hazelnut shells, remains of brassica, vetch and false oat-grass seed, along with a fragment of bracken. The second fill (370107) also produced 14 sherds of a single Beaker vessel with twisted cord decoration (Chapter 4.2, P37.9), and one broken flint scraper. The later fills yielded a quantity of carbonised hazelnut shells and barley grain.

Immediately adjacent was pit 370068, which measured 0.87m long, 0.86m wide and 0.33m deep. Both pits contained similar charcoal-flecked silty clay fills. The single fill (370067) of pit 370068 produced no dateable artefacts.

Some 60m to the west a solitary, possibly contemporary pit (370069), measuring 0.62m long, 0.56m wide and 0.33m deep, produced 19 sherds of a single Beaker vessel with twisted cord decoration (Chapter 4.2, P37.10) of a similar date to the pottery from 370106, and a single flint flake.

Site 44 (Fig. 2.9)
A small excavation was carried out on the western bank of the River Taf, immediately to the east of Site 25, to investigate the floodplain stratigraphy and any possible earlier river course development.

Coarse grey gravel (440005) was exposed at a depth of 2m from present ground level, overlain by an orange brown silty clay (440003) layer measuring 1m deep. A further 0.75m layer (440002) of lighter yellowish brown silty clay sealed layer 440003, and the sequence was completed by a 0.25m layer of topsoil.

A worked timber 440004, 3m in length, up to 0.4m in width and 0.2m in thickness, was recovered lying horizontally, and oriented north-east to south-west. This was broadly on the same alignment as the present course of the River Taf at this point, and approximately 5m from the present western bank. The timber was lying at the base of the alluvial clay (440003) at its interface with the gravel (440005). The timber is a half-round log, with one roughly flat face, and several poorly defined tool marks close to one end. A radiocarbon date from the timber obtained a date of 2034–1890 cal BC (SUERC-64559). The function of the timber is currently uncertain. A processed sample of waterlogged river gravel 440005 in association with the timber yielded a large quantity of waterlogged twigs and organic material, including a small number of whole hazelnuts and hazelnut shells.

Early Bronze Age

The burnt mound: Site 32 (Fig. 2.10)
Site 32 was located on gently sloping ground immediately south of the A477 near Red Roses. The western side was adjacent to a watercourse.

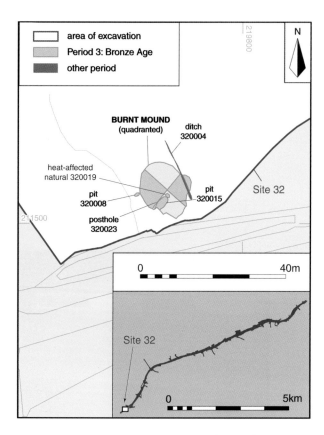

Fig. 2.10   Site 32 Bronze Age: Period 3. Scale 1:1000

Removal of a shallow (*c.* 0.1m) layer of topsoil and the subsoil revealed a sequence of related features, the earliest being two sub-rectangular pits or troughs, both oriented south-west/north-east and situated perpendicular to the line of a north-west/south-east water course. The smallest of these features (320008) measured 1.35m long, 0.85m wide and 0.35m deep, with steep sides and a flat base. No evidence of a puddled clay or wooden lining was noted. Its single fill (320009), which produced no artefactual evidence, was a dark grey silt with a high charcoal content and numerous inclusions of small stones, many reddened by burning. A radiocarbon date on charcoal from this fill produced a date of 1878–1661 cal BC (SUERC-61264). The feature lay close to the western edge of a large sub-circular mound comprising a mix of dark grey sandy silt, charcoal and burnt stone measuring approximately 15m long by 12.3m wide. Initially the southern and northern quadrants (320012 and 320017) of the mound were excavated (Fig. 2.11).

Excavation of the southern quadrant revealed a second trough or oval pit (320015), measuring 3.37m long, 2.17m wide and 0.46m deep, with steep sides and a flat base. As with the smaller trough 320008, no evidence of a lining was revealed. However, a posthole 320023 and a stakehole 320011 (not shown on plan) were revealed on either side of trough 320015, which suggest

Fig. 2.11   Site 32 The burnt mound (quadranted), looking north-west. 2m scale

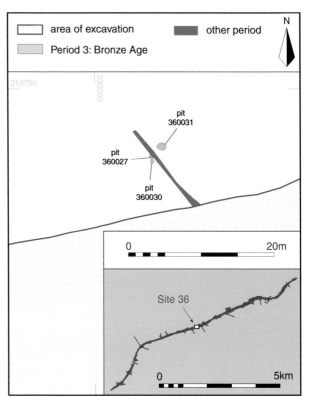

Fig. 2.13   Site 36 Bronze Age: Period 3. Scale 1:500

Fig. 2.12   Site 32 The burnt mound, southern quadrant with trough 320015 and area of burning. 1m scale

some structure associated with its use. Its fill (320016) comprised a similar material to that from trough 320008, a very dark silty clay with a high proportion of charcoal and inclusions of burnt stone. A radiocarbon date from charcoal within this fill produced a date of 1634–1503 cal BC (SUERC-50322), significantly later than that from the smaller trough, suggesting that the activity associated with the mound possibly extended over a considerable period. At the north-eastern end of pit 320015 an area of approximately 1m in diameter (320019) of the underlying silty clay natural was coloured a pinkish red, a legacy of the effects of intense heat (Fig. 2.12). Excavation of the remaining two quadrants did not uncover any other features.

The excavation revealed that the mound material was deposited in three clear episodes. The initial layer (320022) of dark grey silt, charcoal and burnt stone, survived to a maximum depth of 0.34m at the centre of the mound. This was overlaid by a layer of redeposited natural brown silty clay (320021), visible in the section exposed alongside the larger trough 320015, and suggesting that layer 320021 represented the upcast from the excavation of trough 320015. This layer of clay was not present in the rest of the mound

to the south and east. Sealing this upcast was the upper layer of mound material 320020, comprising a layer of charcoal and burnt stone in a silty clay matrix. No artefacts or animal bone evidence was recovered from any part of the mound material, and no other contemporary archaeological features were identified in the vicinity. A later shallow post-medieval boundary ditch cut (320004) across the eastern edge of the mound, but caused minimal damage to the mound structure.

Bronze Age

Site 36 (Fig. 2.13)

A close group of three shallow features (360027, 360030 and 360031) were identified in the eastern part of the site. Pit 360027 measured 0.52m long, 0.2m wide and 0.14m deep. Possible pit or scoop 360030 measured 0.35m long, 0.3m wide and 0.03m deep; pit 360031 measured 1.15m long, 0.95m wide and 0.4m deep. None yielded any dateable artefacts, although all three features contained silty clay fills with numerous burnt stones and charcoal, and pit 360031 also yielded hazelnut shells. The presence of burnt stones, charcoal and hazelnut shells are characteristic inclusions in numerous other pits within the road scheme corridor that contained Bronze Age dating or were in close proximity to features of Bronze Age date, and these features have been tentatively assigned to this period on that basis.

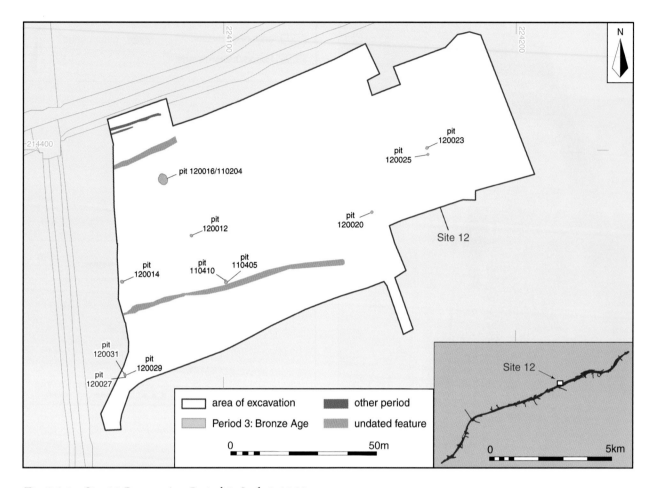

Fig. 2.14   Site 12 Bronze Age: Period 3. Scale 1:1250

Site 12 (Fig. 2.14)

A total of eleven pits on this site have been tentatively ascribed to the Bronze Age period. Two contained dateable pottery described below. The remainder of the pits were undated, but are assumed to be of Bronze Age date because of the similarity of their fills to the features with pottery, and their proximity to features of this date both on this site and Site 18 to the east.

A sub-circular pit 120025, in the eastern part of this area contained a single abraded sherd of potentially Early to Middle Bronze Age pottery, most likely from a Collared Urn (Chapter 4.2). Characteristics of the fill of this pit, namely the presence of charcoal and heat-affected stones were shared with pit 110405 which contained nine undiagnostic sherds of prehistoric pottery. A sample taken from fill 110407 of pit 110405 recovered large amounts of charred hazelnut shell, and a smaller number of brassica-type seeds (Chapter 5.3).

Pit 120016/110204 was an unusually large oval pit, over 3m in length, and up to 0.65m deep, but shared a similar type of silty clay fill to the remainder of the pits, which were of similar size, between 0.7m and 1m in diameter.

Sites 13 and 18 (Figs 2.15, 2.16 and 2.21)

Note: cremation burials and related activity from this area are included within the description of Site 26 (Chapter 2.5)

Approximately 70 pits were scattered along the extent of the plateau that extended approximately 1km westward from the cremation area. The pits appear to represent a continuation of pit-digging activity previously identified within Site 12 (see above), extending southward downslope from the plateau and also eastward to the area of the Early Bronze Age cremation cemetery examined as Site 26 (see below). The pits mostly measured between 0.6m and 1.2m in diameter and averaged approximately 0.5m deep, although some irregular and shallow features were likely to be tree throws. A further 20 postholes and stakeholes were also identified. Little artefactual material was recovered from the pit fills; in the absence of artefactual evidence, the phasing on Site 18 is based upon the similarity of feature fills – typically a mid brown silty clay with stone inclusions, many showing evidence of burning.

Contemporary linear features were not evident, the exception being an amorphous curving linear feature

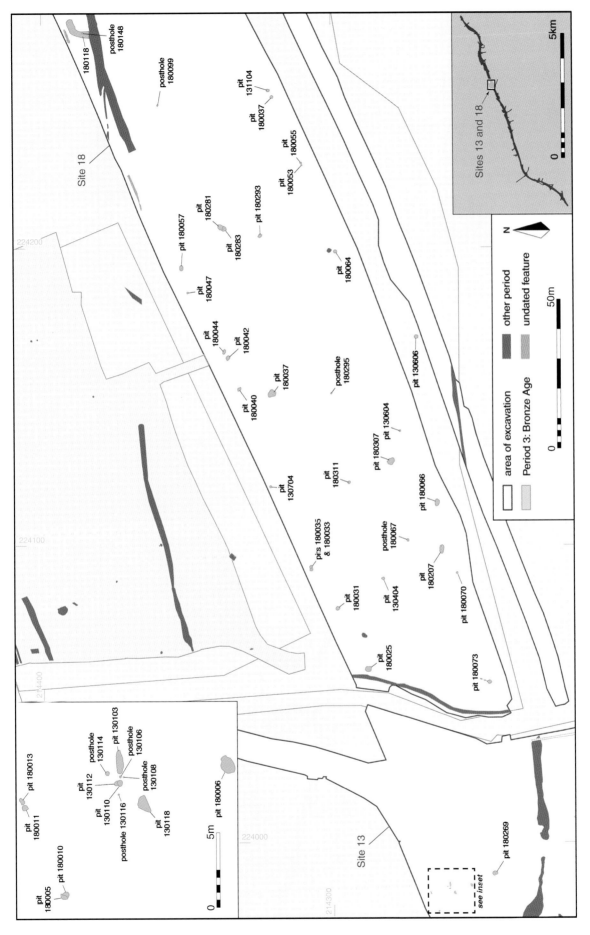

Fig. 2.15   Sites 13 and 18 (west end) Bronze Age: Period 3. Scale 1:1250

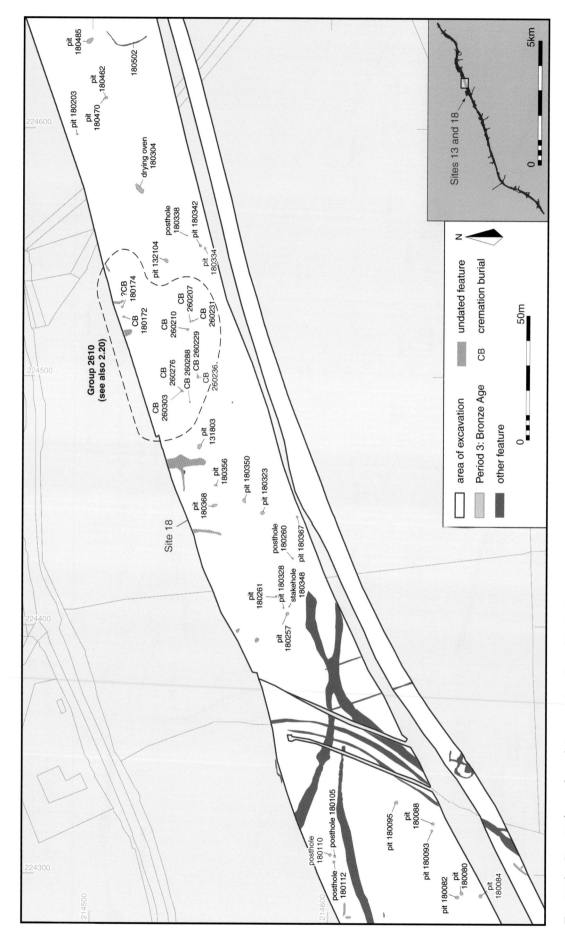

Fig. 2.16   Site 18 (central area) Bronze Age: Period 3. Scale 1:1500

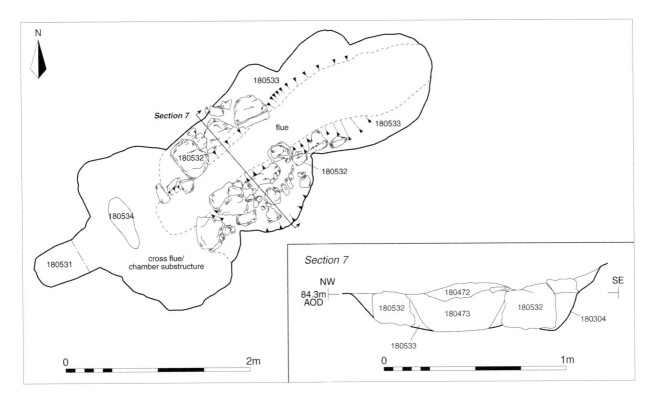

Fig. 2.17   Plan and section 180304 Bronze Age. Scale: plan 1:40, section 1:20

(180118) (Fig. 2.15), cut by an undated posthole 180148 and a later feature, which produced from its upper fill 14 sherds from a rock-tempered vessel that may be of Early Bronze Age date (Chapter 4.2). No clear evidence was found throughout the site of a building, or even a domestic focus, despite several of the

features containing significant inclusions of charcoal or burnt stone. However, a few small groups of features might suggest the presence of a structure – for instance postholes 180110, 180112 and 180105 all displayed stone packing (Fig. 2.16), and four postholes 130106, 130108, 130114 and 130116 found at Site 13 (Fig. 2.15, inset) may denote a structure, although its form could not be determined.

In regards to dating the Bronze Age settlement evidence in the area (excepting the archaeology relating to the burial activity) a significant feature is the stone-lined pit or trough 180304, which may represent the remains of a drying oven (Figs 2.16–2.18). Though clearly heavily truncated and disturbed by ploughing and overburden machining, it survived as a roughly rectangular pit 4.85m long by 1.3m wide, and up to 0.3m deep. The central part of the pit was lined with large stone blocks (180532), and soil backfill (180533) creating a channel approximately 0.5m wide and up to 1.9m long interpreted as a flue. A deposit of ashy silt (180473) filled the centre of the channel. At either end the channel or flue opened out to a shallow hollow. At the south-west end the hollow measured 1.8m by 1.2m, with a projecting patch of compacted grey silt (180531) extending further to the south-west. At the north-east end of the channel, the hollow extended up to 1.5m from the channel, and was up to 1m wide. None of the exposed faces of the stones in the channel were reddened by burning, and yet some of the charcoal recovered from ashy deposit 180473 had been heated

Fig. 2.18   Feature 180304, looking south-west. From bottom to top: scales 0.5m, 0.3m and 1m

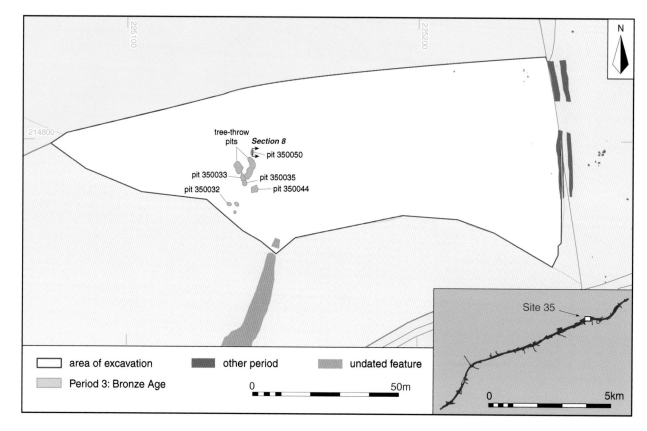

Fig. 2.19   Site 35 Bronze Age: Period 3. Scale 1:1250

to such a high temperature it had a coal-like shine. The charcoal from basal layer 180526 (not shown on plan) indicated that the principal fuel used in the structure was gorse/broom and oak.

From this same basal fill (180526) of the north-east hollow, a radiocarbon date of 1513–1414 cal BC (SUERC-50314) was obtained, suggesting that the structure significantly post-dates the cremation activity – both to the south-west and north-east. No contemporary finds were recovered from the structure, although two intrusive sherds of late 16th to 18th-century pottery were recovered from the upper fill of the north-eastern hollow. While the structure shows close affinities to similar structures of a similar date found in Ireland, themselves interpreted as crop- or corn dryers, there are aspects of this structure which invite a more nuanced interpretation. The function of this structure is considered further in Chapter 6.

Site 19 (Fig. 2.21)

Site 19 was a strip of land to the south of Site 18, stripped for an access road. Five shallow sub-circular pits (190020, 190022, 190111, 190114 and 190117), up to 1.2m long, 0.8m wide and 0.15m deep, were recorded at the eastern end of the site. Burnt stone and charcoal was evident in their fills, but no dating evidence was forthcoming. A sample processed from pit 190111 contained a single barley grain and some brassica-type seeds and pit 190114 a single hazelnut shell. The pits appear to be part of the same pattern of scattered pits found in Site 18.

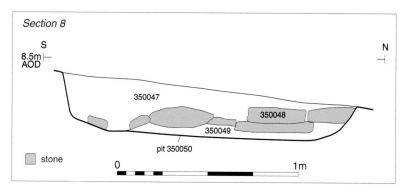

Fig. 2.20   Pit 350050 section. Scale 1:20

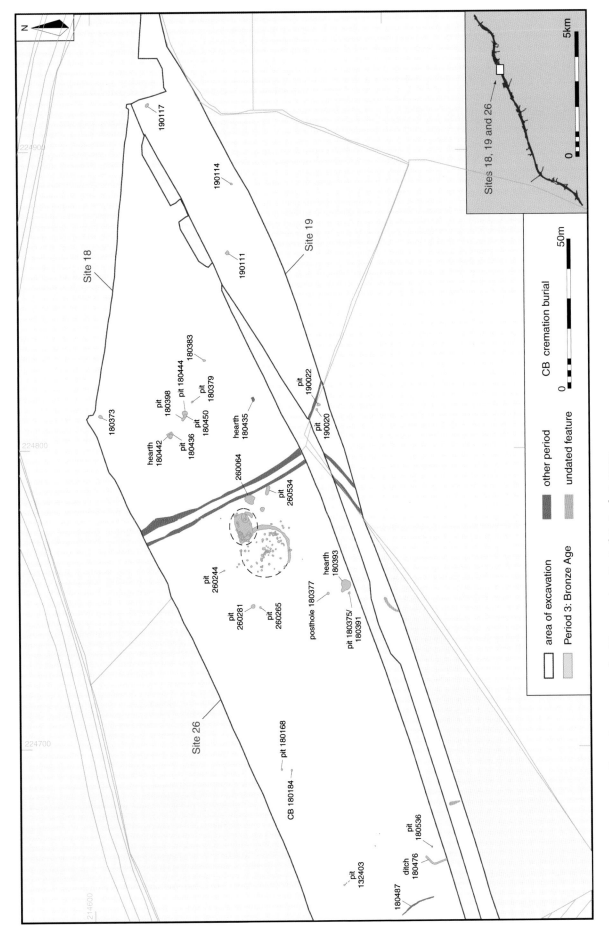

Fig. 2.21   Site 18 (east end), and Sites 19 and 26 Bronze Age: Period 3. Scale 1:1250

Site 35 (Fig. 2.19)

A group of features were identified at the west end of the site; over an area approximately 15m square. In the northern part of this area a number of large features displayed an irregularity which suggested they were of natural origin, perhaps tree throws, but backfilled with material derived from human activity, including burnt stones and charcoal. To the north of these was an elongated oval pit 350050, measuring 1.75m by 0.65m and 0.3m deep with a lower fill 350049 rich in charcoal, above which a number of flat stones appeared to have been deliberately laid horizontally (Fig. 2.20). To the south of these features, three pits (350033, 350044 and 350035) averaged approximately 1.2m in diameter and up to 0.3m deep. All three contained further large quantities of burnt stone and charcoal, and may have an anthropogenic origin. Lying to the south of these a group of three smaller pits also contained high concentrations of charcoal and burnt stone. All the features were filled with a dark grey sandy silt with a high concentration of burnt stone and charcoal identified in samples from pit 350033 as deriving from a mix of wood species including alder, hawthorn, hazel and oak (Chapter 5.3). The fills clearly derive from an activity nearby which included the deliberate or accidental burning of stones, but none of the pits suggested burning *in situ*. No artefactual evidence was recovered from this group

of features, although a radiocarbon date was recovered from charcoal within the fill 350034 of pit 350033, of 1525–1419 cal BC (SUERC-61265).

2.5 Period 3 Bronze Age: cremation cemetery

Site 26 (including related parts of Site 18) (Fig. 2.21)

The focus of burial activity was an area of approximately 500 sq m. This comprises the entirety of Site 26 and most of the eastern part of Site 18, considered here as a single continuous site.

The burial evidence comprised both urned and unurned cremations in individual pits, each belonging to one of three groups:

Group 261: the 'barrow'
Group 268: the 'pyre hollow'
Group 2610: the western group

The disposition of the largest group of these pits (Group 261) initially invited the interpretation that many were either sealed by, or cut through, a round barrow. Close study of the stratigraphy indicated that, due to historical and modern ploughing, any trace of a barrow mound, or a surrounding ditch, would have been almost completely removed. Nevertheless some

Fig. 2.22   Site 26 barrow area from the north after first phase of machining Bronze Age: Period 3. 1m scales

aspects of the evidence do suggest the original presence of a round barrow, possibly with a surrounding ditch (Figs 2.21–2.24).

A further concentration of cremation and burial activity (Group 268) was identified adjacent to the barrow area to the north-east (Figs 2.21, 2.23 and 2.33).

Truncation
The combined depth of topsoil and ploughsoil in this area was reasonably consistent at 0.3–0.4m. However, there was a significant variation in the natural stratigraphy across the area of cremation burials. On Site 26 the natural subsoil (260003) typically was a pale reddish brown silty clay and sand mix, with numerous inclusions of sandstone/limestone rubble derived from the degraded bedrock. After machine removal of the overburden the visibility of discrete features cut into this indistinct horizon was very variable, and heavily dependent on both the light levels and the moisture content of the exposed surface (Fig. 2.22).

The original archaeological horizon exposed on Site 26 was very uneven and disturbed, and had to be lowered by a further 0.1m to ensure that all discrete features were identified. Therefore, although assessing the degree of surface truncation of the site as a whole by

agricultural activity cannot be precisely calculated, the reduction in some of the cremation urns to little more than their bases or rims (depending on their original orientation) gives some archaeological indication of the topography of the cremation burial area at the time of its use as a burial place.

In contrast to the situation on Site 26, the natural below the topsoil and ploughsoil in the north and west of the area (Site 18) was typically intact or only slightly degraded bedrock, with isolated pockets of silty clay and stone fragments. This played a significant part both in the depth and shape of the cremation pits, but also their susceptibility to damage from later ploughing.

The varied character of the landscape stratigraphy and the part it played in aspects of the burial culture here is further considered in Chapter 6.

Chronology and phasing
Radiocarbon dating of selected burials indicated a period from approximately 2000 BC to 1650 BC during which these burials took place. The absence of any stratigraphic relationship between the archaeological remains relating to Groups 261 and 268, and the relative isolation of Group 2610, means that phasing of the burial groups is problematic. However, Bayesian

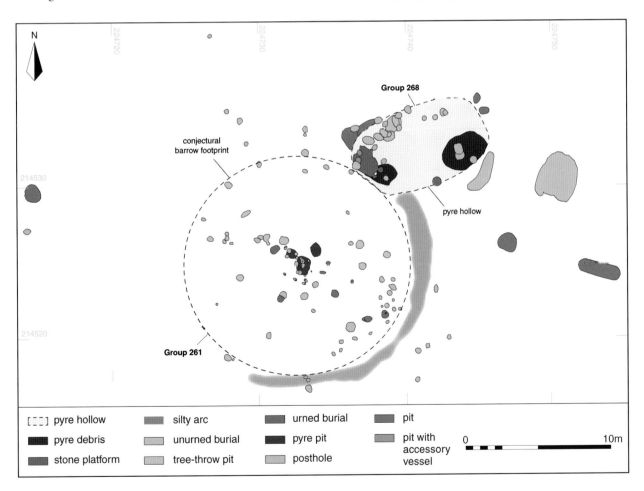

Fig. 2.23   Site 26 barrow Group 261 and pyre hollow Group 268 Bronze Age: Period 3. Scale 1:250

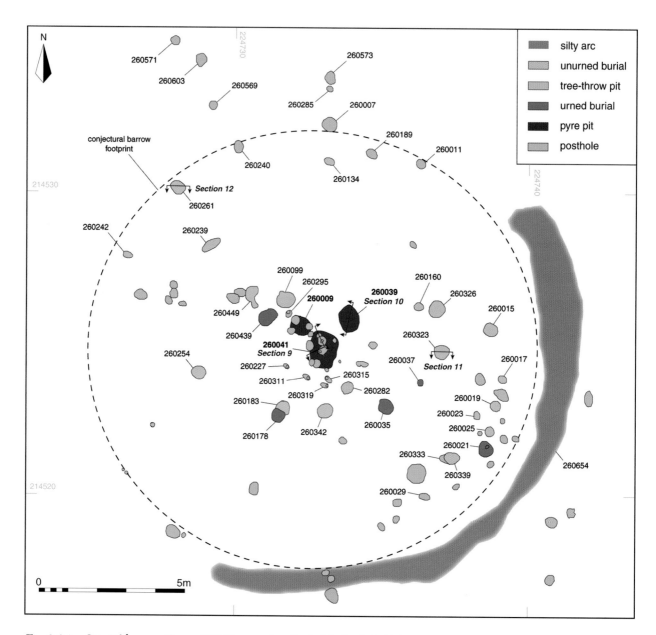

Fig. 2.24   Site 26 barrow Group 261 Bronze Age: Period 3. Scale 1:125

analysis of the calibrated radiocarbon dates suggests that burials in Group 261 began before, and ended after the burials in Group 268 (see Chapter 5.5). The two radiocarbon dates obtained from Group 2610 can only indicate that burials in that group probably took place during the same overall period.

Group 261: the 'barrow'

The focal point of this activity was a group of three closely spaced shallow bowl-shaped pits, 260009, 260041 and 260039 (Figs 2.23 and 2.24). Pit 260009 measured 0.8m long by 0.63m wide by 0.11m deep; pit 260039 measured 1.21m by 1.02m by 0.1m, and pit 260041 measured 1.23m by 0.96m by 0.11m (Fig. 2.26, Sections 9–10). One of the pits (260039) contained a few indeterminate pieces (23.6g) of human bone.

Between them these three pits displayed 16 postholes/ stakeholes (averaging 0.15m in diameter and 0.25m deep) cutting through their fills of grey ashy silt with charcoal inclusions and evidence of burning. One of these features, a posthole (260295) on the north-west side of pit 260009, contained a postpipe and 6.2g of indeterminate and redeposited human bone. In pit 260041, a postpipe (260147) suggests a post, inserted after fill had accumulated in the feature (Fig. 2.26, Section 9). Significantly, the initial mechanical removal of the overburden had made visible two substantial areas of dark grey ashy silt corresponding with the location of these features (Fig. 2.22), suggesting that their upper fills had been considerably more ash- and charcoal-rich. Four further postholes with postpipes were identified immediately to the south of pit 260041 (260227,

Fig. 2.25   Burial 260439. 0.2m scale

260311, 260315 and 260319). It is suggested that the three shallow pits represent a stage in the funerary rite, possibly as pyre pits themselves, or as a place where the newly cremated bones and ash were brought from a pyre elsewhere, here to be separated and deposited in an urn or container, for subsequent burial. The evidence of the postholes and postpipes in and around the three pits suggests perhaps successive construction had taken place of small timber structures directly related to this part of the process, in or over one or more of the three pits.

A swathe of discrete features was identified, extending away from these pits in all directions, but particularly to the east and south-east. These comprised a number of cremation burials (23 in total) and in addition 29 pits and postholes/stakeholes. The eastern edge of this group seemed to follow a south-west/north-east line, and during the initial cleaning of the machined surface a very faint change in surface colour was noted here, defining a possible arc of slightly greyer sandy silt (260654) beyond the limit of the features' extent (Fig. 2.24). There was no depth to this feature, or definable edges, so it cannot represent the surviving base of a ditch, but it is conceivable that if there were a ditch above this point, its silty fill may have percolated down into the loose and friable natural below, leaving an echo of a now completely truncated feature. No trace of such a feature was identified to the north and west of the area, yet, ephemeral though the arc 260654 was, its radius was

Fig. 2.27   Site 26 accessory vessel within cremation pit 260254 Bronze Age: Period 3. 0.1m scale

fairly constant, and suggests a radial centre point at, or very close to the three pyre pits described above.

Spreading to the west and north-west of this arc, a slightly greyer colour was noted in the machined archaeological horizon. Again, this was initially interpreted as the remains of a barrow mound, but the truncation of the site must have removed all trace of a mound; it is most likely that later and modern disturbance of the site incorporated the ashy material in the upper layers of the three pits in the centre of the area (see above) into the surrounding area.

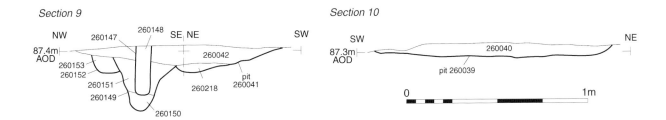

Fig. 2.26   Site 26 sections of north-west quadrant of pit 260041 and pit 260039 Bronze Age: Period 3. Scale 1:20

Fig. 2.28   Site 26 cremations 260178 and 260183 with urn and packing Bronze Age: Period 3. 0.3m scale

An urned cremation (260439) was identified immediately west of the three pits (Figs 2.24 and 2.25). The urn was inverted and set within a vertically sided flat-bottomed pit (measuring 0.35m in diameter by 0.25m deep) with redeposited natural backfilling the pit. Although the base of the urn was slightly truncated by post-burial activity, the quantity of bone recovered was the third highest (at 986.5g) of the burials in the area. The bone produced a radiocarbon date of 2022–1882 cal BC (SUERC-50367), the earliest date obtained from all the cremation burials on the site, and suggests this may have been the primary burial, at least in this group. Sufficient bone was recovered to establish that the burial was that of a mature or elderly woman suffering from joint degeneration.

To the south-west a single cremation pit (260254) was located, measuring 0.5m in diameter and 0.24m deep. It contained an unurned burial of an adult, under an upper sealing layer of stone rubble, along with an inverted accessory vessel (Fig. 2.27; Chapter 4.2, P26.20). A radiocarbon date of 1887–1697 cal BC (SUERC-61119) was obtained from the bone.

To the north two unurned cremations were located (260099 and 260449). The former, in a pit measuring 0.5m in diameter and 0.4m deep, was covered by a shale stone cap (one of two visible on Fig. 2.22, nearest to camera), and contained 77.6g bone from a young adult. The latter was very shallow (presumably truncated), measuring 0.3m in diameter and 0.09m deep and yielding only a small quantity (4.6g) of human skull fragments.

To the south of burial 260439 were two unurned burials (260342 and 260183). The former, in a pit measuring 0.39m in diameter and 0.25m deep, contained 344.5g of adult bone, and a radiocarbon date from the bone returned a date of 2022–1782 cal BC (SUERC-61118). Burial 260183 contained 670.6g of the bones of an adult, contained within a pit measuring 0.45m in diameter and 0.39m deep, and sealed by a flat limestone slab (visible on Fig. 2.22, furthest from camera). Slightly truncating the south side of the burial pit was an urned burial 260178, containing a virtually complete upright vessel (Fig. 2.28; Chapter 4.2, P26.6), in a pit measuring 0.35m in diameter and 0.32m deep, with stone packing placed in the top to seal the 73.2g of bone from an individual that had possibly not reached adulthood (Fig. 2.28). A fragment of the rim of another vessel (Chapter 4.2, P26.2) was also found within the urn.

To the east two more urned burial pits were located (260035 and 260037), the former, a pit measuring 0.5m in diameter and 0.3m deep, containing an inverted vessel, slightly truncated (Fig. 3.3; Chapter 4.2, P26.5).

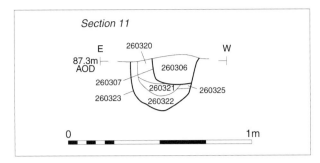

Fig. 2.29 Site 26 features 260207 and 260323 Bronze Age: Period 3. Scale 1:20

Burial 260037, a heavily truncated pit measuring 0.28m in diameter and 0.11m deep, contained an upright vessel, of which only the base remained (Fig. 3.4, Chapter 4.2, P26.17). The former contained 1183.4g of the bones of an adult female; the latter, because of its truncation, yielded only 0.7g of very small and undiagnostic bone fragments.

To the north of these features, three unurned cremation burials were located (260323, 260015 and 260326). Two were of adults: burial 260015, in a pit measuring 0.45m in diameter and 0.2m deep, contained 189.2g of adult bone; burial 260326 contained 343.3g of the bones of an older adult in a pit measuring 0.49m by

0.3m deep. Burial 260323, comprising a pit measuring 0.38m in diameter and 0.31m deep containing 144.9g of bone, may have been a non-adult. These particular bones returned a radiocarbon date of 1869–1628 cal BC (SUERC-61273). A notable characteristic of this burial was a small pit (260307) cut into the upper fill of pit 260323, possibly representing the setting of a grave marker (Fig. 2.29, Section 11). Finally, unurned burial 260160, located to the west of burial 260326 and measuring 0.38m in diameter and 0.25m deep, contained 386.5g of the bones of a 4 to 12-year-old child.

To the east, and forming part of the arc of features that appeared to define the eastern edge of the 'barrow', were four more truncated and unurned cremation burials, three of adults (260023, 260017 and 260025) and one of an infant over one year old (260019) (Fig. 2.24). Burial 260017, a pit measuring 0.4m in diameter and 0.16m deep contained 82.9g of adult bones, along with fragments of an accessory vessel (Chapter 4.2, P26.24). Burials 260023 and 260025 contained 23.2g of adult bones and 944.1g older male bones in pits measuring 0.26m in diameter and 0.25m deep, and 0.33m in diameter and 0.26m deep respectively. Immediately to the south of these was a pit (260021), containing an urned burial, surviving as an upright bowl-like vessel, surrounded by packing stones in a pit measuring 0.38m

Fig. 2.30 Site 26 cremation 260339 Bronze Age: Period 3. 0.3m scale

in diameter and 0.36m deep (Fig. 3.2; Fig. 4.6, P26.3). The burial comprised 264.4g of non-adult bones, which produced a radiocarbon date of 1744–1560 cal BC (SUERC-61275). The backfill into the pit was a mix of charcoal and ashy silt, suggesting it may have been part of the pyre debris itself. The cremation pit cut an earlier stakehole (260187), possibly a setting for a marker.

To the south-west, an unurned cremation (260339) was located, comprising a pit measuring 0.35m in diameter and 0.36m deep containing a small stone cist fashioned from unworked pieces of sandstone, constructed to contain the bones (Fig. 2.30), the whole being sealed with stone rubble. The quantity of bone recovered (of an adult male) from the cist was the second-heaviest of all the burials, 1650.5g. Given that no fragments of bone were found below the floor of the cist, this suggests that the cremation bone was possibly placed within a bag before deposition in the cist. Cutting into the west side of the cremation pit was a possible setting for a grave marker (260333). The stones on the west side of the cist had collapsed slightly into the fill of this feature, presumably as the post rotted away.

Among these urned and unurned cremations along the east side of the barrow were several small sub-circular features, typically approximately 0.2m in diameter and between 0.1m and 0.15m deep (Fig. 2.24). They did not appear to form any regular line, and may represent postholes for individual grave markers, although none appeared to be directly adjacent to any identified burial. Several similar small and shallow features were located outside the silty arc 260654 to the east.

One further truncated oblong pit was located to the south-west (260029), measuring 0.3m long, 0.17m wide and 0.11m deep, containing sherds of an accessory vessel (SS26002) (Chapter 4.2, P26.21), along with significant plant remains. These yielded a radiocarbon date of 1771–1623 cal BC (SUERC-61282). On the western edge of the barrow footprint a possible cremation burial 260242 was located, as a severely truncated pit (measuring 0.25m in diameter and 0.12m deep) yielding just 17.5g of probably adult bone.

A total of three unurned cremations were located to the north-west of the centre point of the 'barrow', although there was no clear indication that their placement respected a perimeter, as was the case on

the east side. A unurned burial (of an adult) in an oblong pit (260239), measuring 0.75m long, 0.35m wide and 0.24m deep, was located approximately 3m from the centre of the barrow. The charcoal and silty clay backfill of the pit was sealed by a packing layer of stone rubble. A radiocarbon date of 1943–1763 cal BC (SUERC-61274) was obtained from a sample of the 936.7g cremated adult male bone. To the north-west another sub-circular pit (260261), measuring 0.52m in diameter and 0.18m deep which was clearly substantially truncated, but nevertheless contained at least part (202.4g) of an unurned burial of an adult (Fig. 2.31).

Four more small and shallow pits were identified extending to the north-west (260240, 260569, 260603 and 260571). While charcoal traces were found in their fills, none showed any trace of human bone, so cannot be confidently interpreted as cremation burials. To the east of these five further small pits or postholes were located (260573, 260285 and 260007, 260189 and 260011), and one unurned cremation burial (260134), in a pit measuring 0.36m in diameter and 0.22m deep, containing 463.5g of the bones of a probable male adult.

Two more related features were identified: the first, a small pit (260244), approximately 5m further to the north, well beyond the area of the possible barrow. Measuring 0.3m in diameter and 0.11m deep, it yielded less than 1g human bone from the pit backfill, but contained an upright slightly truncated accessory vessel (Chapter 4.2, P26.14), which itself contained no human bone at all (Figs 2.21 and 2.32). The second was a large tree-throw pit (260064) which contained the sherds of an accessory vessel (Chapter 4.2, P26.22). It is possible that the disturbance caused by the tree had destroyed an earlier pit.

Finds associated with the cremation burials

Grave goods
With the single exception of the ceramic beads and copper-alloy awl fragments from cremation burial 180172, in Group 2610, the only grave goods recovered were accessory vessels. These were found, some inverted, some upright – some intact on deposition, some clearly fragmentary. These are described in more detail in Chapter 4.2 below.

Charcoal from the burial pits
The charcoal from a total of 16 cremation burials and a number of other pits and postholes across the entire area of cremation activity (Sites 18 and 26) was analysed, revealing that the range of species exploited was relatively narrow, consisting predominantly of oak, with smaller quantities of alder/hazel, hazel, cherry species and blackthorn also recorded (see Chapter 5.3 for further details).

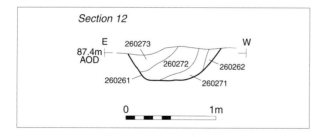

Fig. 2.31 Site 26 cremation pit 260261 Bronze Age: Period 3. Scale 1:40

Charred plant remains in significant quantities and species were found in only two burials; burial 260254

Fig. 2.32   Site 26 pit 260244 and accessory vessel Bronze Age: Period 3. 0.3m scale

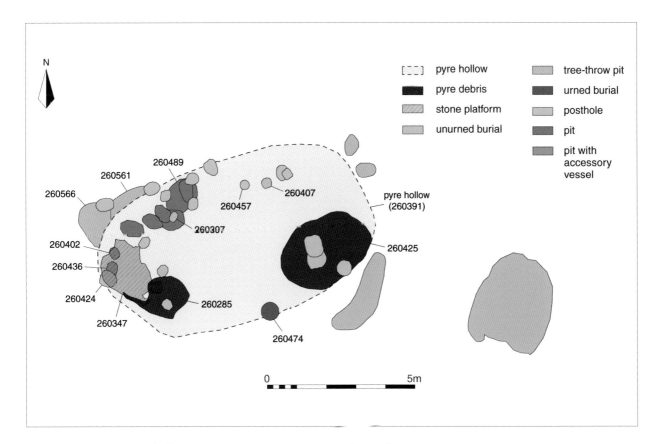

Fig. 2.33   Site 26 pyre hollow Group 268 Bronze Age: Period 3. Scale 1:125

produced a quantity of sloe pips from within the accessory vessel accompanying the cremation, along with hazelnut shells, grass stems, culm node, straw, an indeterminate cereal grain fragment, and a cleavers seed. Burial 180172 yielded (from its inverted accessory vessel) hazelnut shells, an acorn cup, a crab apple pip, cherry species pip fragments, a large number of grass stems and roots and a small amount of vitrified material which has been tentatively identified as fruit flesh. These are potentially the remains of food or plants placed on the pyre along with the body, although they could equally represent accidental/intentional inclusions of fruit and nuts still attached to branches used for the pyre. However they do indicate the season of the pyre as summer, when these fruits are available (see Chapter 5.3).

Group 268: the 'pyre hollow' (Figs 2.33 and 2.34)

Immediately north of the barrow footprint, a substantial but poorly defined oval feature was identified (260391), measuring approximately 8.5m by 4.3m, and up to 0.3m deep. It appeared to be a hollow, possibly originating as one or more tree throws, or possibly a quarry for material for the barrow to the south, and then evolving as the site of repeated and varied burial-related activity, including the possible preparation and use of cremation pyres, and the burial of four, or possibly five, completed cremations (one feature was severely truncated), with posthole evidence suggesting associated grave markers and/or funerary structures.

The earliest features identified were three inter-cutting shallow pits (260566, 260561 and 260456), the largest (260561) measuring 1.85m long, 1.44m wide and 0.66m deep. Each was filled with silty clay and mudstone fragments, and possibly represent tree throws, or small quarry pits. A few hazelnut fragments were recovered from fill 260553 of pit 260561, yielding an Early Bronze Age radiocarbon date of 1930–1755 cal BC (SUERC-61280).

Concentrations of charcoal suggestive of pyre debris were found at the eastern end of the hollow (260425), and at the western end (260285). While the centre of the hollow remained clear of features, other than spreads of charcoal, the perimeter of feature 260391 became defined by a scatter of postholes, pits and four cremation burials. One of the larger features, oval pit 260489, contained a fill (260490) of mid brown silty clay which yielded a small quantity of redeposited human bone, and a fragment of hazel charcoal which produced a radiocarbon date of 1880–1688 cal BC (SUERC-61281). Some of the small circular features contained charcoal-rich fills, like 260457 on the north side of feature 260391, but no trace of bone. It is reasonable to interpret them as postholes relating to pyre structures, rather than cremation burials themselves.

None of the cremations contained any grave goods or dateable artefacts other than (where present) an urn or an accessory vessel. The radiocarbon dating of these cremations suggests the activity fell within the same period as that of the barrow to the south.

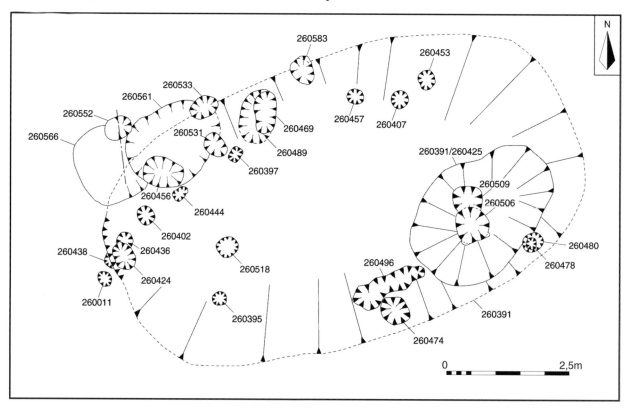

Fig. 2.34   Site 26 detail of pyre hollow after excavation Bronze Age: Period 3. Scale 1:75

On the southern edge of hollow 260391, pit 260474 contained an untruncated and inverted urn (Chapter 4.2, P26.8) containing a burial of an older adult male weighing 1795.2g. Towards the opposite edge of the hollow unurned burial 260407 was located, which comprised 739.7g of an older adult. A radiocarbon date of 1946–1771 cal BC (SUERC-50368) was obtained from the bone.

To the west, cut into the fill of an earlier pit, was a truncated possible unurned burial pit (260397) measuring 0.6m in diameter and 0.3m deep, containing approximately 5g of adult bone. Further west, pit 260402, measuring 0.4m in diameter and 0.16m deep, contained a fragmented accessory vessel (Chapter 4.2, P26.10) and just 5g of (probably infant) bone. Close by, unurned burial 260424 contained 361g of adult bones within a pit measuring 0.45m in diameter and 0.26m deep, from which was obtained a radiocarbon date of 2017–1777 cal BC (SUERC-61120). Cut into the northern edge of pit 260424, and possibly part of the same burial rite, was a small pit (260436), containing an inverted accessory vessel (Fig. 2.36; Chapter 4.2, P26.11).

Several small shallow pits or postholes were identified (Fig. 2.33) within the extrapolated perimeter of the hollow; while some contained charcoal-rich dark silty fills, and were thus provisionally considered as possible cremation burials, none produced meaningful quantities (i.e. more than 0.1g) of bone to confirm this interpretation. They appear to have been (as were the other shallow pits described above), evidence of burial-related features. They may have been postholes for above-ground structures, or linked to the cremation rite, perhaps as small pits in which to deposit pyre debris.

Sealing the cremation burial 260424 and the adjacent accessory vessel pits 260436 and 260402, along with the western part of the charcoal and ash layer 260285, was a layer or platform measuring approximately 1.9m by 1.2m formed of large unworked limestone slabs (260347) (Figs 2.33 and 2.35). No clear evidence of arrangement or structure was evident, although later disturbance by ploughing must have taken place. The possible function of this feature is considered in Chapter 6.

A mixed deposit (260364) of silty clay and coarse sand, with inclusions of mudstone fragments and flecks of charcoal was recorded as filling the hollow of feature 260391. A monolith (260306) taken from the stratigraphy of the deposits filling the feature suggests there was no hiatus while the hollow remained open (see Chapter 5.4). This suggests that either the hollow was levelled out and infilled with possibly redeposited material in one operation, or that the sides of the hollow eroded rapidly to fill the space.

Group 2610: cremations west of the barrow area

A number of cremations were found to the west of the barrow area; the nearest single cremation was approximately 60m away (Fig. 2.21), the remainder at a distance

Fig. 2.35   Site 26 limestone slabs 260347 Bronze Age: Period 3. 1m scales

Fig. 2.36   Site 26 accessory vessel buried in pit 260436 alongside cremation pit 260424 Bronze Age: Period 3. 0.2m scale

of 200m to the south-west (Fig. 2.16). The single unurned cremation (180184), 60m west of the 'barrow' was deposited in a pit measuring 0.5m in diameter and 0.12m deep. A solitary shallow pit (180168) was located approximately 5m to the north. It contained a signif- icant amount of charcoal in its silty clay fill, suggesting an associate function to the cremation burial 180184.

A scatter of nine further cremations were identified some 200m south-west of the 'barrow', in an area of approximately 1200 sq m (Fig. 2.16). Six of the crema- tions were contained in urns (two inverted), the rest inserted in small pits. All the urns, whether upright or inverted, had suffered truncation by historical or modern ploughing, as had the unurned burials, and the weights of surviving human bone reflect that. No evidence of a barrow or other funerary structure was identified in the area and there was no suggestion in the cremations' distribution of a focal point for the group, although there may have been a feature to the north or south of the excavated strip which would explain the choice of location. The burials were widely spaced, but notably six of the cremations were located in pairs.

The most northerly located within the confines of the excavated area was unurned cremation burial 180172, in a shallow pit measuring 0.44m in diameter and 0.17m deep. Within the pit was also placed an accessory vessel

(Chapter 4.2, P18.1) along with five ceramic beads and two fragments of a copper-alloy awl (Chapter 4.3; Figs 4.13 and 4.14). The cremated bone weighed 176.2g in total and represented an adult burial and a sample of bone was radiocarbon dated 1948–1766 cal BC (SUERC-61255). A shallow scoop close by (180174), contained a dark grey very charcoal-rich silt; this was possibly a heavily truncated cremation (although no bone remained), or may have had a function associated with the burial process.

Approximately 23m to the south lay one of the pairs of burials (260207 and 260231), both urned and located within 0.8m of each other, both placed in shallow and severely truncated pits dug into the degraded bedrock of the area. The former, in a pit measuring 0.49m in diameter and 0.11m deep, contained the rim of an inverted urn, containing 141.3g of the bones of an adult female (Fig. 3.6; Chapter 4.2, P26.7). The latter contained the base of an upright urn containing 442.1g of the bones of a probable adult female, all contained within a pit measuring 0.39m in diameter and 0.11m deep (Fig. 3.9; Chapter 4.2, P26.18).

Four metres to the west of 260207 and 260231 was urned burial 260210, surviving in a shallow pit measuring 0.6m diameter and 0.1m deep cut into the degraded bedrock, containing 725.8g of the bones of an adult probable male, contained within the shattered (but complete) remains of an urn (Fig. 3.7; Chapter 4.2, P26.9). A radiocarbon date of 2020–1779 cal BC (SUERC-61122) was obtained from the bone.

Approximately 20m to the west of 260210, a second pair of burials were located (260229 and 260236), both surviving as shallow pits (measuring 0.45m in diameter and 0.19m deep, and 0.45m in diameter and 0.09m deep respectively) cut into the degraded bedrock. The former was contained within the remains of a shattered upright urn (Fig. 3.8; Chapter 4.2, P26.12), comprising 355.3g bone of a probable male adult. The latter was unurned, and produced 71.6g of bone of an older adult.

The third pair of burials (260276 and 260303) was situated some 8m to the north-west of the second pair and *c*. 3m from cremations 260207 and 260231. Both were contained in shallow pits cut into the degraded bedrock. Burial 260276 survived as 746.3g of the bones of an older female adult, within the lower part of an upright urn (Fig. 3.10; Chapter 4.2, P26.15) in a pit measuring 0.36m in diameter by 0.21m deep. Burial 260303 was unurned and consisted of 493.2g of the bones of an adult probable male, contained within a pit measuring 0.8m in diameter and 0.14m deep.

Approximately five metres to the south-west of the third pair was a very shallow (less than 0.06m deep and 0.21m in diameter) hollow in the bedrock (260288) from which was recovered 4.7g of indeterminate human bone. Charcoal flecks were noted in the fill, so it could represent an extremely truncated and unurned cremation burial, although it may more probably be the result of bone from another cremation nearby being dragged, by ploughing, into a natural hollow.

Other possible cremation-related activity (Fig. 2.21)
Two possible hearth sites were identified in proximity to the 'barrow'. Hearth 180442 approximately 50m north-east of the 'barrow', survived as a carefully set layer of burnt stone with raised edges around the side. The structure (measuring 1.9m long, 0.97m wide and 0.19m deep) was set on an accumulation of the remnants of previous hearths, seemingly periodically dug up and reset as required, the whole originally constructed in a pit (180436). No finds were recovered from any of the fills, and charcoal was not common except in the matrix of the upper layer of burnt stones.

Approximately 20m south-west of the 'barrow' area a second hearth was identified (180393), surviving as an oval setting of burnt stones surrounded by the remnants of a stone kerb, the whole measuring 1.6m long and 1.1m wide. Adjacent to the west side of this feature was a small pit from which eight undiagnostic worked flint flakes were recovered. A single posthole (180377) was located nearby.

Although these hearths are possibly related to the cremation activity, they do not contain dateable material and it is also possible that these features date to activity of

a different period. It may be pertinent to note that a third feature resembling a hearth (180435) approximately 30m to the south of hearth 180442 returned a radiocarbon date of the early 11th to early 13th century AD.

2.6 Periods 4 and 5 Post-Bronze Age and undated features: a summary

Archaeological evidence of activity along the road corridor of a later date than the Bronze Age was sporadic. Evidence for Roman activity was extremely sparse; the majority of dating came from the medieval and post-medieval periods. Aside from a single concentrated focus of occupation to the north of Red Roses (Site 31), and a scatter of medieval pits and post-medieval field

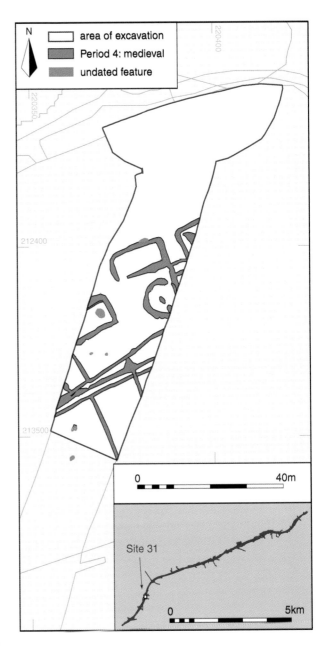

Fig. 2.37   Site 31 medieval: Period 4. Scale 1:1000

boundaries along the route, most of the activity was concentrated at the eastern end of the road scheme to the north of Llanddowror at Sites 18, 19 and 41. Just to the south-west of St Clears lies the Dolgarn Moated Site (Site 17) where medieval dating was obtained. The sites of the most notable post-Bronze Age and undated features are summarised here, ordered from west to east along the road corridor. A fuller report on these findings will be published in the journal *Archaeology in Wales* (Hart and Alexander forthcoming).

Site 31 (Fig. 2.37)

Approximately 0.7km north of Red Roses, a cluster of ditches and robbed-out foundation trenches indicate the location of a farmstead, comprising at least two rectangular houses and one circular structure situated close to the buildings, with a network of associated paddock and field ditches extending to the south-east. Pottery from the features gave a date range of the 13th to the 14th centuries AD. An assemblage of charred plant remains from the ditch of the circular structure provides information on diet, crop processing and the local environment of the farmstead.

Site 27

Part of a large enclosure was revealed within the excavated area, which yielded a Roman radiocarbon date but no other dating evidence. A scatter of largely undated ditches suggest agricultural exploitation of the high ground overlooking the River Taf, probably of medieval or post-medieval date. A single pit yielded two sherds of 12th to 14th-century pottery.

Sites 18 and 19

A scatter of field boundary ditches were identified with a confluence of them south of Pentrehowell Farm, and a nearby small ditch hollow and possible wall foundation yielding 12th to 16th-century pottery. Further east an isolated sub-rectangular enclosure that may have been a sheepfold was dated by pottery to the 12th to 16th century AD. Some later post-medieval ditches were identified, which could be related to boundaries marked on the 1888 OS map. Towards the west end of Site 18 charcoal from an isolated pit returned a radiocarbon date of cal AD 387–537 (SUERC-50313).

Site 41

Within a woodland that fringes the sharp slope down to the floodplain, a large ditched and banked enclosure was revealed by LiDAR and photographic survey. Part of the bank was revetted by a drystone wall. No dating

was recovered from the feature, and it does not appear on any map; it is likely to have had an agricultural function.

Site 17 (Fig. 2.38)

Excavation of the southern part of the Dolgarn Scheduled Monument revealed a large surrounding ditch (170024); radiocarbon dating from the basal fill of the ditch (cal AD 1059–1263 (SUERC-50312)) indicated that it was dug in the 11th–13th centuries AD. Other dating from the subsoil indicated a 13th to 14th-century date, although there was no indication of significant occupation of the enclosure in any period. No prehistoric or Romano-British evidence was found to support an earlier construction date for the monument.

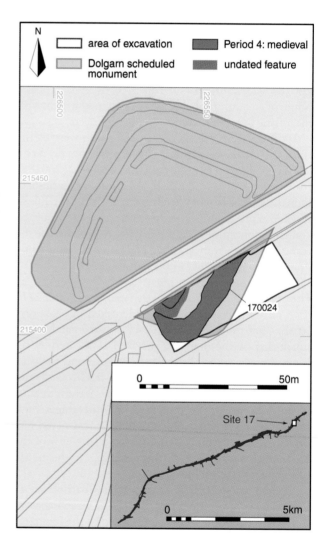

Fig. 2.38   Site 17 medieval: Period 4. Scale 1:1250

Chapter 3
Cremation Burial Catalogue

(dimensions: diameter × depth)
Ra. = registered artefact

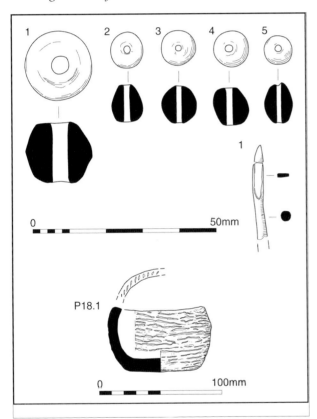

Fig. 3.1   Burial 180172. Scale 1:1 and 1:3

Burial 180172 Site 18 (Group 2610); Fig. 3.1
Grave: Unurned, truncated. 0.44m × 0.17m.
Cremated bone total weight: 176.2g.
Age/sex/pathology: Adult.
Artefacts: Five ceramic beads (Fig. 4.14), two copper-alloy awl fragments (Fig. 4.13), accessory vessel Ra. 18.01 (Fig. 4.2, P18.1).
C14 dating: 1948–1766 cal BC (SUERC-61255; 3534 + 30 yr BP).

Burial 180184 Site 18 (Group 2610)
Grave: Unurned. 0.5m × 0.12m.
Cremated bone total weight: 162.9g.
Age/sex/pathology: Adult.
Artefacts: None.
C14 dating: None.

Burial 260015 Site 26 (Group 261)
Grave: Unurned, truncated. 0.45m × 0.2m.
Cremated bone total weight: 189.2g.
Age/sex/pathology: Adult.
Artefacts: None.
C14 dating: None.

Burial 260017 Site 26 (Group 261)
Grave: Unurned, truncated. 0.4m × 0.16m.
Cremated bone total weight: 82.9g.
Age/sex/pathology: Adult.
Artefacts: Accessory vessel SS26009 (P26.24).
C14 dating: None.

Burial 260019 Site 26 (Group 261)
Grave: Unurned. 0.29m × 0.21m.
Cremated bone total weight: 31.7g.
Age/sex/pathology: Child over 1 year.
Artefacts: None.
C14 dating: None.

Burial 260021 Site 26 (Group 261); Fig. 3.2
Grave: Urned. 0.38m × 0.36m.
Cremated bone total weight: 264.4g.
Age/sex/pathology: Non-adult.
Artefacts: Urn Ra. 1 (Fig. 4.6, P26.3).
C14 dating: 1744–1560 cal BC (SUERC-61275; 3363± 30 yr BP).

Burial 260023 Site 26 (Group 261)
Grave: Unurned, truncated. 0.26m × 0.25m.
Cremated bone total weight: 23.2g.
Age/sex/pathology: Adult.
Artefacts: None.
C14 dating: None.

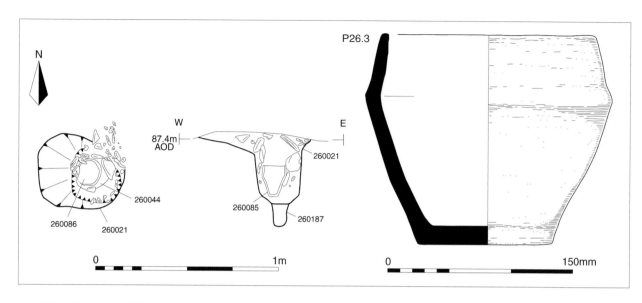

Fig. 3.2   Burial 260021. Scale 1:20 and 1:3

Burial 260025 Site 26 (Group 261)
Grave: Unurned. 0.33m × 0.26m.
Cremated bone total weight: 944.1g.
Age/sex/pathology: Older adult, ?male.
Artefacts: None.
C14 dating: None.

Burial 260035 Site 26 (Group 261); Fig. 3.3
Grave: Urned. 0.5m × 0.3m.
Cremated bone total weight: 1183.4g.
Age/sex/pathology: Older adult, ?female.
Artefacts: Urn Ra. 5 (Figs 4.4 and 4.6, P26.5).
C14 dating: 2011–1774 cal BC (SUERC-61276; 3555 ± 30 yr BP).

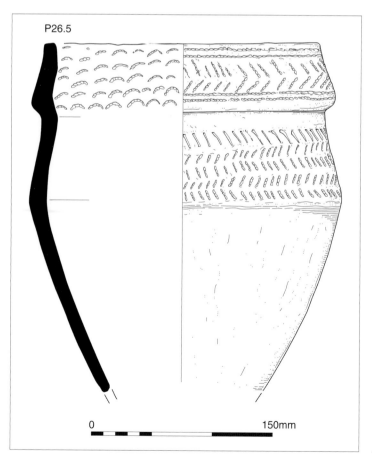

Fig. 3.3   Burial 260035. Scale 1:3

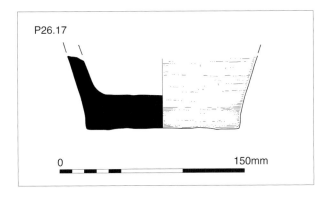

P26.17

0   150mm

Fig. 3.4   Burial 260037. Scale 1:3

Burial 260037 Site 26 (Group 261); Fig. 3.4
Grave: Urned, truncated. 0.28m × 0.11m.
Cremated bone total weight: 0.7g.
Age/sex/pathology: Indeterminate.
Artefacts: Urn Ra. 6 (Fig. 4.11, P26.17).
C14 dating: None.

Burial 260099 Site 26 (Group 261)
Grave: Unurned. 0.5m × 0.4m.
Cremated bone total weight: 77.6g.
Age/sex/pathology: 18–20 years.

Artefacts: Shale stone capping.
C14 dating: None.

Burial 260134 Site 26 (Group 261)
Grave: Unurned, truncated. 0.36m × 0.22m.
Cremated bone total weight: 463.5g.
Age/sex/pathology: Adult, ?male.
Artefacts: None.
C14 dating: None.

Burial 260160 Site 26 (Group 261)
Grave: Unurned. 0.38m × 0.25m.
Cremated bone total weight: 386.5g.
Age/sex/pathology: 4–12 years.
Artefacts: None.
C14 dating: None.

Burial 260178 Site 26 (Group 261); Figs 2.29 and 3.5
Grave: Urned. 0.35m × 0.32m.
Cremated bone total weight: 73.2g.
Age/sex/pathology: ?Non-adult.
Artefacts: Urn Ra. 7a (Figs 4.5 and 4.6, P26.6), Vessel rim Ra. 7b (P26.2) within Urn Ra. 7a.
C14 dating: None.

Burial 260183 Site 26 (Group 261); Figs 2.29 and 3.5
Grave: Unurned. 0.45m × 0.39m.

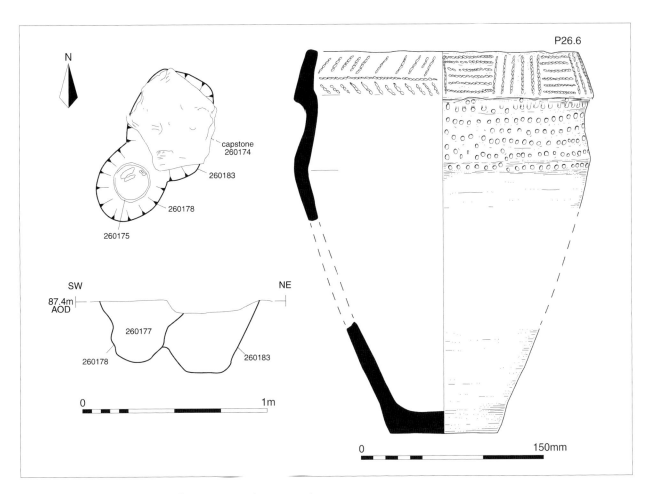

Fig. 3.5   Burials 260178 and 260183. Scale 1:20 and 1:3

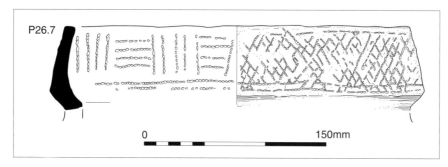

Fig. 3.6   Burial 260207.
Scale 1:3

Cremated bone total weight: 670.6g.
Age/sex/pathology: Adult.
Artefacts: None, although sealed by a limestone slab; abraded bodysherds (P26.1) probably an accidental inclusion.
C14 dating: None.

Burial 260207 Site 26 (Group 2610); Fig. 3.6
Grave: Urned, truncated. 0.49m × 0.11m.
Cremated bone total weight: 141.3g.
Age/sex/pathology: Adult, ?female.
Artefacts: Urn Ra. 9 (Fig. 4.7, P26.7).
C14 dating: None.

Burial 260210 Site 26 (Group 2610); Fig. 3.7
Grave: Urned, truncated. 0.6m × 0.1m.

Cremated bone total weight: 725.8g.
Age/sex/pathology: Adult, ?male.
Artefacts: Urn Ra. 8 (Figs 4.7 and 4.9, P26.9).
C14 dating: 2020–1779 cal BC (SUERC-61122; 3567 ± 29 yr BP).

Burial 260229 Site 26 (Group 2610); Fig. 3.8
Grave: Urned, truncated. 0.45m × 0.19m.
Cremated bone total weight: 355.3g.
Age/sex/pathology: Adult, ?male.
Artefacts: Urn Ra. 11 (Fig. 4.7, P26.12).
C14 dating: None.

Burial 260231 Site 26 (Group 2610); Fig. 3.9
Grave: Urned, truncated. 0.39m × 0.11m.
Cremated bone total weight: 442.1g.

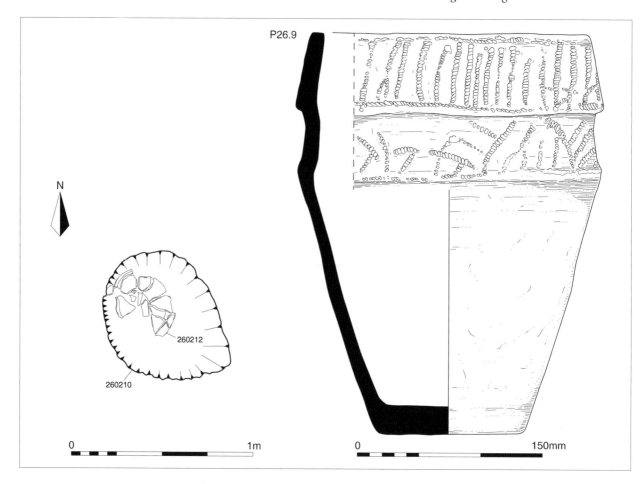

Fig. 3.7   Burial 260210. Scale 1:20 and 1:3

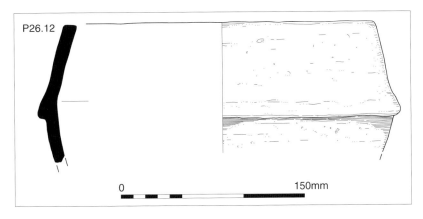

Fig. 3.8 Burial 260229. Scale 1:3

Age/sex/pathology: Adult, ?female.
Artefacts: Urn Ra. 10 (Fig. 4.11, P26.18).
C14 dating: None.

Burial 260236 Site 26 (Group 2610)
Grave: Unurned, truncated. 0.45m × 0.09m.
Cremated bone total weight: 71.6g.
Age/sex/pathology: Mature–older adult.
Artefacts: None.
C14 dating: None.

Burial 260239 Site 26 (Group 261)
Grave: Unurned. 0.75 × 0.35m × 0.24m.
Cremated bone total weight: 936.7g.
Age/sex/pathology: Adult, ?male.
Artefacts: None.
C14 dating: 1943–1763 cal BC (SUERC-61274; 3530 ± 30 yr BP).

Burial 260242 Site 26 (Group 261)
Grave: Unurned. 0.25m × 0.12m.
Cremated bone total weight. 17.5g.
Age/sex/pathology: Adult.
Artefacts: None.
C14 dating: None.

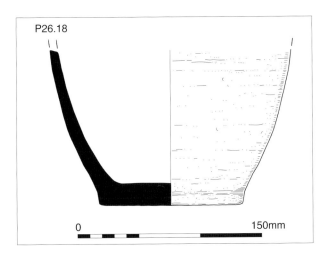

Fig. 3.9 Burial 260231. Scale 1:3

Burial 260254 Site 26 (Group 261); Fig. 2.27
Grave: Unurned. 0.5m × 0.24m.
Cremated bone total weight: 165.6g.
Age/sex/pathology: Adult.
Artefacts: Accessory vessel Ra. 3 (Fig. 4.11, P26.20).
C14 dating: 1887–1697 cal BC (SUERC-61119; 3479 ± 29 yr BP).

Burial 260261 Site 26 (Group 261); Fig. 2.31
Grave: Unurned, truncated. 0.52m × 0.18m.
Cremated bone total weight: 202.4g.
Age/sex/pathology: Adult.
Artefacts: None.
C14 dating: None.

Burial 260276 Site 26 (Group 2610); Fig. 3.10
Grave: Urned, truncated. 0.36m × 0.21m.
Cremated bone total weight: 746.3g.
Age/sex/pathology: Older adult, ?female.
Artefacts: Urn Ra. 13 and 19 (Fig. 4.11, P26.15).
C14 dating: None.

Burial 260303 Site 26 (Group 2610)
Grave: Unurned, truncated. 0.8m × 0.14m.
Cremated bone total weight: 493.2g.
Age/sex/pathology: Adult 20–40 years, ?male.
Artefacts: None.
C14 dating: None.

Burial 260323 Site 26 (Group 261); Fig. 2.29
Grave: Unurned. 0.38m × 0.31m.
Cremated bone total weight: 144.9g.
Age/sex/pathology: ?Non-adult.
Artefacts: None.
C14 dating: 1869–1628 cal BC (SUERC-61273; 3414 ± 30 yr BP).

Burial 260326 Site 26 (Group 261)
Grave: Unurned, truncated. 0.49m × 0.3m.
Cremated bone total weight: 343.3g.
Age/sex/pathology: Mature older adult, ?male.
Artefacts: None.
C14 dating: None.

Burial 260339 Site 26 (Group 261); Fig. 2.30
Grave: Unurned. 0.35m × 0.36m.
Cremated bone total weight: 1650.5g.

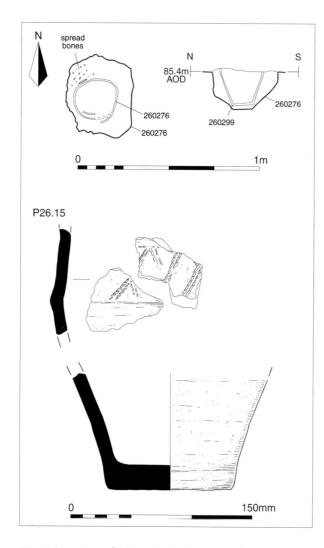

Fig. 3.10   Burial 260276. Scale 1:20 and 1:3

Age/sex/pathology: Adult, male.
Artefacts: Stone capping.
C14 dating: 1751–1619 cal BC (SUERC-61272; 3390 ± 30 yr BP).

Burial 260342 Site 26 (Group 261); Fig. 3.11
Grave: Unurned. 0.39m × 0.25m.
Cremated bone total weight: 344.5g.
Age/sex/pathology: Adult.
Artefacts: None.
C14 dating: 2022–1782 cal BC (SUERC-61118; 3571 ± 27 yr BP).

Burial 260397 Site 26 (Group 268)
Grave: Unurned, truncated. 0.6m × 0.3m.
Cremated bone total weight: 5g.
Age/sex/pathology: Adult.
Artefacts: None.
C14 dating: None.

Burial 260407 Site 26 (Group 268)
Grave: Unurned. 0.34m × 0.21m.
Cremated bone total weight: 739.7g.

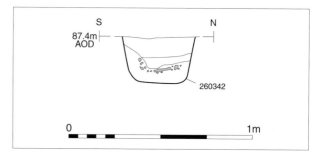

Fig. 3.11   Burial 260342. Scale 1:20

Age/sex/pathology: Older adult.
Artefacts: Capping.
C14 dating: 1946–1771 cal BC (SUERC-50368; 3537 ± 27 yr BP).

Burial 260424 Site 26 (Group 268); Figs 2.36 and 3.12
Grave: Unurned, truncated. 0.45m × 0.26m.
Cremated bone total weight: 361g.
Age/sex/pathology: Adult, ?male.
Artefacts: Accessory vessel Ra. 16 (Fig. 4.7, P26.11).
C14 dating: 2017–1777 cal BC (SUERC-61120; 3563 ± 29 yr BP).

Burial 260439 Site 26 (Group 261); Fig. 3.13
Grave: Urned. 0.35m × 0.25m.
Cremated bone total weight: 986.5g.
Age/sex/pathology: Older adult, female.
Artefacts: Urn Ra. 17 (Figs 4.3 and 4.6, P26.4).
C14 dating: 2022–1882 cal BC (SUERC-50367; 3580 ± 25 yr BP).

Burial 260449 Site 26 (Group 261)
Grave: Unurned, truncated. 0.3m × 0.09m.
Cremated bone total weight: 4.6g.
Age/sex/pathology: ?Adult.
Artefacts: None.
C14 dating: None.

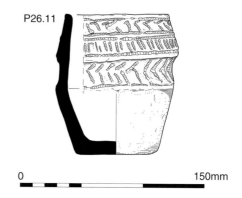

Fig. 3.12   Burial 260424. Scale 1:3

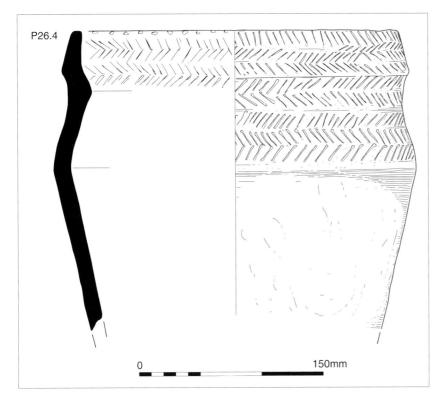

P26.4

0   150mm

Fig. 3.13   Burial 260439.
Scale 1:3

Burial 260474 Site 26 (Group 268); Fig. 3.14 on following page
Grave: Urned. 0.55m × 0.47m.
Cremated bone total weight: 1795.2g.
Age/sex/pathology: ?Older adult, ?male.
Artefacts: Urn Ra. 18 (Figs 4.7 and 4.8, P26.8).
C14 dating: 1948–1771 cal BC (SUERC-61121; 3538 ± 27 yr BP).

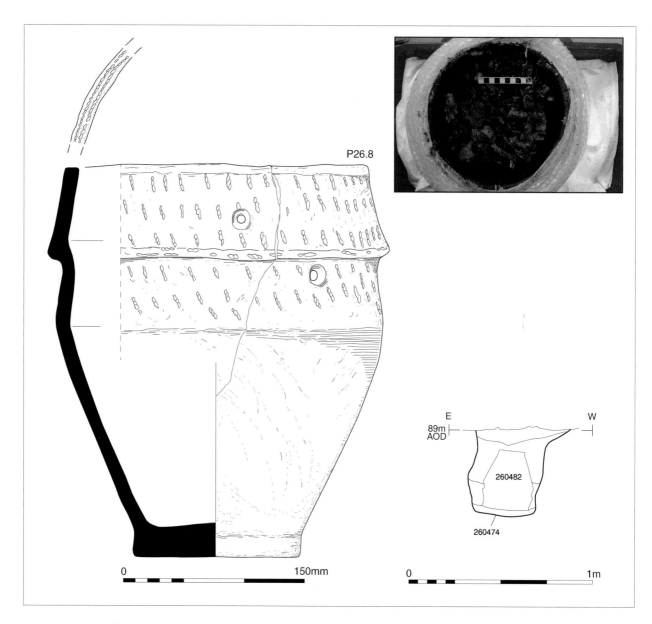

P26.8

E   W

89m
AOD

260482

260474

0   150mm

0   1m

Fig. 3.14   Burial 260474. Scale 1:20 and 1:3 (inset 100mm scale)

Chapter 4
Finds

4.1 Worked flint and chert
Jacky Sommerville

Introduction and methodology

Lithics totalling 284 worked items, and 14 pieces of burnt, unworked flint, were recovered from excavations at eight sites, mostly in the north-eastern half of the road corridor. Lithics were recovered from 39 separate deposits and as unstratified finds. The majority were hand-recovered, with 24 items retrieved from bulk soil sampling of 12 deposits. The bulk of the assemblage (215/76%) was recovered as unstratified, topsoil or subsoil finds. Where flint was found in large numbers in the subsoil (Sites 25 and 35) these were plotted to identify the presence of clusters.

The artefacts were recorded according to broad artefact/debitage, general condition noted and dating attempted where possible. Full details are available in the archive. At sites where flint was found in large numbers in the topsoil, the flints were plotted.

Raw material and condition

In all but one case the raw material is flint. One blade from fill 250142 of Period 2 pit/tree throw 140404/250141 (Site 25) was made on Greensand chert, which outcrops in the region of the Devon/ Somerset border. A closer source (if travelling by land) is Abbots Leigh on the south side of the River Avon, close to Bristol although this is still *c*. 240km/150 miles from St Clears. A collection of fieldwalked tools and debitage made from Greensand chert, from Chapel Pill Farm, Abbots Leigh, includes handaxes and other material of Lower Palaeolithic date (Lacaille 1954).

The flint is mostly of moderately good quality and grey in colour. Only 6% features brown or honey-coloured staining. A degree of cortication was noted on just over half of the flints and it was moderate to heavy on approximately half of these. Where cortex is present, it is abraded or 'chattered' (i.e. pitted from battering)

in 78% of cases and this material was clearly derived from pebbles. As chalk flint does not outcrop in Wales (Burrow 2003, 12) the source is likely to be the beach gravels of the south Welsh coast. Cortex is chalky on 21% of cases, suggesting this portion of the raw material had been imported from primary sources (chalk/clay with flints) further afield.

Range and variety

Primary technology
The quantification of the assemblage by site is set out in Table 4.1. A proportion of the primary material is suggestive of Mesolithic or Early Neolithic flintworking technology, including evidence of platform preparation on seven items and the presence of two core rejuvenation flakes. The 15 cores are of mixed type (six multi-platform, six single-platform and three dual-platform) and 11 are very small and worked out. Two feature blade/bladelet scars in addition to flake scars.

Secondary technology
Pieces with secondary working amount to 17 items (6%), including three microliths and four leaf-shaped arrowheads. Three of the arrowheads are very small, measuring a maximum of 20mm in length.

Sites 12, 17, 18 and 27

A total of 17 pieces of debitage was recovered across these four sites. Of these the only item which permits narrower dating than 'prehistoric' is a broken blade (most likely Mesolithic/Early Neolithic) from fill 270170 of an undated ditch 270169. However, this item is considered to be residual.

Site 25

At 203 items, Site 25 produced the largest number of worked flints. Of these, 118 (58%) were retrieved from the interface between subsoil 250001 and the natural 250002. The latter lithics include: 15 items of Mesolithic

Table 4.1   Quantification of the flint assemblage by site

Category Type	Site 12	Site 17	Site 18	Site 25	Site 26	Site 27	Site 35	Site 37	Total
Burnt unworked	–	–	–	9	2	–	2	1	14
Primary									
Blade	–	–	–	10	–	1	1	1	13
Bladelet	–	–	–	14	–	–	4	–	18
Chip	1	–	1	7	–	–	–	5	14
Core	–	–	–	13	–	–	2	–	15
Core fragment	–	–	–	2	–	–	–	–	2
Core rejuvenation flake	–	–	–	2	–	–	–	–	2
Flake	2	3	9	128	4	–	18	13	177
Shatter	–	–	–	12	–	–	–	–	12
Secondary									
Arrowhead (leaf- shaped)	–	–	–	–	–	–	1	3	4
Knife (plano-convex)	–	–	–	–	–	–	–	1	1
Microlith	–	–	–	2	1	–	–	–	3
Retouched blade	–	–	–	1	–	–	–	1	2
Retouched bladelet	–	–	–	1	–	–	–	–	1
Retouched flake	–	–	–	1	1	–	1	–	3
Retouched fragment	–	–	–	1	–	–	–	–	1
Scraper (straight/concave)	–	–	–	–	–	–	–	1	1
Scraper (end?)	–	–	–	–	–	–	–	1	1
Total	**3**	**3**	**10**	**203**	**8**	**1**	**29**	**27**	**284**

date (bladelets, microliths (Figs 4.1, Nos 1 and 2) and a flake/bladelet core); and eight of Mesolithic or Early Neolithic date (blades, one of which is retouched, and a core rejuvenation flake). The obliquely blunted microlith (Fig. 4.1, No. 1) is a type which featured throughout the Mesolithic period. Broad blanks (8mm or more) tend to date to the Early Mesolithic (Jacobi 1976, 67); however, this dating cannot be securely applied to a single item.

Amongst the 68 unstratified flints from Site 25 a further five Mesolithic items were identified: two bladelets, one retouched bladelet and two flake/bladelet cores.

Of the 17 lithics from stratified deposits in this site, the only diagnostic types are a core rejuvenation flake from Period 2 pit 250103; and the complete blade and blade fragment (the latter on Greensand chert) from fill 250142 of Period 2 pit/tree throw 250141. The technology accords with an Early Neolithic date, although the rolled and edge-damaged condition of the core rejuvenation flake suggests that it may have been redeposited.

Illustration catalogue (Fig. 4.1)

1. *Microlith, subsoil 25000.* An obliquely blunted microlith, belonging to Clark's Group A1 (1934, 56). The retouch along the left dorsal edge is fine, steep and regular, and the base has broken off. Made on a blade of pale grey/honey-coloured flint, measuring 13mm at its widest point.

2. *Microlith, subsoil 25000.* A particularly small (13mm long × 3mm wide) crescent microlith belonging to Clark's Group D2a (sub-geometric arc-blunted) (ibid., 57). This intact microlith has been made on pale grey flint.

Site 26

Lithics from this intervention consist of four flakes, one retouched flake and one microlith fragment. Four of the flakes (including the retouched example) are burnt and these, along with the microlith and two pieces of burnt unworked flint, were recovered from Period 3 cremation pits 260134, 260183 and 260339. All were recovered via bulk soil sampling. The microlith fragment is a pointed tip which displays fine, semi-abrupt retouch along both dorsal edges. It is most likely an obliquely blunted type (Group A2b, B2 or B4) or scalene triangle type (D1b) (Clark 1934, 56–7). The microlith is clearly residual; however, the other items are not closely dateable.

Site 35

A total of 27 worked flints (and two burnt, unworked) were recorded in this intervention: all from topsoil or subsoil. Diagnostic items include four Mesolithic bladelets, one Mesolithic/Early Neolithic blade and one flake/blade core, and an Early Neolithic leaf-shaped arrowhead (Fig. 4.1, No. 3).

Illustration catalogue (Fig. 4.1)

3. *Leaf-shaped arrowhead, subsoil 350001.* An arrowhead which most closely matches Green's Type 3Aj (Green 1980, 71) but is slightly flatter at the base. Made on a dark grey flint flake. It has been invasively flaked on the dorsal face of the flake blank; on the ventral face several flakes have been removed from the right hand side of the base, with a little retouch along the opposing edge. A small portion has broken off the left-hand side of the retouched face, close to the base, and the break surface has subsequently been retouched.

Site 37

Worked flints totalling 26 items were retrieved from this intervention: half via bulk soil sampling. All are from stratified deposits: the majority from Period 2 pit and posthole fills; and two from Period 3 pits. Early Neolithic radiocarbon dates have been returned on two of the pits: fill 370021 of pit 370019 (3696–3531 cal BC; SUERC-61271) and fill 370035 of pit 370037 (3771–3651 cal BC; SUERC-61270).

The Period 2 features containing lithics consist of ten pits and one posthole. A total of 24 flints are spread across these features including six retouched tools, which is a high proportion at 25%. A figure of *c.* 6% is more typical of assemblages in southern Britain and closer to 10% in areas where flint resources are not readily available (Lamdin-Whymark pers. comm., 2015) The tools comprise three leaf-shaped arrowheads (Fig. 4.1, Nos 4–6), a plano-convex knife (Fig. 4.1, No. 7) and two scrapers (including Fig. 4.1, No. 8). Of the 11 features, six (pits 370017, 370019, 370037, 370043, 370119 and 370153) also contain Early Neolithic pottery and/or fragments of hazelnut shell. A small number of wheat grains was also present in pits 370019,

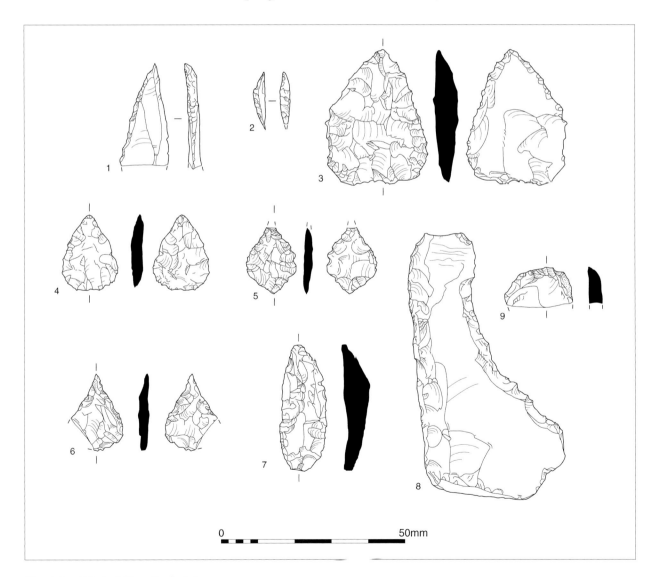

0   50mm

Fig. 4.1   Worked flint. Scale 1:1

370037 and 370153, in addition to crab apple remains in pit 370019. The number of lithics in each pit is small: between one and six items.

Lithics from Period 3 features are restricted to: a flake of very coarse flint from pit 370069; and a burnt fragment from a scraper (Fig. 4.1, No. 9) from pit 370106, found associated with Beaker pottery. Classification of the scraper has not been possible due to breakage and burning. However, what remains does not feature the invasive retouch and/or domed profile of a typical Early Bronze Age/Beaker thumbnail scraper.

Illustration catalogue (Fig. 4.1)

4. *Leaf-shaped arrowhead, Fill 370035 of Period 2 pit 370037.* A Type 4A (Green 1980, 72) arrowhead, made on pale beige/grey rather coarse, cherty flint. It is intact and has been fully bifacially retouched.

5. *Leaf-shaped arrowhead, Fill 370021 of Period 2 pit 370019.* A particularly small and thin arrowhead made on pale grey flint, measuring 17mm in length, with the very tip missing. It has been retouched across both faces and is classified as a Green Type 4 (ibid., 72).

6. *Leaf-shaped arrowhead, Fill 370056 of Period 2 pit 370054.* A Type 4Ac (ibid., 72) arrowhead with a slightly elongated tip, made of mid grey flint. The retouch is fully bifacial and a portion has broken off the base on one side.

7. *Plano-convex knife, Fill 370084 of Period 2 posthole 370083.* A very small knife (33mm × 18mm) made on a blade or flake of mid grey flint. The ventral face is unworked and the dorsal features steep, invasive retouch along both lateral edges, forming a triangular cross-section.

8. *Straight/concave side scraper, Fill 370155 of Period 2 pit 370153.* This tool has been made on a flake of very pale, opaque, slightly coarse-grained flint. The retouch is semi-abrupt and quite regular, forming a straight scraping edge on the left-hand edge and a concave edge on the right-hand edge, both on the dorsal face. The tip is missing.

9. *Scraper fragment, Fill 370107 of Period 3 pit 370106.* A burnt fragment with fine, semi-abrupt retouch along a convex dorsal edge.

Discussion

Mesolithic

Mesolithic flints were recovered from Sites 25, 26 and 35 along the road corridor. Those from subsoils 250001 and 350001 of Sites 25 and 35 were plotted to see if any clusters were evident; however, they were broadly scattered across the areas. The number of items of certain Mesolithic date recorded from subsoil 250001 is low (15) but a proportion of the 103 other items retrieved is also likely to be of this date. The Mesolithic items recovered are not suggestive of particular activities (and key elements such as scrapers and micro-denticulates are absent). The Mesolithic material from this project adds to the dataset of activity in South Wales, and in particular Carmarthenshire, during that period, however, only in the form of background scatters.

Other Mesolithic sites in the area include Marros Sands, Eglwyscummin, Carmarthenshire (c. 5km south of Red Roses), where lithics scatters including chipping floors were recorded associated with a submerged forest (RCHAMW 2014, Marros Sands).

Neolithic

Fills of several of the pits and postholes at Site 37 contain a range of materials which includes pottery, polished stone axe fragments, flaked stone, worked flints and substantial amounts of charred plant remains. It has been suggested that the contents of some of these features may be the result of 'structured' deposition, rather than purely waste disposal (Chapter 4.2, Chapter 5.3). This is the deliberate placement of artefactual and/or environmental material within a feature (Thomas 2012, 2). The purpose of such action is unclear but may include association with an event of ritual importance (Robinson 2000, 87) or for aesthetic reasons (Pollard 2001). The flint assemblage from Site 37 features is small (26 items) but includes a high proportion of tools (23%). Several of these tools may represent part of structured deposits, for example, in pit 370019 (which contains Early Neolithic pottery, hazelnut shells and two flaked stone items, along with a leaf-shaped flint arrowhead) and pit 370037 (containing a leaf-shaped flint arrowhead, a sherd of Early Neolithic pottery and a large amount of hazelnut shell).

Structured deposition has been suggested for similar Neolithic pit assemblages elsewhere in Wales, for example at Upper Ninepence, Walton Basin, Powys where lithics, Peterborough ware and/or Grooved ware pottery, hazelnut shells and occasional emmer wheat were associated in 19 pits of Middle and Later Neolithic date. Five of the pits contained upwards of 100 fragments of hazelnut shell (Gibson 1999, 73–9). At Capel Eithein, Anglesey, a small cluster of pits of Later Neolithic date contained Grooved ware, flints, charred hazelnut shells and cereal grains. The lithics included a denticulated knife made on a blade and a possible flint axe fragment (Pannett 2012, 130; Burrow 2003, 72–91).

Two examples of probable structured deposits in pits of Early Neolithic date are known in Carmarthenshire. Coygan Camp (c. 9km from St Clears) featured a single pit containing an Early Neolithic bowl, lithics, hazelnut shells and cattle and sheep/goat bones. The lithics included a fragmentary leaf-shaped arrowhead, and a radiocarbon date of 3950–3700 cal BC was returned on the hazelnut shells (Wainwright 1967). At Cwmifor three out of four pits which formed an arc contained Early Neolithic pottery and small amounts of lithics, emmer wheat and hazelnut shells (Pannett 2012, 137).

4.2 Neolithic and Bronze Age pottery
E.R. McSloy with thin-section analysis
by Rob Ixer

Prehistoric pottery which was hand-recovered from the excavations amounts to 988 sherds (24kg). An additional 1072 sherds (1.03kg) were recovered from bulk soil samples. The pottery derives from five areas of excavation along the road scheme corridor.

The condition of the hand-collected assemblage is mixed; the Early Neolithic pottery from Sites 25 and 37 is heavily fragmented and the mean sherd weight is moderately low at 6.6g. The preservation of sherd surfaces among this group tends to be good although the common vesicular fabric VES is characterised by abundant voids in the surfaces and break resulting from the chemical leaching or burning away of organic inclusions. The pottery retrieved from soil sample residues is very heavily fragmented and sherd surfaces commonly poorly preserved. For the Beaker and Early Bronze Age group, surfaces tend to be well-preserved, although for a number of vessels the outer surface is poorly preserved with the result that decoration, if present, can be indistinct.

Pottery of Early Bronze Age from Sites 18 and 26 mainly comprise urns and accessory vessels associated with cremation burials. Most or all are likely to have been deposited intact, the larger vessels serving as receptacles for the cremated human remains. All were subject to conservation treatment by University of Cardiff Conservation Services and some vessels reconstructed. A number of vessels survive only as base/lower body or rim portions, and it is assumed this is the result of later truncation and the survival of upper or lower elements depending on whether they were originally deposited in an upright or inverted position.

Methodology

The assemblage has been fully recorded, and quantified using sherd count and weight per fabric. Vessel form/ rim morphology and type/location of decoration are recorded, as are evidence for use (residue type/location), sherd thicknesses, and burning/'re-firing'. Pottery fabric definitions are based on primary/secondary inclusions. Fabrics analysis and identification of source has been informed by a programme of thin-section analysis, the results of which are presented below. The main body of the report is set out according to area (Site) and includes catalogue descriptions for the complete or substantially complete vessels and selected featured (rim or decorated) sherds.

Pottery fabrics
Early Neolithic
Fabric ARG. Argillaceous fabric (Site 37)
Light brown throughout or with darker core. Soft, with finely irregular fracture and smooth/soapy feel. Common, moderately sorted, sub-rounded mudstone/soft rock or clay pellet 1–2mm.
(Not sampled for thin-section analysis).

Fabric QT1. Coarser quartz/quartzite-tempered (Sites 25 and 37)
Buff/yellow brown exterior surface with dark grey-brown core and interior. Soft, with slightly sandy feel and irregular fracture. Common poorly sorted clear/white quartz mostly 1–3mm, but up to 5mm.
(Thin section: sample #1: Site 37 posthole 370006 (fill 370005)).

Fabric QT2. Finer quartz/quartzite-tempered (Site 37)
Light brown exterior surface with dark grey-brown core and interior. Soft, with slightly sandy feel and irregular fracture. Common moderately sorted angular white quartz mostly 2–2.5mm.
(Thin section: sample #5: Site 37 pit 370017 (fill 370018)).

Fabric VES. Vesicular fabric (Sites 25 and 37)
Dark grey brown throughout or with red-brown core. Soft, with irregular fracture and smooth feel. Common rounded/sub-rounded vesicles 0.5–2mm.
(Thin section: sample #6: Site 25 pit 250176 (fill 250177)).

Fabric QIR1. Quartz erratics-tempered (Site 37)
Dark red brown throughout or with grey-brown core and internal surface. Soft, with irregular fracture and smooth feel. Common, moderately sorted angular quartz (<0.5mm) and sparse black rock up to 1mm.
(Thin section: samples #2, #3, #4: Site 37 pit 370119 (fill 370120), pit 370041 (fill 370040) and posthole 370083 (fill 370084)).

Late Neolithic/Beaker
Fabric GR1. Fine/medium grog-tempered (Sites 25 and 26)
Grey brown and typically with buff exterior surface. Soft, with finely irregular fracture and smooth/soapy feel. Common, moderately sorted sub-angular grog 1–2mm.
(not sampled for thin-section analysis).

Fabric BKG. Beaker fine grog-tempered (Sites 25, 26, 37)
Variable colouration; may be light brown/ orange-pink throughout or grey with red-brown surfaces. Soft, with irregular fracture and smooth feel. Common, well-sorted, self-coloured sub-angular grog (0.5–1.5mm). May contain rounded quartz (0.5–1mm) and sparse black rock up to 1mm.
(Thin section: sample #7: Site 37 deposit 370070).

Early Bronze Age
Fabric GRm. Grogged glacial erratics-tempered (Site 26)
Reddish-orange exterior surface and medium dark grey core/interior surface. Soft, with irregular fracture and smooth feel. Sparse, poorly sorted inclusions of quartz, sandstone and red-brown, buff or black-coloured grog up to 3mm.

(Thin section: samples #12, #13, #14: Site 26 cremation pits 260276 (fill 260299), 260439 (260440), 260035 (fill 260166)).

Fabric IR2. Coarser igneous rock/glacial-tempered (Site 18)
Reddish-orange exterior surface and medium grey core and interior surface. Soft with irregular fracture and rough feel. Abundant, well-sorted black and white-coloured, angular igneous rock 2–4mm.
Thin section: sample #11 (Site 18 ditch 180118 (fill 180116)).

Fabric IR3. Igneous rock/glacial erratics-tempered (Sites 12, 18 and 26)
Reddish-orange exterior surface and pale yellowish-brown interior surface. Soft, with irregular fracture and rough feel. Common, pale and dark, angular rock clasts up to 3mm and rounded quartz up to 0.7mm. Mica (muscovite) rich.
Thin section: samples #8, #9, #10 (Site 26 cremation pits 260210 (fill 260212), posthole 260005 (fill 260078), and 260231 (fill 260233)).

Fabric QZ1. Fine quartz/organic (Site 26)
Dark grey/black throughout. Soft with fine fracture and smooth feel. Common, fine/silt-size quartz and voids from burnt-out organics (vegetable-derived). Not sampled for thin-section analysis.

Summary

Six sites along this 9.5km road scheme produced prehistoric pottery (Table 4.2), the majority ascribable to chronologically discrete styles. Early Neolithic (Site 25 and 37) and Early Bronze Age (Sites 25 and 26) styles are best represented and the fabrics among these provide further material evidence for regionally discrete potting traditions. There are significant absences from this sample of substantive Middle or Late Neolithic, and Middle Bronze Age material. Similarly there is a dearth of evidence from the pottery assemblage for 'domestic' activity contemporary with the Early Bronze Age funerary evidence from Sites 25/26. The possible reasons for this, whether as the result of environmental or cultural factors, are discussed in the report conclusions (Chapter 6).

Meaningful inter-site comparisons of the prehistoric pottery are largely invalidated by variable group sizes and differences in the nature of the assemblages. Early Neolithic groups from Sites 25 and 37 reflect what appears to be a pattern within south-west Wales for deposition within pits. The larger group, from Site 37, provides some evidence for 'structured' deposition – particularly when considered together with other artefact classes. Clearly 'structure' is also at play within the Early Bronze Age funerary groups from Sites 25 and 26. Some evidence is provided from these groups for changing funerary practices, with interment within ceramic vessels only the most 'visible'. The Collared Urns, which form the majority of vessel styles in use at Site 26, for the most part exhibit earlier stylistic traits. Radiocarbon dating associated with such vessels is consistently early in the accepted range for the style, within the 20th to 18th centuries BC range. A Biconical Urn (P26.3) is a notably rare instance of a later style, the radiocarbon determination associated with this indicating a date in the mid 18th to mid 16th centuries BC. A number of the burials from Sites 25 and 26 were unurned, but furnished with accessories which vary from inexpertly made 'thumb pots' to highly decorated miniature vessels. There is some evidence suggesting burials with accessories are later than the main Collared Urn group.

Pottery catalogue and discussion by site
E.R. McSloy

Site 12

A thick-walled sherd (58g) in igneous rock-tempered fabric IR3 from pit 120025 is considered of Early Bronze Age. It is abraded but features indistinct, possibly corded decoration and probably belongs to the Collared Urn style.

Table 4.2 Prehistoric pottery summary by site

Area	Ct.	Wt.(g)	EVEs	Date*	Notes
–	9	9	–	EN?	Unstratified sherds
12	1	58	–	EBA	Stray Collared Urn sherd
18	15	209	1.03	EBA	Accessory
25	66	235	0.22	EN; BKR	EN plain bowl; Beaker coarsewares
26	1594	22701	9.54	EBA; LN	Collared Urn cremation burials; stray Beaker and Grooved ware
27	1	16	–	EBA?	Stray sherd
37	374	1993	1.06	EN; BKR	Plain bowl; Beaker finewares
Total	**2060**	**25221**	**11.85**		

*EN = Early Neolithic; LN = Late Neolithic; BKR = Beaker; EBA = Early Bronze Age

Site 18

Two features produced quantities of Early Bronze Age pottery (180172 and 180118). The simple, cup-like form of the complete accessory vessel (P18.1) is similar to vessels known from the region, including from Cwm Cadlan, Rhondda Cynon Taf and Nantcwnlle, Ceredigion (Savory 1980, fig. 71). The fabric for this vessel appeared visibly similar to IR3 utilised for vessels from Site 26. Cremated bone recovered in association with vessel P18.1 provided a radiocarbon date in the range 1948–1766 cal BC (SUERC-61255).

Other pottery from Site 18 is restricted to 14 sherds (60g) in a coarse rock-tempered fabric (IR2) from ditch 180118. This vessel was undecorated and dating (to the Early or Middle Bronze Age) is tentative. Fabric IR2 was visibly coarser compared to those characterising the Early Bronze Age vessels from Site 26 and was selected for thin-section analysis (Ixer, this report).

Catalogue

P18.1 Complete accessory vessel (149g) Fabric IR3. Red-brown surfaces. Simple cup-like form with simple/squared rim. Decoration consists of all-over horizontal deep scoring to the vessel's walls and extending over the base. The rim top exhibits impressed decoration using a small circular-sectioned implement. Thickness 4mm. Cremation burial/pit 180172 (fill 180173). Fig. 4.2.

P18.2 Rim sherd (15g) Fabric IR3. Buff-brown. Rim sherd from thick-walled vessel with slightly incurved rim with squared rim top. Undecorated. Thickness 13mm. Ditch 180118 (fill 180116). *Not illustrated.*

Site 25

This area was characterised by widely scattered, mainly pit-like features. Radiocarbon determinations returned for four features suggested dating in the Mesolithic, Late Neolithic, Early Bronze Age and post-Roman periods (Table 2.1). The pottery from Site 25 was typically very fragmentary, a factor hindering classification.

Early Neolithic

Pottery of this period (33 sherds, weighing 110g) was recorded from two pit-like features. The 27 sherds from pit 250103 (fill 250104) were very fragmentary and identification is based on fabric alone. Those from pit 250176 included rim sherds from three vessels (below).

The simple bowl forms from this feature (P25.1–3) are characteristic of Welsh material of the earlier Neolithic (Burrow 2003, 54–5), including the larger group from Site 37 (P37.1). Vessel P25.2 exhibits decoration, sometimes referred to as 'impressed burnish' also seen with the Site 37 group.

Catalogue (Fig. 4.2)

P25.1 Two rim sherds (45g) Fabric VES. Grey-brown. Simple bowl form with thickened rim. Thickness 8–9mm. Pit 250176 (fill 250177).

P25.2 Two rim/bodysherds (23g) Fabric VES. Dark grey-brown. Bowl with externally expanded rim. The rim features decoration as lightly impressed radial strokes to the top surface. Thickness 6mm. Pit 250176 (fill 250177).

P25.3 Small rim sherd (3g) Fabric QT1. Dark grey-brown. Bowl (?) with simple/rounded rim. Thickness 6mm. Pit 250176 (fill 250177).

Beaker (?)

All of the pottery ascribed to this period (29 sherds, weighing 107g) relates to features (pits) grouped in the westernmost portion of the site. One radiocarbon determination from pit 250063, which was part of this cluster, but which did not contain pottery, returned dating 2456–2201 cal BC (SUERC-50317).

If this dating is accepted for this group of features, this places the activity at end of the British Neolithic, a period which sees the introduction of the first Beaker pottery, but also when use of Grooved ware may still be current (most indications are that the style lingered until *c.* 2200 BC (Garwood 1999; Needham 2005)).

Due to its small size and fragmentary condition, attribution with confidence is difficult, although Beaker attribution is preferred based on a number of factors. All of the pottery from this group (from pits 250073, 250079, 250091 and 250093) occurs in a similar fine grog-tempered fabric, appropriate for (although not exclusive to) Beaker assemblages. The bifid form and stabbed decoration of the single rim sherd (P25.4) is matched by Beakers described by Savory from Llandow, Vale of Glamorgan (Savory 1980, fig. 52, no. 371.1), Talbenny, Pemb. (ibid., no. 372) and Caldey, Pemb. (ibid., no. 508). That the majority of sherds is undecorated is perhaps surprising, although undecorated Beaker 'coarsewares' are a feature of domestic assemblages, including the group from Stackpole Warren, Dyfed (Benson *et al.* 1990, 212).

Catalogue (Fig. 4.2)

P25.4 Two rim sherds (15g) Fabric GR1. Grey-brown with reddish brown exterior surface. Beaker coarseware vessel? Shallow collared/bifid rim. Impressed decoration in chevron design to lower rim with sharp-tooled implement. Thickness 8mm. Pit 250091 (fill 250092).

P25.5 Base sherd (23g) Fabric GR1. Dark grey-brown with buff exterior surface. Beaker coarseware vessel? Undecorated. Thickness 8mm. Pit 250093 (fill 250096).

Site 26

The pottery from this area largely comprises vessels associated with a poorly preserved barrow monument, including those deposited within 'pyre-hollow' 260391. A total of 36 cremation burials are catalogued (Chapter 3), the majority of which were unurned. Only 11 of the vessels listed in the catalogue (P26.3; P26.4; P26.5; P26.6; P26.7; P26.8; P26.9; P26.12; P26.15; P26.17;

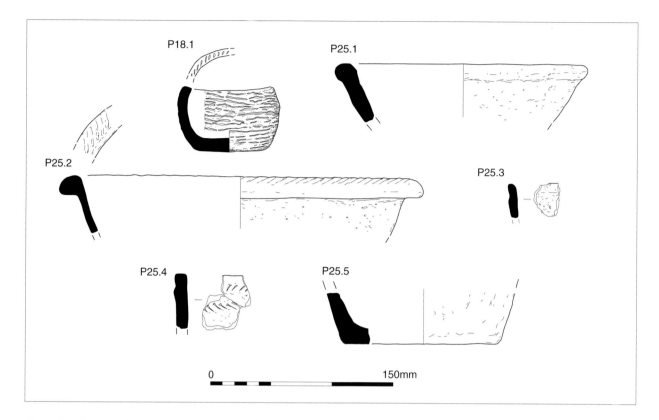

Fig. 4.2   Pottery. P18.1, P25.1–P25.5. Scale 1:3

P26.24) were associated with significant quantities of cremated human bone and functioned as receptacles for this material or were accessories to unurned cremation burials. Cremated material was scarce (P26.10) or not noted at all in association with the remainder (P26.11; P26.14; P26.20; P26.21; P26.22; P26.23); and two vessels (P26.1–2) are not thought to be contemporary with associated cremation deposits and are probably disturbed from earlier activity. Of the (seven) vessels where cremated remains were not present or very scarce, it is probably significant that six comprise small (P26.10–11) or miniature (P26.20–23) forms. It seems likely that these represent disturbed/truncated, 'cenotaph-type' memorials, or perhaps infant interments where little or none of the skeletal material has survived. The further possibility that these are non-funerary 'structured' deposits might also be considered.

The group of Collared Urns and other vessels from Site 26 is among the largest known from Wales. Most vessels occur in fabrics containing igneous and other rock types probably derived from glacial sands, and variable quantities of grog (see Ixer, this report). All appears to be local to the area. Preservation is variable, probably reflecting truncation relative to depth of burial. For a number of vessels (P26.14–18), where the diagnostic upper portions are absent, stylistic attribution has not been possible. In describing the decoration and formal characteristics of the Collared Urns, terminology employed by Longworth in his corpus (Longworth 1984) has been employed. In discussing chronology

relative to stylistic/formal traits, Burgess's scheme (1986) is preferred. The stylistic traits exhibited by this group which are thought to be reflective of relative chronology are set out in Table 4.4.

The Collared Urn series in Britain is long-lived; Needham's estimates of *c.* 2200/2100 to *c.* 1600/1500 (Needham 1996), more recently narrowed to *c.* 1950 to *c.* 1550/1500 (Needham *et al.* 2010) are based on evaluation of the available radiocarbon determinations. Four of the Collared Urns from the Site 26 group were associated with radiocarbon determinations obtained from cremated bone samples (Chapter 5.5; Table 2.1). All are within the range 2022–1771 cal BC, dating which would agree with an 'Early' or 'Middle' range suggested by the stylistic traits.

Significantly, undecorated bipartite vessel P26.3 (feature 260021) and miniature vessel P26.21 (feature 260029) were each associated with radiocarbon determinations which support later dating compared to that of the Collared Urn burials (below), and hint at changing vessel styles and burial traditions within the life of the monument.

Catalogue

?Grooved ware

P26.1   Fifteen abraded bodysherds (32g) some of which join. Fabric GR1. Patchy buff/grey-coloured surfaces with dark grey core and inner surface. All of the larger sherds show decoration in the form of grooves including vertical zones infilled with scored diagonals. Thickness 5–6mm. Feature 260183 (fills 260181 and 260185). *Not illustrated.*

Two deposits (fills of 'cremation pit' 260183) produced sherds probably representing a single vessel. All sherds were recovered from bulk soil samples and the poor condition of the sherds is in part at least an effect of the soil sampling process. The fragmentary nature of P26.1 would support its being an accidental incorporation within feature 260183, probably relating to activity pre-dating the barrow construction.

The fragmentation of P26.1 precludes its fullest classification. The vertical zoned decoration matches the widely distributed Durrington Walls style (Wainwright and Longworth 1971). The overall paucity of Grooved ware from Wales has been remarked on (Gibson 2014a, 35) and until recently findspots have been confined to central and north Wales (Burrow 2003, 98–9). The recovery of Grooved ware from Llandeilo, Carmarthenshire and Steynton, Pembrokeshire (Gibson 2013, 17–19; Gibson 2014a, 35) indicates that the style was more widely distributed than has been appreciated.

Collared Urn (Figs 4.3 and 4.6)

P26.4 Tripartite Collared Urn (Ra. 17). Base portion missing. Fabric GRm (thin-section sample #13). Consistent light brown external surface with grey-brown core and interior. The surfaces of the upper vessel are hard and well-smoothed. The tripartite form is not well defined, although the profile is variable over its circumference. The collar section is short (*c.* 30mm), approximately vertical, with its internal face concave and the rim top simple/rounded. Decoration to the exterior extends from the collar zone to the neck and comprises an interrupted herringbone design executed with 'linear incisions'. The same pattern is also repeated on the interior of the collar. The inside edge of the rim features regularly spaced small circular impressions. Rim diam. 240mm; Thickness 8–9mm. Feature 260439 (fill 260440).

Discussion: Vessel P26.4

The very short, ill-defined collar of P26.4 is an untypical feature within the Site 26 group. The collar depth, use of short line motifs and, particularly, the decorated internal moulding are stylistic traits shared by Burgess's 'early' urns (Burgess 1986, 345). The radiocarbon dating returned for associated cremated bone from this vessel (SUERC-50367: 2022–1882 cal BC) would support a broadly 'early' date (Table 4.3). The short line 'herringbone' is a scheme which is common on Welsh urns. Examples with herringbone executed in linear incisions include examples from Trefeglwys, Powys (Savory 1980, 210, no. 426) and Brackla Hill, Coity, Glamorganshire (ibid., no. 433).

Catalogue (Figs 4.4 –4.7)

P26.5 Tripartite Collared Urn (Ra. 5) (Figs 4.4 and 4.6). The base portion of this vessel is missing and the surfaces

Fig. 4.3 Collared Urn P26.4. 100mm scale

Fig. 4.4 Tripartite Collared Urn P26.5. 100mm scale

of lower body are pitted, probably as the result of differential preservation. Fabric GRm (thin-section sample 14). Pale orange external surface with grey core and interior. The surfaces of the upper vessel are hard and well-smoothed; the lower portion is pitted, seemingly the result of poorer preservation. There is a thin and patchy carbonaceous deposit to the lower interior. The vessel's collar is short (45mm), close to vertical and with simple/flattened rim top. Decoration at the collar comprises a double border

Table 4.3   Site 26 Collared Urns. Comparisons using Burgess's 'early' and 'middle/late' features and correspondence with radiocarbon determinations

Vessel	Ra.	Early traits	Middle and late features	Remarks	C14 (at 95% confidence)
P26.4	17	Shallow collar; Internal decoration; Below-collar decoration 'Short line' decoration	–	–	2022–1882 cal BC
P26.5	5	Shallow collar; Internal decoration; Internal moulding; Whipped cord decoration; Below-collar decoration 'Short line' decoration	–	–	2011–1774 cal BC
P26.6	7a	Shallow collar; Internal decoration; Internal moulding; Below-collar decoration	Complex/'bold' decoration	–	–
P26.7	9	Shallow collar; Internal decoration; Internal moulding;	Complex/'bold' decoration	Collar zone only	–
P26.8	18	Whipped cord decoration; Below-collar decoration 'Short line' decoration	–	–	1948–1771 cal BC
P26.9	8	Below-collar decoration Slender proportions/Irregular internal profile	Complex/'bold' decoration	–	2020–1779 cal BC
P26.10	15	Below-collar decoration; 'Short line' decoration Whipped cord decoration	–	Small	–
P26.11	16	Below-collar decoration; 'Short line' decoration Whipped cord decoration	–	Small	–
P26.12	11	–	–	Undecorated; collar zone only	–
P26.13	4b	–	–	Very fragmentary	–

of continuous twisted cord containing a chevron pattern formed from whipped cord (Longworth's motif 'F'). The interior face of the collar is decorated with 4 × rows of U-shaped whipped cord impressions. Decoration to the neck consists of a 5 × line herringbone motif, the uppermost line from 'linear incisions' made with a sharp implement and with whipped cord below. Rim diam. 220mm; Thickness 8–9mm. Feature 260035 (fill 260166).

P26.6   Tripartite Collared Urn (Ra. 7a) (Figs 4.5 and 4.6). Probably complete to full height, but not fully reconstructable. Fabric GRm. Light brown exterior surface, grey-brown interior hard and well-smoothed. Patchy carbonaceous internal residue. The collar (45mm) is well-formed, angled inwards at *c.* 65° and with a concave internal moulding and simple/rounded rim. Decoration to the collar exterior consists of a corded hurdle pattern of alternating horizontal (5–6) and vertical (4–6) lines. Decoration to the inside of the collar consists of a central horizontal continuous

Fig. 4.5   Tripartite Collared Urn P26.6. 100mm scale

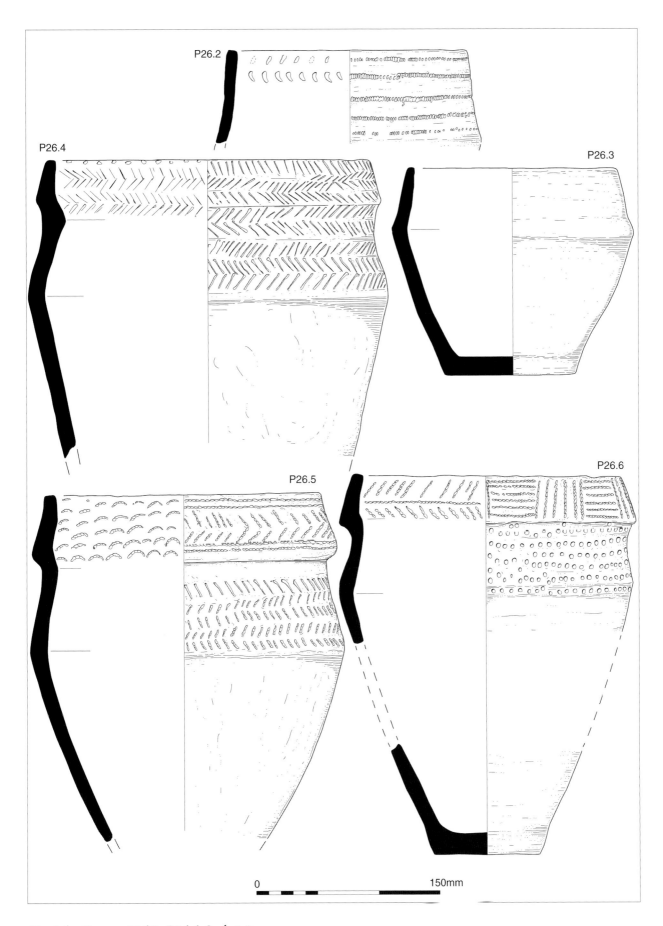

Fig. 4.6 Pottery. P26.2–P26.6. Scale 1:3

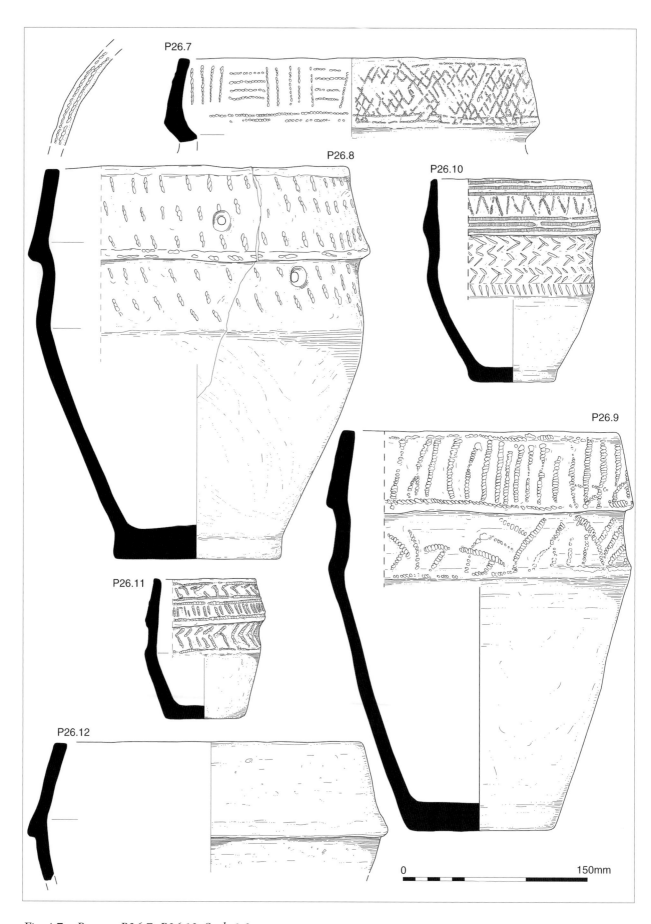

Fig. 4.7   Pottery. P26.7–P26.12. Scale 1:3

corded line with oblique-angled cord impressions above and below forming a running chevron design. Decoration to the neck and just below the shoulder angle comprises 6–7 rows of small circular impressions. Rim diam. 220mm; Base diam. 80mm; Thickness 8mm. Feature 260178 (fill 260177).

P26.7   Tripartite(?) Collared Urn (Ra. 9) (Fig. 4.7). Fragments representing the full circumference of the vessel, surviving just below the collar. Fabric GRm. Patchy light orange to mid-brown surfaces. The exterior is well-smoothed, the interior rough. Light brown exterior surface, grey-brown interior hard and well-smoothed. The collar (60mm) is angled inwards at *c.* 80° with a concave internal moulding and simple/flattened rim. Decoration to the collar exterior consists of a poorly impressed double twisted cord border, within which is two lines of crossed twisted cord producing an interrupted lattice design. Decoration to the interior moulding comprises a corded hurdle pattern of alternating horizontal (8–10) and vertical (5) lines. Decoration to the small area of the neck which survives consists of oblique-angled whipped cord impressions. Rim diam. 230mm; Feature 260207 (fill 260208).

Discussion: Vessels P26.5–7

Vessels P26.5–7 share features of tripartite form, with short collars and decoration internal to the collar zone, and with the inner face of the collar concave. These and the tall, slender (projected) proportions of P5 and P6 are 'early' traits according to Burgess's scheme (Burgess 1986, 345). The short line motifs, and use of whipped cord on P26.5 (Ra. 5), are further traits consistent with Burgess's early or middle groupings and radiocarbon dating (2011–1774 cal BC) derived from cremated bone from this vessel accord with the 'stylistic' dating (Table 4.3). The combined use of incised line and whipped cord in the main (neck) design of P26.5 appears unusual, the short line herringbone is a feature common to Welsh vessels. The U-shaped impressions to the interior of this vessel (P5) are unusual in a Welsh and wider context. They are doubtless a variant of Longworth's 'horseshoes, loops or rings' (Motif 'M') which occur typically on the outside collar or neck of the vessel, as for example a vessel from Llanboidy, Carmarthenshire (Savory 1980, 216, no. 417.3). The use of similar 'U-shaped' motifs do, however, occur as bordering elements (Longworth 1984, 13, fig. 10).

The complexity/'boldness' of the corded decoration seen with P26.6 and P26.7 is a trait that Burgess considered common to middle and late vessels in the series (Burgess 1986, 345–6). The scheme exhibited by P26.6 cannot be matched exactly from among Savory's Welsh corpus (1980) or among the large group from Steynton, Pembrokeshire (Gibson 2014a). The individual design elements, the hurdle motif and the small circular impressions do occur with Welsh Collared Urns, the former on a vessel from Carew, Pembrokeshire (Savory 1980, 218, no.

432.2) and the latter at Abergynolwyn, Gwynedd (ibid., 209, no. 411).

Vessel P26.7 (Ra. 9) was very fragmentary, the survival of the collar zone an indication of inverted deposition. Tripartite form is indicated by the concavity below the collar. The lattice-like corded design is recorded on vessels from Rhoscrowther, Pembrokeshire (Savory 1980, 420) and Cross Hands, Llanboidy, Carmarthenshire (ibid., 418.2). The internal corded 'hurdle' appears on a vessel from Carew, Pembrokeshire (ibid., 432.2).

Catalogue (Figs 4.7–4.9)

P26.8   Tripartite Collared Urn (Ra. 18) (Figs 4.7 and 4.8). Complete. Fabric GRm. Patchy light brown/grey-brown surfaces, grey-brown interior. The exterior surfaces are hard and well-smoothed. There are some linear marks to the lower body possibly indicating the use of a forming 'paddle'. The collar (70mm) is angled inwards at *c.* 70°, the rim top square with double continuous twisted cord impressions. The base is pushed-out/expanded from the line of the lower body (Longworth's base angle B). Decoration to the collar and neck (exterior) consists of oblique-angled whipped cord impressions. There is also a line of horizontal whipped cord to the collar overhang. Two post-firing perforations are positioned either side of a crack running obliquely through the upper part of the vessel; these probably used to affect a repair using a leather or rawhide thong. There is distortion to the rim circumference which is probably post-depositional, though likely to have been made worse by the original break. Height 315mm; Rim diam. 260–70mm; Base diam. 130mm; Thickness 9–10mm. Feature 260474 (fill 260482).

Fig. 4.8   Tripartite Collared Urn P26.8. 100mm scale

Fig. 4.9   Tripartite Collared Urn P26.9. 100mm scale

P26.9   Tripartite Collared Urn (Ra. 8) (Figs 4.7 and 4.9). Complete to full height. Fabric 1R3 (thin-section sample #8). Red-orange surfaces, hard and well-smoothed. The collar (65mm) is well-formed with a partial overhang, the interior plain and the rim top simple/flattened. Decoration to the collar consists of horizontal bands of continuous twisted cord with close-set repeated vertical lines of twisted cord. Decoration to the neck zone comprises a line of continuous twisted cord at the base, above which is with an irregular and close-set pattern of obliquely crossed lines of twisted cord. Height 315mm; Rim diam. 230mm; Base diam. 115mm; Thickness 9–10mm. Feature 260210 (fill 260212).

Discussion: Vessels P26.8 and P26.9

Vessels P26.8 and P26.9 are tripartite vessels and share characteristics of a comparatively deep, well-defined collar which lacks decoration to its interior surface. Although some 'early' features exhibited by other vessels from Site 26 are absent for P26.8 and P26.9 (Table 4.3), they do not conform to Burgess's 'late' vessels grouping, characterised by a very deep/overhanging collar, absence of decoration to the neck and 'squat' proportions with narrow base. In its 'short line' decorative scheme and use of whipped cord P26.8 matches Burgess' 'early' vessel styles. Radiocarbon dating was provided for both vessels from cremated bone samples and the determinations: 1948–1771 cal BC for P26.8 (SUERC-

61121) and 2020–1779 cal BC (SUERC-61122), are consistent with dating appropriate to the early/middle range for the Collared Urn series (Table 4.3).

Whipped cord is a technique seen commonly with Welsh Collared Urns, although most typically employed as a herringbone design (Savory 1980, 412, 441). P26.8 (Ra. 18) is the largest vessel from the Site 26 group, though its dimensions are not unusually large for the Collared Urn series (Longworth 1984). The expanded base, presumably for increased stability on a flat surface, is a feature of a minority of Collared Urns (Longworth 1984, 7) and one which has been recorded on a number of Welsh vessels (Savory 1980). The apparent repair to vessel P26.8 appears to be an unusual feature for a vessel of this class; Longworth, in noting the absence of repaired vessels in Collared Urn burials (1984, 8), considered that the selection of vessels for burial purposes from among domestic assemblages meant that defective vessels were not used.

The complex, if messy, corded decoration exhibited by P26.9 accords with the 'bold' designs considered by Burgess to be common to 'middle' and 'late' vessels. The repeated horizontal corded decoration to the rim (Longworth's motif 'B') would seem uncommon from Wales, although it is seen on a vessel from Llandysul, Carmarthenshire (Savory 1980, 213).

Catalogue (Figs 4.7 and 4.10)

P26.10   (Small) Tripartite Collared Urn (Ra. 15) (Figs 4.7 and 4.10). Complete to full profile. Fabric GRm. Consistent light brown external surface with grey-brown core and interior. The exterior surfaces are hard and well-smoothed; the interior is pitted possibly due to inclusion of corrosive materials and

Fig. 4.10   (Small) Tripartite Collared Urn P26.10. 50mm scale

there is a light and patchy carbonaceous internal residue. Proportionally, the collar section is fairly deep (*c*. 45mm), near vertical and the rim top simple/rounded. Decoration to the collar consists of a border of three lines of continuous whipped cord, between which is a repeated 'V' motif also from whipped cord. Decoration below extends from the neck to just below the shoulder and comprises a herringbone design executed as 'linear incisions' using a rounded-ended implement. Height 160mm; Rim diam. 130mm; Base diam. 66mm; Thickness 8–9mm. Feature 260402 (fill 260401).

P26.11 (Small) Tripartite Collared Urn (Ra. 16) (Fig. 4.7). Complete. Fabric IR3. Consistent pale orange external surface with grey-brown interior. The exterior surfaces are hard and fairly well-smoothed. Proportionally, the collar section is fairly deep (*c*. 35mm) and the neck shallow. The collar is angled inwards at *c*. 70°, the rim top with a slight but irregular bevel. Decoration at the collar (exterior) consists of an upper zone bordered with continuous single rows of horizontal whipped cord and containing oblique-angled 'T' motifs; and below this a zone of close-set vertical whipped cord, also bordered by rows of continuous whipped cord. Decoration to the neck consists of obtuse-angled chevrons from whipped cord and with a continuous line of whipped cord at the shoulder angle. Height 110mm; Rim diam. 80mm; Base diam. 70mm; Thickness 6–7mm. Feature 260436 (fill 260434).

Discussion: Vessels P26.10 and P26.11
Vessels P26.10 and P26.11 are grouped together as small examples of the Collared Urn class. They are also alike in respect of their slack, cup-like profile and decoration combining zoned and 'short line' designs. An unusual technical feature of P26.10 and P26.11 is the use of repeated contiguous whipped cord impressions to create the horizontal zones in preference to continuous lengths of cord. In their use of whipped cord, short line motifs and decoration which extends (just) below the shoulder, P26.10 and P26.11 are stylistically 'early' according to Burgess's scheme (1986, 345).

Small Collared Urns are not uncommon across the Britain (Longworth 1984) and vessels of comparable size and smaller are known from Wales (Savory 1980, nos 419, 425, 427, 493; Gibson 2014a). Longworth (1984) recorded heights in the range 75mm to over 500mm and his scatter diagrams comparing vessel diameter/height show an even (unclustered) progression for both his Primary and Secondary series.

Catalogue (Figs 4.7 and 4.11)
P26.12 Collared Urn (Ra. 11) (Fig. 4.7). Fabric GRm. Consistent light brown external surface colour with dark grey core/interior. Patchy carbonaceous residue to the interior and in a band below the rim exterior. Only the upper portion is preserved and it is unclear whether P26.12 is of tripartite or bipartite form. The collar (80mm) is angled inwards at approximately 70° and its lower edge well defined. The rim top is simple/flattened. Rim diam. 220mm; Thickness 9mm. Feature 260229 (fill 260230).

P26.13 Collared Urn (Ra. 4b) (Fig. 4.11). Fabric IR3. Fragmentary; consists of the base portion and detached sherds, including portion of vessel collar. Brown external surface colour with dark grey core/interior. Surfaces are poorly preserved and rough. The small part of the collar surviving features twisted cord decoration. Base diam. 64mm; Thickness 7mm. Feature 260005 (fill 260078).

Discussion: Vessels P26.12 and P26.13
Vessels P26.12 and P26.13 are fragmentary, the preservation of portions of the collar zone permitting identification as of this series. Neither is sufficiently complete to determine details of profile (tripartite or bipartite form) or usefully refine dating relative to style.

P26.12 is the only undecorated Collared Urn from this group. Plain Collared Urns are relatively common from the principality (possibly more so than across the Britain); nine occur among the *c*. 50 in Savory's catalogue (Savory 1980) and a further two examples come from the Steynton barrow group (Gibson 2014a, 39–40). An absence of decoration (added to the incompleteness of P26.12) means that attribution to early or middle/late groups using Burgess's criteria becomes problematical. There appear to be no grounds for considering undecorated vessels either an early or late phenomenon.

Biconical Urn (Fig. 4.6)
P26.3 Bipartite carinated form. (Ra. 1). Complete. Fabric IR3. Light brown surfaces. The exterior surfaces are hard, though are not well-smoothed. The neck section is fairly irregular (50–60mm deep), the rim top is simple/rounded and also irregular. The base is slightly pushed-out/expanded from the line of the lower body. Height 163mm; Rim diam. 160mm; Base diam. 130mm; Thickness 8–9mm. Feature 260021 (fill 260085).

The Biconical Urn tradition would seem on current evidence to belong to the later part of the Early Bronze Age with indications that the period of use overlaps with that of Collared Urns. The style may have emerged first as a 'continental intrusion' (Tomalin 1988) and in Britain is largely confined to the south. The style is certainly present in domestic assemblages, known variously from East Anglia, Dorset and Somerset (see discussion in Bell 1990, 126). Evidence for the style in Wales is limited, and hitherto confined to the south-east (Savory 1980, 84–5). A domestic group linked to this style is that from Lesser Garth Cave, Radyr, Glamorgan (ibid., fig. 72, 505).

Fabrics utilised for Biconical Urn groups appear to vary according to region and the availability of suitable clays and tempering materials. In this instance the coarse igneous fabric, is comparable to the other (Collared Urn and miniature) vessels from the group and suggestive of a local technological continuum.

Radiocarbon dating utilising a sample of cremated human bone associated with P26.3: 1744–1560 cal BC (SUERC-61275) (Table 4.4) indicates the vessel is among the latest from the monument and significantly later than the burials associated with Collared Urn vessels (Table 4.3). The dating indicated P26.3 is within the range indicated for Biconical Urns elsewhere, for example a domestic group from Brean Down, Somerset: 1861–1422 cal BC (Bell 1990).

That P26.3 is the single example of this style from the monument, among other burials sharing comparable dating, hints that interment within ceramic vessels may have been more the exception than the norm at this time, and possibly, that burials were more typically unaccompanied or contained miniature/accessories (below). Whether this pattern extends beyond the locality is unclear, although the scarcity of Biconical Urns from burials in Wales and the preponderance of miniature vessels as the only pottery present in the grave (Savory 1980, 86) may be evidence for this.

Indeterminate (Figs 4.6 and 4.11)

P26.2   (Ra. 7b) (Fig. 4.6). Vessel P26.2 is present only by a portion of its rim (0.12 EVEs). Fabric GRm. Light brown surfaces with grey core. The exterior surface is well-smoothed, the interior though is rough and pitted, making the decoration to the interior indistinct. The rim top is simple/rounded. Decoration to the exterior consists of fairly widely spaced continuous horizontal cording. This is well executed and the impressions distinct. Decoration to the rim interior appears to consist of a row of whipped cord, and below this an opposed row of whipped cord or possibly 'bird bone'-type impressions, both angled to create a running chevron design. Rim diam. 190mm; Thickness 8–9mm. Feature 260178 (fill 260177).

Table 4.4 Site 26 Non-Collared Urn forms and correspondence with radiocarbon determinations

Vessel	Ra.	Class	C14 (at 95% confidence)
P26.3	1	Biconical Urn	1744–1560 cal BC
P26.2	7b	Indet.	
P26.14	12	Indet.	
P26.15	19/13	Indet.	
P26.16	4a	Indet.	
P26.17	6	Indet.	
P26.18	10	Indet.	
P26.20	3	Accessory	
P26.21	–	Accessory	1771–1623 cal BC
P26.22	–	Accessory	
P26.23	–	Accessory	
P26.24	–	Accessory	

P26.14   ?Tripartite vessel (Ra. 12) (Fig. 4.11). Fragmentary; comprising 25 sherds (225g) from upper part of the vessel. Fabric GRm. Light brown/grey-brown surfaces and grey-brown core and interior. The surface of the vessel is much degraded and much of the decoration is unclear. The collar is angled inwards at *c.* 70°, the lower edge ill-defined. The rim top is not present. Decoration to the collar (exterior) consists of a lightly impressed pattern of repeated vertical cord impressions. There is decoration to the neck as paired diagonals also of twisted cord. Thickness 8–9mm. Feature 260244 (fill 260247).

P26.15   ?Tripartite vessel (Ras. 13 and 19) (Fig. 4.11. Fragmentary; comprising 51 sherds (970g) from base and portion of the neck. Fabric GRm. Consistent brown exterior surface and grey-brown core and interior. Hard, well-smoothed surfaces. Internal carbonaceous residue. Decoration to the neck consists of paired diagonal lines of twisted cord over which are lighter-impressed paired twisted cord diagonals and single horizontal twisted cord line above. Thickness 8–9mm. Feature 260276 (fill 260299).

P26.16   Urn (Ra. 4a) (Fig. 4.11). Base portion and bodysherds. Fabric GRm. Consistent light brown external surface with grey-brown core and interior. Surfaces are hard and well-smoothed. One bodysherd exhibits decoration as whipped cord arranged in herringbone pattern. Hard and well-smoothed surfaces. Base diam. 70mm; Thickness 6–7mm. Feature 260011 (fill 260012). *Not illustrated.*

P26.17   Urn (Ra. 6) (Fig. 4.11). Base portion only (surviving to height of *c.* 60mm). Fabric GRm. Consistent light brown external surface with grey-brown core and interior. Hard and well-smoothed surfaces. Base diam. 120mm; Thickness 12mm. Feature 260037 (fill 260172).

P26.18   Urn (Ra. 10) (Fig. 4.11). Base portion only (surviving to height of *c.* 110mm). Fabric IR3. Consistent brown external surface with grey-brown core and interior. Surfaces are hard and moderately well-smoothed. Lower part of interior surface with carbonaceous residue. Base diam. 118–120mm; Thickness 8–9mm. Feature 260231 (fill 260233).

Discussion: Vessels P26.2 and P26.14–18

Vessel P26.2 (Ra. 7b) was recovered in association with tripartite Collared Urn P26.6 (Ra. 7a). Due to its incompleteness and a number of unusual features stylistic attribution is unclear. The surviving decorated neck zone would be untypically deep should this be representative of a 'Collar' and the banded, twisted cord decoration and use of fine grog-tempered fabric, would similarly be unusual if compared to the Collared Urn vessels in this group. The fabric, together with the vessel's constant thickness and shallow 'S'-shaped profile, are indications that it is of the Beaker series. As a stray sherd it is possible that it represents either a disturbed earlier burial, or might relate to earlier non-funerary activity.

The remainder are severely truncated/fragmentary vessels, with only P26.14–15 surviving (partially) to

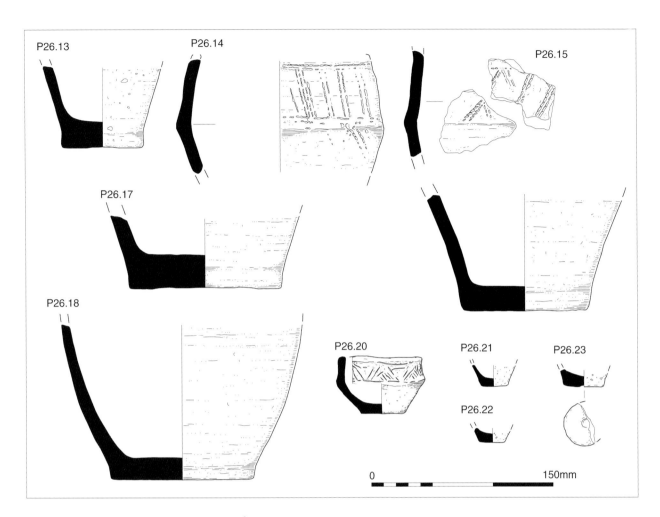

Fig. 4.11   Pottery. P26.13–P26.23. Scale 1:3

neck level. P26.14 and P26.15 are almost certainly of the Collared Urn series and tripartite form vessels.

Miniature ('accessory') vessels (Fig. 4.11)

P26.20 Accessory vessel (Ra. 3). Complete. Fabric IR3. Orange-brown surfaces with grey core surfaces grey-brown interior. The exterior surfaces are hard and fairly well-smoothed. The vessel is bowl-like in its proportions, bipartite in form, with the neck section slightly concave and the rim top simple. Decoration is limited to the neck zone and consists of an irregular incised geometric pattern of repeated diagonals within single or paired horizontal lines. Height 45mm; Rim diam. 66mm; Base diam. 35–38mm; Thickness 5–6mm. Feature 260254 (fill 260004).

P26.21 Accessory vessel (Soil sample 26002). Incomplete. Fabric QZ1. Dark grey throughout. The surfaces are degraded, in part to due to the processes resultant from bulk environmental sampling. The vessel is of pinch-pot type, possibly of simple conical form and undecorated. Base diam. 25mm; Thickness 3mm. Feature 260029 (fill 260030).

P26.22 Accessory vessel (Soil sample 26011). Incomplete. Fabric IR3. Light orange-brown throughout. The surfaces are with coarse rock inclusions protruding.

The vessel is of pinch-pot type probably with a simple curving profile and undecorated. Rim diam. c. 50mm; Base diam. 25mm; Thickness 3–4mm. Feature 260064 (fill 260065).

P26.23 Accessory vessel (Soil sample 26014). Incomplete. Fabric IR3. Light orange-brown throughout. The surfaces are again rough, the result or coarse rock inclusions protruding. The profile is indeterminate, but seemingly simple pinch-pot type. The underside of the base features a central fingertip impression. Base diam. 28mm; Thickness 3–4mm. Feature 260007 (fill 260008).

P26.24 Accessory vessel? (Soil sample 26009). Incomplete. Fabric IR3. Light orange-brown throughout. Small sherds only and the form indeterminate. Probably undecorated. Thickness 3–4mm. Feature 260017 (fill 260047). *Not illustrated.*

Discussion: Vessels P20–24

As is usual for miniature vessels from Wales (Savory 1980, 86), those from Site 26 were all from otherwise unaccompanied (unurned) cremation burials. Only P26.21 is associated with a radiocarbon determination indicating dating 1771–1623 cal BC (SUERC 61282) (Table 4.4), this being appreciably later than those for the Collared Urn accompanied burials, and also that for accessory vessel P18.1.

The shallow, biconical form and incised geometric decoration seen with the only substantially complete vessel of this type, P26.20, are features common with Welsh examples described by Savory (1980, 219, fig. 71). On such bipartite vessels decoration can be to both upper and lower portions, or as with P26.20, confined to the neck (ibid., nos 425.2; 473). Vessels P26.21–24 were identified only following the processing of bulk soil sampling to recover the cremated human remains. Their incomplete and degraded condition owes much to the sampling process and it is likely that these vessels were substantially complete when first deposited. None appear to be burnt suggesting they were added at the time of interment. Stylistically these appear to be simple, undecorated vessels and are significantly smaller than P26.20. P26.21 (SS26002) was unusual in occurring in a fine sandy fabric. Its form may be similar to the simple, conical forms from Llanfihangel Nant Brân, Powys and Holt, Wrexham (Savory 1980, 219, fig. 71, nos 477.39 and 468). Vessels P26.22 and P26.23 appear to be more globular in form, more akin to a vessel from Cwm Cadlan, Penderyn, Rhondda Cynon Taf (ibid., 219, fig. 71, no. 380.4). P26.23 is alone in exhibiting some elaboration, as a single fingertip impression to its base.

Savory considered that the origins of the Welsh accessory vessels may have been with the Food vessel/ Encrusted Urns from Ireland (ibid., 86–7) and noted a tendency in findspots (particularly for vessels of greater elaboration), to areas of west Wales, closest to the Irish Sea coast. Gibson has also noted the similarities of form of some miniature vessels with Food vessels (2002, 104). It should be noted however that the squat/bipartite form of P26.20, whilst being reminiscent of some Food vessel forms, is also similar that of Biconical 'urns', represented here by P26.3. This being the case, and bearing in mind the equivalence of the absolute dating relating to (Biconical Urn) P26.3 and (accessory vessel) 26.21, it is tempting to see both as a related, contemporaneous tradition. On the, albeit limited, evidence from this group it seems likely that such a tradition extends later than that of burials accompanied by Collared Urns.

Site 37 (Fig. 2.3)

Early Neolithic
The Neolithic pottery from this area amounted to 341 sherds, weighing 1894g (0.99 EVEs). Most was hand-collected, although a sizeable proportion (92 sherds, weighing 114g) was recovered from bulk soil samples.

The assemblage relates to 16 discrete features interpreted as pits/postholes. The largest group (108 sherds), from pit 370119, is composed primarily of sherds from a single, well-fragmented vessel (P37.1). Similarly, the majority of sherds from larger groups, including from 370019 and 370054, are made up of single vessels. Among these, a vessel from 370054 is notable in being

burnt. Radiocarbon determinations from three pits (370153, 370037 and 370019), located across the excavated area, were indicative of activity in the range 3771–3466 cal BC (Chapter 5.5), dating which is consistent with the stylistic dating.

Form and decoration
The group includes rim sherds from eight vessels, which are described (P37.1–8). Although the level of fragmentation means that in no instance was the profile fully reconstructable, most vessels are identifiable as bowls, with a single vessel (P37.8) possibly of deeper, 'baggy' jar proportions. Vessels with thickened/D-shaped rims (P37.1–3) and simple/rounded rims (P37.6–7) are representative of open forms with curving walls and a gently rounded base (equivalent to Cleal's simple bowl forms: Cleal 2004, 174, fig. 4). Vessels with rolled-over/ thickened rims (P37.4–5) might derive either from carinated or simple/open forms; an absence in the assemblage of angular shoulder fragments is probably significant, and the heavy character of rims P37.3–4 suggests all belong to simple bowl forms.

Typically for ceramics of this period, vessels are well-made with surfaces smoothed and possibly burnished. Three vessels (P37.1–3) exhibit decoration which takes the form of lightly tooled, 'impressed burnish' to the rim. Notably the three decorated vessels are located in close proximity, from a cluster of pits close to the western limit of the site (features 370119, 370123, 370153) (Cluster 1). One vessel (P37.3 from pit 370123) features two small post-firing perforations below its rim, most likely to facilitate suspension, a feature known elsewhere from the region from Clegyr Boia, Pembrokeshire (Burrow 2003, 55, fig. 21, no. 4).

Stylistic affinities and dating
Burrow's (2003, 53, fig. 19) distribution map for Early Neolithic pottery from Wales shows few sites in the south-west, with only a single pit group from Coygan Camp, Laugharne within 20km of the sites under discussion. This picture has been expanded by more recent work, most notably pipeline excavations, where new material, including some large groups (Gibson 2014b–d), has been identified from 12 findspots from Pembrokeshire, Carmarthenshire, Powys and Ceredigion. The Welsh groups are typically small and pit-derived, the largest from Clegyr Boia, Pembrokeshire amounting to 500 sherds (Burrow 2003, 52–5). A narrow range of fabrics types would seem to characterise the Welsh material, with vesicular, crushed quartz types seemingly most prominent. Variable recording and uncommon use of petrography or other analyses means that the origin of fabrics materials is rarely known, although, as with this group (see Ixer, this report), there is no evidence for longer-distance movement of pottery.

The earlier Neolithic ceramic traditions of Wales remain imperfectly understood, although development would seem to reflect wider patterns across the British Isles. A 'primary' tradition of undecorated carinated bowls, which is commonly associated with vesicular fabrics, would, on the basis of a recent radiocarbon dating programme (Whittle *et al.* 2011), span a longer period, *c.* 3800–3400 cal BC, than had been thought. On this evidence there is scope for overlap with non-carinated, heavier-rimmed forms commonly regarded as representing a secondary or *post-inception* phase, dating after *c.* 3600 BC (Gibson 2002, 72).

Most indications are that the group described here (and that from Site 25) falls within the 'secondary' tradition, defined by simpler bowl or jar-like forms, commonly with heavier rims, the occasional use of decoration and an expanded range of fabrics. The three radiocarbon determinations noted above, including *c.* 3765–3466 cal BC (SUERC-61266) from the pit (370153) containing vessel P37.2, would be consistent with the secondary phase dating. Close contemporaneity of all of the ceramics from Site 37 cannot be demonstrated and there are perhaps suggestions from the stylistic variability relating to spatial distribution that this is not the case: vessels with decorated thickened/D-shaped-rims (P37.1–3) occur only from the westernmost feature cluster, whereas those with rolled-over (P37.4–5) and simple rims (P37.6–7) are absent from this group but occur among the scattered features east of this group and in Cluster 2. Variability relative to pottery fabric would seem also seem to relate in part to (spatial) distribution; this is most obviously seen in the absence of igneous (QIR1) rock-tempered fabrics from features within the easternmost part of the site (Table 4.5).

Discussion

The nature of the activity represented at Site 37 is difficult to interpret, the full extent of the 'site' being unknown, and the levels of truncation likely to be significant. It is unclear whether the clustering of the pit-like features in the western portion of the excavation area relates to discrete areas of habitation/other activities, although this seems possible. Discussion regarding the non-utilitarian nature of Neolithic pits highlights the apparently 'structured' character of the associated artefacts and faunal/environmental materials (Thomas 1999, 66). The evidence for this is widespread and incidences from Wales include from Coygan Camp, Carmarthenshire (Burrow 2003, 56), which included a mixed deposit of pottery, hazelnut shell, animal bone and lithics. The character of structured deposits can be very different; however, a unifying feature would seem to be the indications of deliberate selection 'from more substantial deposits' (Thomas 1999, 68). Lithics present can include a high ratio of tools to waste, are typically 'fresh' and sometimes deliberately broken. Tools commonly include arrowheads or axes of flint or stone. Where pottery is deposited it is rarely as complete vessels, but more often consists of portions of a larger number of vessels. Viewed in this light, aspects of the pit groups from Site 37, notably the inclusion of arrowheads and axe flakes, accord with 'non-utilitarian' deposition of the kind described. The

Table 4.5   Site 37. Pottery incidence by fabric (shown as sherd count), and min. no. vessels per feature

Group	Feature	ARG	QIR1	IR2	QT1/2	VES	Totals	Min. no. vessels
Cluster 1	370123	–	2	–	–	3	5	5
(west)	370119	–	108	–	–	–	108	2
	370153	–	2	–	–	8	10	4
	370121	–	–	–	–	13	13	5
Cluster 2	370037*	–	–	–	–	1	1	1
(east)	370049		–	1	–	–	1	1
	370083	–	1	–	–	2	3	3
	370052	–	2	–	–	11	13	2
Dispersed	370085	–	1	–	–	2	3	3
(western	370073	–	–	–	–	7	7	1
area)	370017	–	1	–	11	2	14	5
	370041	–	1	–	–	7	8	4
	370043	–	5	–	–	16	21	5
Dispersed	370006†	–	–	–	1	–	1	1
(eastern area)	370019*	2	–	–	–	81	83	11
	370054*†	–	–	–	–	47	47	2
(subsoil)	370001	–	–	–	-	3	3	3
Totals		**2**	**123**	**1**	**12**	**203**	**341**	**58**

* feature contained leaf-shaped arrowhead   † feature contained flake from stone axe

evidence from the pottery is however equivocal; whilst group size expressed as sherd count (Table 4.3) is seemingly variable, the numbers of vessels (sherd families) represented is typically low and would be in keeping with a group 'selected' for a purpose. There is no evidence for the selection of vessels based on decoration, size or technology (fabric).

Catalogue (Fig. 4.12)

P37.1   Ninety-seven sherds (539g). Fabric QIR1. Red-brown with dark grey surfaces which are well-smoothed. Open bowl form with thickened/ D-shaped rim. Decoration to top part of the rim consists of (lightly impressed) paired impressions. Thickness 6–9mm. Pit 370119 (fill 370120).

P37.2   Two sherds (18g). Fabric QIR1. Red-brown throughout, with well-smoothed surfaces. Bowl with D-shaped/triangular rim. The rim features decoration as lightly impressed strokes to the top surface. Thickness 8mm. Pit 370153 (fill 370155).

P37.3   Three sherds (39g) Fabric VES. Dark grey-brown throughout. Bowl with thickened/D-shaped rim. Decoration to the top surface of the rim as lightly impressed strokes. Thickness 6–7mm. Pit 370123 (fill 370124).

P37.4   One sherd (32g) Fabric VES. Dark grey-brown throughout. Bowl with rolled-over rim. Undecorated. Thickness 9mm. Pit 370041 (fill 370040).

P37.5   One sherd (28g) Fabric VES. Grey throughout (burnt/re-fired). Bowl with rolled-over rim/externally expanded rim. Undecorated. Thickness 9mm. Pit 370019 (fill 370021).

P37.6   Two sherds (13g) Fabric VES. Dark grey throughout. Simple open (curving walls) bowl with rounded rim. Undecorated. Thickness 6mm. Pit 370017 (fill 370018).

P37.7   Eleven sherds (83g) Fabric VES. Dark grey throughout. External carbonaceous residue below rim. Simple open (curving walls) bowl with rounded rim. Undecorated. Thickness 8mm. Pit 370052 (fill 370053).

P37.8   One sherd (6g) Fabric VES. Dark grey throughout. Jar/deep bowl with globular body and externally expanded rim. Undecorated. Thickness 4–5mm. Pit 370019 (fill 370021).

Beaker (Site 37) (Fig. 2.7)

Pottery of Beaker type amounts to 33 sherds (99g/0.07 EVEs), recorded from pits 370069 and 370106, both located in the western portion of Site 37. Two fineware vessels are represented, each occurring in a similar fine grogged fabric. Both vessels are highly fragmented with the result that the vessel profiles are unclear. Decoration consists of bands of twisted cord decoration, which is indistinct for the vessel from feature 370067, due to surface weathering.

Catalogue (Fig. 4.11)

P37.9   Fourteen sherds (47g) Fabric BK G. Light yellow brown throughout. Beaker fineware vessel with expanded/triangular rim. Decoration as horizontal bands of impressed twisted cord. Thickness 6mm. Pit 370106 (fill 370107).

P37.10   Nineteen bodysherds (45g) Fabric BK G. Light yellow brown throughout. Beaker fineware vessel with (indistinct) horizontal banded decoration, probably of impressed twisted cord. Thickness 6mm. Pit 370069 (fill 370070). *Not illustrated.*

Thin-section analysis
Rob Ixer

Fourteen Neolithic, Beaker and Early Bronze Age sherd samples were provided for petrographical examination. They were from excavated material and from various locations within Sites 18, 25, 26 and 37. Details of the methodology employed and a full catalogue description of each sample is contained in the archive. The emphasis of the report is on providing detailed petrographical characterisation of the samples with some discussion on their manufacture and the geographical provenance of the raw materials. Where it is possible, the origin of the raw materials used in the manufacture of the pot is geographically sourced, and divided into local (less than 10km), regional (50km) or exotic with reference to the pottery sherd findspot.

Definitions
In this report 'chert', 'autogrog' and 'grass' are defined below. It is possible to distinguish flint and chert macroscopically, but as they cannot be distinguished petrographically under the microscope, the more generalised geological term for any very fine-grained/cryptocrystalline quartz rock, namely chert, has been adopted in this report. This should not conflict with any pottery being described as flint-tempered in hand specimen. Many prehistoric pots carry grog/grog-like areas that share the same petrographical characteristics as the main clay but display a different firing colour or internal orientation (its petrographical fabric) to the main clay. These are informally called 'autogrog' and may be adventitious or intentionally added dried clay, rather than true grog, namely, intentionally added, crushed, fired pot. Grass is used in its broad botanical sense and so would include all cereal crops. Its presence is recognised by hollow culms seen in cross-section and longitudinal striae along the culm length. Some grasses show cut edges; this also aids identification. Petrographical fabric is used in its geological sense and so is to be distinguished from the usual archaeological term 'fabric'.

Petrographical summary
Macroscopically the Early Neolithic potsherds have been divided into four fabric codes namely QT1, QT2, QIR1 and VES. Their thin-section petrography is in much agreement with these codes. The single Beaker sherd is described as Fine Grog (BK G) and there is petrographical agreement.

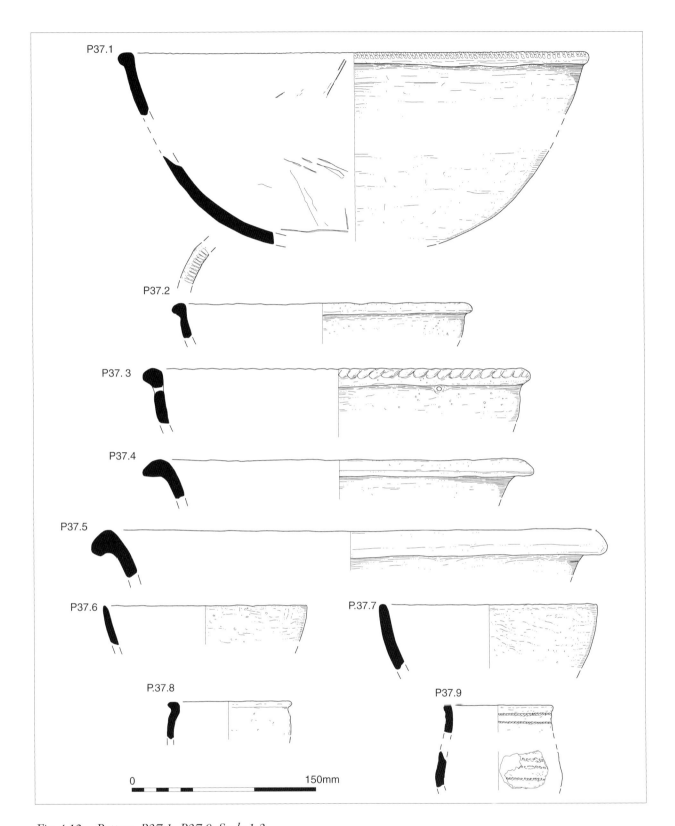

Fig. 4.12 Pottery. P37.1–P37.9. Scale 1:3

The seven Early Bronze Age potsherds have been divided into four groups namely IR3, IR3g, IR2, and GRm. These divisions are less clear in thin section and the potsherds include a range of grogged or ungrogged, igneous and meta-sedimentary erratic-tempered wares.

Discussion of results

Early Neolithic. Quartz/quartzite-tempered QT1 and QT2
Thin-section petrography on samples #1 QT1 and #5 QT2 supports the separation of the two sherds macro-

scopically; however, petrographically this is mainly based on differences between the two main pastes rather than their tempers. Sample #5 (Site 37 deposit 370018) is a very well-made quartz-tempered pot probably using local raw materials. The main paste is extremely clean and the angular temper is almost exclusively monolithic, namely, coarse-grained, strained quartz. This suggests a crushed rock was added to a cleaned clay. Despite local siltier areas in the main paste the pot has a high preparation index as defined by Ixer and Lunt (1991).

Sample #1 (Site 37 deposit 370005) QT1 has a slightly silty clay tempered with angular, coarse-grained quartz. The temper is almost exclusively monolithic, namely coarse-grained, strained quartz. This suggests crushed rock added to a (natural), silty (grains <187μm in diameter) clay.

Early Neolithic. Quartz erratics-tempered QIR1
Thin-section petrography on samples #2 (Site 37 deposit 370120), #3 (Site 37 deposit 370040) and #4 (Site 37 deposit 370084) confirms that they form a coherent group. All three have a sandy/silty main paste and coarse-grained non-plastics that are dominated by angular strained quartz, altered monocrystalline feldspar and fine-grained altered rocks including quartz ± feldspar ± muscovite ('granite') clasts. As other lithologies are present the non-plastics are polylithic in composition. There is some variation within the group; #4 has the clearest bimodal size distribution and #3 the least, as here the coarser non-plastic clasts have a wider size range. In sherds #2 and #3 feldspars are altered to fine-grained white mica but in #4 they are altered to epidote and perhaps prehnite. All three pots could have been manufactured by adding crushed quartz rock to a roughly washed, local, fine- to medium- grained (mainly 375μm in diameter, medium sand size), sandy glacial clay.

Early Neolithic. Vesicular VES
Sample #6 (Site 25 deposit 250177) VES is distinctive. Coarse-grained vesicles, some of which may have held cellular plant matter rather than grass are enclosed within a fine-grained (187μm in diameter), sandy main paste, quartz grains in this paste have a restricted size range.

Beaker. Beaker fine grog-tempered BK G
Sample #7 (Site 37 deposit 370070) BK G is difficult in thin section. A very clean clay (<<187μm in diameter) carries few natural non-plastics dominated by sparse, monocrystalline quartz. Areas that show a different firing colour to the main paste and different birefringence colours in crossed polars are probably grog but any other grog is hard to recognise and if present is 'autogrog'. The very rare non-plastics include altered igneous and fine-grained metamorphic rocks.

Early Bronze Age. Coarser igneous rock IR3 and coarser igneous rock with grog IR3g
In thin section the three sherds would be designated #8 IR3g, #9 IR3 and #10 IR3. Samples #8 (Site 26 deposit 260212), IR3, #9 (Site 26 deposit 260078), IR3 and #10 (Site 26 deposit 260233) IR3g, share general characteristics but only #8 is intentionally grogged. Grog is not recognised from #9 and 'autogrog' is minor, if present, in #10, and both these sherds show signs of poor mixing, with siltier layers within the main paste. All have a clean clay (<187 to <<187μm in diameter) tempered with coarse-grained meta-sandstones, mainly arkose to litharenite in composition, plus igneous rocks dominated by micro-porphyry in #9 and very altered, phenocrystic feldspar in a fine-grained feldspathic matrix in #10 but by ophitic dolerite in #8. Sherd #10 is almost monolithic and the temper is angular, suggesting perhaps crushed rock.

Early Bronze Age. Medium igneous rock IR2
Sample #11 (Site 18 deposit 180116) is ungrogged and its non-plastics have a bimodal size distribution, with a temper comprising altered igneous rocks dominated by altered ophitic dolerite and meta-sediments, mainly coarse-grained sandstone and arkosic sandstone, in a dark clean (187μm in diameter, fine sand size) clay.

Early Bronze Age. Medium/coarse grog GRm
Samples #12 (Site 26 deposit 260299), #13 (Site 26 deposit 260440) and #14 (Site 26 deposit 260166) are all grogged but especially #13 and #14; much of the grog in #12 is very small 'autogrog'. In all three sherds a clean (<187μm in diameter) clay carries grog and erratic rock fragments comprising altered igneous rocks and meta-sediments; these differ in lithologies between the three sherds. In #12 pale-coloured, clean 'autogrog' and dark grog is accompanied by altered ophitic dolerite and litharenite, in #13 'autogrog'/grog is accompanied by altered diorite and meta-sandstone and siltstone and #14 a number of different grogs are accompanied by fine-grained quartz-feldspar/rhyolite and meta-litharenite.

Manufacture

Grogging
None of the Early Neolithic sherds (thin sections #1–6) show signs of grogging. The Beaker fineware sample #7 (Site 37 deposit 370070) is grogged but this is quite difficult to see in thin section. The Early Bronze Age sherds vary in the amount of recognised grog, from none (thin sections #9 (Site 26 deposit 260078) and #11 (Site 18 deposit 180116) to very minor, possible 'autogrog' (sample #10 (Site 26 deposit 260233)) to very clean, clay-rich areas and minor grog (sample #12 (Site 26 deposit 260299)) to being distinctly grog-tempered (Site 26 samples #8 (deposit 260212), #13 (deposit 260440) and #14 (deposit 260166)). In sherds

#13 and #14 grog is more abundant than rock clasts and #14 is essentially grog-tempered.

In some of the sections where it is present, some possible grog is very similar to the main clay but differs in the orientation of its petrographical fabric and firing colour and this is called 'autogrog': thin sections #8, #13, #14 and possibly #10 and #12. It may be that very minor amounts of dried clay are becoming incorporated into the main clay rather than it being intentionally added, as fired grog. In ungrogged sherd #11 very large areas and streaks of clean clay suggest incomplete mixing. In other sections a number of different grogs are present (recognised by their firing colours, density and type of their non-plastic inclusions) and indeed some of these are themselves grogged (grog-in-grog). This poly-grog temper is noted in sherds #8, #14 and #13. Thin section #8 is unusual as it shows a very clear rim fragment with both pale and dark grog within the same clast suggesting that some of the 'poly-grog' may be from the same vessel.

No exotic (non-local/regional) grog was recognised, all true grog is tempered with quartz or with small erratic clasts and all grog could have been obtained from pots that were themselves locally made.

Tempering

Other than in #6 (Site 25 deposit 250177) and for the use of grog, all tempers are natural and inorganic. Plant matter and bone are extremely rare, if present. The quartz-tempered Early Neolithic pots have crushed quartz added to clean or silty clays. Sherd #6 differs from the other quartz-tempered pots in having a very clean(ed) main paste but with siltier streaks and patches. Other Early Neolithic pots perhaps have crushed quartz added to sandy clays or quartz-natural coarse sand was added to a clean clay.

In the Early Bronze Age pots a wide range of medium-grained igneous and meta-sediments have been chosen as temper, often the temper is bilithic or polylithic suggesting a natural glacial sand, and that crushed single rocks have not been used. Other pots are more monolithic, perhaps suggesting the addition of crushed rock. No specific rock type has been chosen, but in most temper, medium- to coarse-grained igneous or sedimentary rocks dominate (this is less true for #13 (Site 26 deposit 260440) and #14 (Site 26 deposit 260166) as meta-sediments including fine-grained meta-sediments are more numerous than igneous rocks). The local bedrocks do not appear to have been used, nor do any fine-grained rocks.

Origin of the raw materials

Thorpe *et al.* (1991, 145) noted and identified numerous erratics cobbles and boulders (up to metres in diameter) cleared from fields at Lampeter Velfrey just to the west of the findspots; amongst these were Preseli dolerites, rhyolites, pyroclastics and Lower Palaeozoic sediments. Strahan *et al.* (1914) include in their list of erratics

from the Haverfordwest area boulders of hornblende porphyrite (see potsherd #9). Many of these lithologies are present as temper in the pots, especially the Early Bronze Age pots.

For the Early Neolithic pots the main inorganic non-plastics are monocrystalline quartz and this is accompanied by minor amounts of altered feldspar including both plagioclase and potassium feldspar groups alongside quartz-rich 'granitic' rock clasts; intermediate to basic igneous rocks are absent. The lack of any distinctive or diagnostic mineral clasts means it is difficult to provenance either the temper or main paste in these pots but they are probably made from local materials. This is also suggested by the rare occurrence of epidote and perhaps prehnite as alteration products of feldspar.

Sherds #6 (Site 25 deposit 250177) and #7 (Site 37 deposit 370070) have few natural, inorganic non-plastics and so little can be determined with regard to the origin of their raw materials, although the few non-plastics present in #7 might suggest a local source. The grog within sherd #7 is from the same general source as the main paste.

Early Bronze Age sherds #8 (Site 26 deposit 260212), #9 (Site 26 deposit 260078), #10 (Site 26 deposit 260233) and #12 (Site 26 deposit 260299) have silty/sandy main pastes tempered with medium-grained igneous rocks and medium- to coarse-grained meta-sandstones (meta-arkose and meta-litharenite). Sherds #11 (Site 18 deposit 180116), #13 (Site 26 deposit 260440) and #14 (Site 26 deposit 260166) have clean main pastes, especially #13 and #14. The silty/sandy, fine-grained, non-plastics match those of the temper suggesting a common source that is probably local glacial clay. Grog within the potsherds also appears to have been manufactured from local materials.

Erratics from the Preseli Hills were recognised in potsherds #11 and #12, but in general the erratics vary from sherd to sherd and no original outcrop source can be given, other than they could come from west Wales. However, no raw material can be clearly seen to be exotic with reference to its findspot and all the sherds could be manufactured from local (less than 20km) materials.

Final conclusions

All the ceramics could be of local manufacture as there is no evidence for pots being imported from non-local areas characterised by having very different raw materials. There is a strong suggestion that medium- to coarse-grained rather than fine-grained rocks have been selected for tempering agents.

The Early Bronze Age pots could be manufactured from glacial clays, by cleaning the clay and returning (crushed?) size-graded, sandy clasts to the clay or by using crushed, local igneous and meta-sedimentary erratic cobbles and boulders. There is a slight suggestion that some of the grog found in #8 (Site 26 deposit 260212) is tempered only with ophitic dolerite similar to that found at the Stonehenge-related dolerite outcrops in the Preseli Hills. If this could be shown not to be from an erratic it would be the first example of spotted dolerite-tempered ware in either the Neolithic or Bronze Age.

4.3 Copper-alloy object
E.R. McSloy

Fragments from one or possibly two awl or pin fragments of copper alloy were recorded from cremation burial 180172, Site 18, from the fill of miniature pottery vessel P18.1. Other items from the cremation deposit included a group of fired clay beads (Chapter 4.4). Radiocarbon dating of cremated bone samples confirms an Early Bronze Age date: 1948–1766 cal BC.

X-ray fluorescence analysis of the composition of the copper alloy indicates the use of a leaded tin bronze, with zinc fully absent (in archive P. Greaves). The shaft of the larger fragment is bent at the point of its break which hints at deliberate breakage. The object probably represents an awl (or possibly a pin). Such finds are among the more common metal items recorded from funerary contexts, Longworth illustrates 12 associations in his (Collared Urn) corpus and, undoubtedly, more have been lost (Longworth 1984). Comparable Early Bronze Age examples from Wales include an awl from Castell Bryngwyn, Llanidan, Anglesey (Savory 1980, 199, fig. 51, no. 486) and two examples from cremation burials, from Sheephays Farm, Llandow, Vale of Glamorgan (ibid., 199, fig. 51, no. 440.2), and Rhiw-with-Llanfaelrhys, Caernarfonshire (ibid., 199, fig. 51, no. 341.3).

Catalogue (Fig. 4.13)

1   Bronze. Awl or pin fragments. The larger fragment is a round-sectioned shaft and with flattened, pointed terminal. The smaller piece is round-sectioned and with two broken ends. Length: 24mm (larger) and 6mm (smaller); Diam. 2.2mm (larger) and 2mm (smaller). Period 3 cremation burial 180172 (fill 180173).

4.4 Fired clay beads
E.R. McSloy

Five ceramic beads were recorded from soil samples associated with Site 18 cremation burial 180172. All occur in a similar fine, hard, buff-coloured fabric. Bead No. 1 was of significantly larger and of differing (biconical) form compared to the other examples. Cremation burial 180172 was accompanied by a complete pottery accessory vessel of Early Bronze Age type (Fig. 4.2, P18.1) and the cremated bone was radio-carbon dated to 1948–1766 cal BC (SUERC-61255; 3534 ± 30 yr BP). Beads comparable to those described are known elsewhere from Wales from Llanfihangel Nant Brân, Powys (Savory 1980, 199, fig. 51.477:41–2), which were similarly from a burial containing an Early Bronze Age accessory ('pygmy cup').

Catalogue (Fig. 4.14)

1   Bead of truncated biconical form. Height 15mm; max. diam. 13mm; internal diam. 4mm. Area 18 Period 3 cremation burial 180172 (fill 180173); soil sample 1822.

2   Bead of truncated ovoid form. Height 10mm; max. diam. 8.5mm; internal diam. 1.5mm. Area 18 Period 3 cremation burial 180172 (fill 180173); soil sample 1823.

3   Bead of sub-spherical form. Height 10mm; max. diam. 10mm; internal diam. 1mm. Area 18 Period 3 cremation burial 180172 (fill 180173); soil sample 1824.

4   Bead of sub-spherical form. Height 10mm; max. diam. 9mm; internal diam. 1.5mm. Area 18 Period 3 cremation burial 180172 (fill 180173); soil sample 1824.

5   Bead of lentoid form. Height 10mm; max. diam. 8mm; internal diam. 1mm. Area 18 Period 3 cremation burial 180172 (fill 180173); soil sample 1824.

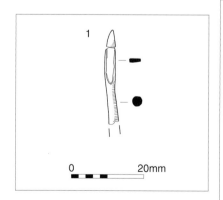

Fig. 4.13   Bronze awl. Cremation burial 180172. Scale 1:1

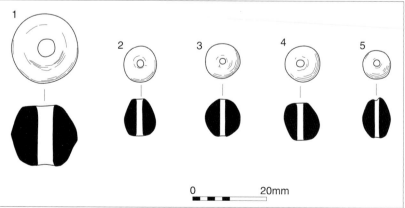

Fig. 4.14   Fired clay beads 1–5. Cremation burial 181072. Scale 1:1

4.5 Worked and utilised stone
Elizabeth Walker [EW], Evan Chapman [EC] and Jana Horák [JH]

Table 4.6 provides a synopsis of the worked or modified stone recorded and a catalogue is included below with a detailed description of items of intrinsic interest. All of the worked items/fragments described relate to Neolithic (Period 2) or Early Bronze Age (Period 3) deposits. The majority comprise ground and polished axe fragments deriving from Welsh sources.

Full details of samples submitted for analysis and including all worked, modified or unmodified and naturally formed pieces, can be found in the archive.

Methodology

Petrological examination of all samples was undertaken following standard methodology detailed in British Standard EN 12407 (2007); initial observation was made with the naked eye followed by use of a x20 achromatic triplet lens, and binocular microscope (Leica MZ 9.5). All observations were restricted to visual identification as no thin sections were produced from these samples. Where appropriate the colour of the rock was estimated using standard Munsell colour charts (Munsell Color 2000) and presented thus (Munsell number [colour name]), and the grain size by standard terminology (e.g. igneous lithologies aphanitic, no crystals visible with the naked eye, phaneritic fine-grained <1mm, medium-grained 1–5mm, coarse 5–50mm and very coarse >50mm; the Wentworth scale has been used for sedimentary lithologies (Table 4.7)).

Geology

The local geology along the St Clears to Red Roses road corridor has a bedrock of Ordovician and Silurian mudstones and limestones, and Lower Devonian sandstones. The lithologies described in this report are dominated by sandstones with a few samples of mudstones and limestone, and several samples of acid volcanic tuffs with a variety of textures. The sedimentary rocks can be broadly attributed to a source in the local bedrock geology but this is not the case for the acid volcanics. Rocks of this composition are present to the west within the Ordovician and Neoproterozoic strata.

These sources lie within the Neoproterozoic Benton Volcanic Group exposed to the north-east of Neyland: approximately 22–37km from the Red Roses to St Clears corridor and to the north-west (approximately 23km) within the volcanic rocks of the Preseli Hills. The Benton Volcanic Group is not particularly well-exposed but does contain siliceous [rhyolitic] volcanic rocks; they are recorded as being dark in colour and typically lavas rather than tuffs. The Preseli acid volcanic tuffs are considered the source of Group VIII axes. These are defined by the Implement Petrology Committee (IPC) as silicified tuff (Clough and Cummins 1988) but it is noted that implements assigned to this group do show some petrographic variation (David and Williams 1995). Axes in this group are typically 'blue or dark coloured, very fine-grained silicic tuffs or lavas, which may be devitrified or recrystallized' (ibid.). Axes with a pale weathered outer surface are however known.

Table 4.6   Synopsis of worked and utilised stone

Site	Period	Context/cut no.	Ra. no.	Status	Lithology
17	–	170002 subsoil		Burnt stone	Clay
18	3	180258/180257		Burnt stone	Sandstone (2 bags)
	3	180262/180261		Burnt stone	Clay (2 bags)
	Unph.	180370/180326		Burnt stone	Calcined limestone
	Unph.	180370/180326		Burnt stone	Calcined limestone
25	3	250064/250063	2501	Whetstone	Sandstone
	2	250104/250103		Burnt stone	Sandstone (3 pieces)
27	5	270119/270120		Burnt stone	Fossiliferous mudstone
30	2	300017/300018	3000	Neolithic ground and polished stone axehead fragment	Microgabbro
31	4	310030/310029	3101	Vitrified stone	Sandstone with vitrified exterior
37	2	370005/370006	3700	Neolithic polished axehead flake	Acid volcanic
	2	370018/370017		Burnt stone	Fossiliferous mudstone
	2	370021/370019		Neolithic denticulated scraper or knife	Acid volcanic
	2	370021/370019		Neolithic stone utilised flake	Acid volcanic
	2	370050/370049		Neolithic stone axehead fragment	Acid volcanic

Key- Unph.= Un-phased. Ra. No.= Registered Artefact number

Identification of samples

The axe fragment from pit 370049, fill 370050 (Cat. No. 3) and a flake from posthole 370006, fill 370005 (Cat. No. 4), both from Site 37, are pale in colour and appear to be pale below the outer surface. From visual identification it would seem that these are therefore not an immediate match to the Group VIII lithology. However an axe and axe fragments more similar to these samples have been described recently from material examined from the Milford Haven to Brecon pipeline excavations (Horák 2014). It may therefore be that the variation within the Group VIII axes has not been fully defined and these are Group VIII examples, or that more than one acid volcanic axe group exists in southern Wales.

The Neolithic ground and polished stone axehead fragment, registered artefact 3000 (Cat. No. 2) from Site 30, pit 300018 is worked from tonalite or leuco-microgabbro. This lithology does not match to any of the axe groups described from South Wales, neither is it readily attributed to a specific geological source.

Worked stone catalogue

Site 25

1   One end of a long, thin rectangular whetstone. This artefact can only be dated to Early Bronze Age by means of its archaeological context [EC]. Arenite. Sandstone, fine-grained, dominated by angular to sub-angular quartz grains. Weathered colour purple/ grey [5YR 6/3] with fresher surfaces closer to pale red [2.5YR 6/2]. The surfaces of this tabular piece of stone are natural in form and bounded by bedding and joint planes. Most likely derivation: local Lower Older Red Sandstone sequence [JH]. Length: 73mm; Width: 35mm; Thickness: 12mm. Period 3 pit 250063 (fill 250064). Registered artefact 2501. *Not illustrated.*

Site 30 (Fig. 4.15)

2   A large fragment of a ground and polished Neolithic stone axehead. The fragment is complete in cross-section and is from a location towards the butt. The axe when complete would have been very large in size and the evidence from the remaining piece indicates that this was a steeply tapering axe, most likely with a pointed butt. The end of the butt is absent and the break at this end is unweathered. This suggests that this break has happened more recently than that at the other end which is weathered and pecked. The axe has a smooth oval cross-section and does not have facets on the sides. Both the sides and the broken blade-end of the axe show possible evidence for pecking. It is possible that once the axe was broken it was reused as a hammer. The pecking is not continuous along both the lengths of the tool suggesting that it is of human origin rather than having been caused by natural processes. The axe surface has been ground and polished [EW]. Microgabbro/microtonalite. Dense medium-grained igneous rock composed of altered

Table 4.7   Udden-Wentworth grain size classification (after Wentworth 1922)

Millimeters		Micrometers µm	Phi ϕ	Wentworth size class		Rock type
4096	4096		−12.0	Boulder		
256	256		−8.0	Cobble	Gravel	Conglomerate/Breccia
	64		-6.0	Pebble		
	4		-2.0	Granule		
	2.00		-1.0	Very coarse sand		
	1.00		0.0	Coarse sand		
½	0.50	500	1.0	Medium sand	Sand	Sandstone
¼	0.25	250	2.0	Fine sand		
¹/₈	0.125	125	3.0	Very fine sand		
¹/₁₆	0.0625	63	4.0	Coarse silt		
¹/₃₂	0.031	31	5.0	Medium silt	Silt	Siltstone
¹/₆₄	0.0156	15.6	6.0	Fine silt		
¹/₁₂₈	0.0078	7.8	7.0	Very fine silt		
¹/₂₅₆	0.0039	3.9	8.0	Clay	Mud	Claystone
	0.00006	0.06	14.0			

plagioclase feldspar and pyroxene. This lithology does not equate to catalogue No. 4 [JH]. Length: 141.2mm; Width: 88.9mm; Thickness: 49.2mm; Weight: 987.9g. Period 2 pit 300018 (fill 300017). Registered artefact 3000. *Fig. 4.15*

Site 37 (Fig. 4.15)

3   Neolithic polished stone axehead fragment. A fragment of what was a ground and polished axehead. There is no certain form to the piece that could indicate precisely where on the original axe the piece originated. It is broad however, and on this basis it would be fair to assume that it may either come from one face of the main body of the axe or alternatively an area towards the blade. The axe is broken; however, the fractured face does not show any certain signs of having been knapped and therefore humanly reworked. There are two scars through the polished surface and neither of these shows any obvious signs of working and there are no traces of any negative bulbs of percussion to either removal [EW]. Acid

tuff. Fine-grained, homogeneous, grey weathering tuff with approximately 7–10% (measured by area) voids formed by the alteration of feldspar crystals [JH]. Length: 58mm; Width: 51.9mm; Thickness: 14.1mm; Weight: 33.1g. Period 2 Pit 370049 (fill 370050). *Not illustrated.*

4   A flake struck from a Neolithic polished stone axehead. The fragment originates from the side of the axe. This edge is facetted. The polished dorsal face of the flake has the remnants of a deep flake scar which was not fully polished out during the manufacture of the axe. This suggests that this axe was not completely regular in form as it gives this face a convex, rather than a concave, section at this specific point. The facetted edge of the axe has a series of distinctive polishing striations which mostly run at right angles to what would have been the axe blade. The position of the bulb of percussion and bulbar scar on the ventral surface indicate that the flake was detached from an already broken piece of axehead, as the striking platform is not on the polished edge

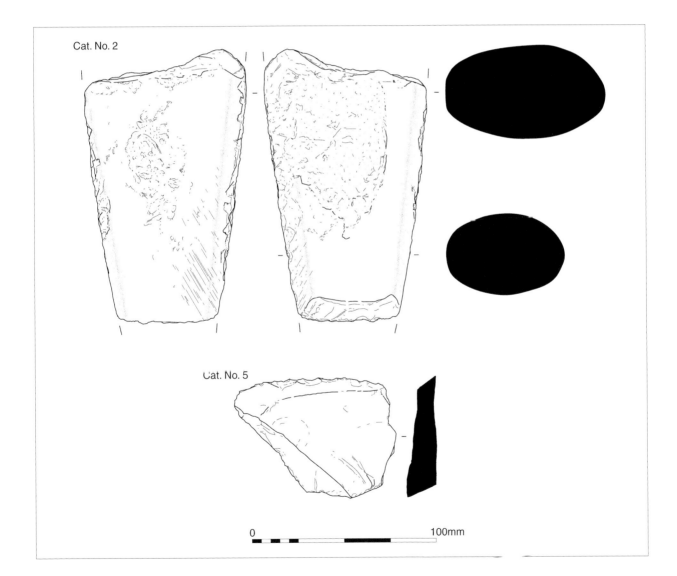

Cat. No. 2

Cat. No. 5

0   100mm

Fig. 4.15   Worked stone. Scale 1:2

which is where it would be if this was a first fracture [EW]. Originally identified as flint this sample is composed of white/cream homogeneous, aphyric acid tuff. A sugary 'saccharoidal' texture has been produced by recrystallisation. The outer surface has a superficial iron staining [JH]. Length: 33.4mm; Width: 18.2mm; Thickness: 6.1mm; Weight: 3.9g. Period 2 Posthole 370006 (fill 370005). Registered artefact 3700. *Not illustrated.*

5   A transverse denticulated scraper or knife. The worked edge is straight and has a series of deep, steep, moderately invasive denticulations running its entire length on the dorsal surface. The dorsal surface has had previous removals taken from it, one of which has a negative bulb of percussion indicating that this flake has been struck from a core. The retouched edge is parallel to the flake's striking platform. The striking platform is thick and plain. On the basis of the tool's form and size it is of probable Neolithic age [EW]. Acid tuff. A fine-grained, grey weathering tuff. This has a homogeneous grain size but

minor colour variations pick out mm to cm scale banding [JH]. Length: 58.2mm; Width: 88.1mm; Thickness: 23.3mm; Weight: 103g. Period 2 pit 370019 (fill 370021). *Fig. 4.15,*

6   A flake with utilisation running along part of one length. The utilised edge is convex in form and the evidence for it only runs along part of the edge. The working is very marginal and is only present on the dorsal surface. The flake has been struck from a core and has no evidence for the original pebble surface surviving. The striking platform is facetted. It has probably been used as a simple cutting tool at some point in its history. The flake size suggests that this may be of Neolithic age [EW]. Acid tuff. Similar but not identical to Ra. 3700. Although generally fine-grained this shows some textural inhomogeneity in the form of ovoid clasts of similar tuff of slightly darker colour [JH]. Length: 68.5mm; Width: 70.1mm; Thickness: 8.5mm; Weight: 31.8g. Period 2 pit 370019 (fill 370021). *Not illustrated.*

Chapter 5
Biological Evidence

5.1 Cremated human remains
Sharon Clough

Osteological analysis was completed on the 62 deposits of cremated human bone recovered from the excavations of Sites 18 and 26 along the St Clears to Red Roses road scheme. Of these, 15 had less than 0.1g of burnt bone recovered and were categorised as accidental inclusions. A further nine deposits had over 1g of cremated bone, but were thought to be redeposited in other features. The remaining 38 deposits were analysed as intentional cremated bone deposits. These were divided into groups by location of burial activity. Twelve samples of the cremated bone and two of charred material from burials were all radiocarbon dated to the Early Bronze Age (Table 2.1). All the cremation burials were contained within a single phase of activity of approximately 220 years. The burials were either contained in an urn or within earth-cut pits, some of which had a stone capping; they varied in size and depth.

Methodology

The cremated bone was examined in accordance with the recommendations by Brickley and McKinley 2004; Mays *et al.* 2004. Each sample was sieved through stacks of 10, 5 and 2mm mesh size. Identifiable bone was further separated into skull, axial, upper and lower limb categories. This was in order to identify any deliberate collection bias and to examine the bone for age, sex and pathological lesions. Animal bone (if identified) was also removed. Age estimations from cremated remains are dependent on the survival of particular age diagnostic elements. Where these survived, reference to standard dry bone methodologies were used. For subadults unerupted teeth, cranial thickness and size of bones help to identify age.

Sex estimation of adult burnt bone relies on the preservation of specific elements and is uncommon

in cremated material. The quantity of warping and shrinkage of the bone during the cremation process must also been taken into consideration when estimating sex using the standard analytical techniques used on dry bone.

Identification of pathological lesions is rarer than in unburnt bone, and where identified standard reference texts are used. Where age at death could be more accurately estimated the burial remains were assigned to the following groups: infant 0–4 years, juvenile 5–12 years, adolescent 13–18 years, young adult 19–25 years, mature adult 26–40 years, older adult 40+ years. Adult, over 20 years, or non-adult, under 20 years, was assigned when no other age indicators were available. Full details of the methodology are available in the project archive.

Results

The cremation burials were divided into three groups (Groups 261: the 'barrow'; 268: the 'pyre hollow'; and 2610: the western group) by spatial location. These are discussed individually; the cremated bone deposits are referred to by the cut number of the feature, also called the cremation burial number. The 15 deposits with less than 1g of bone are considered to be accidental inclusions. They are detailed in Table 5.1, but not discussed further. Deposits of more than 1g, but not intentional deposits have been discussed within their group section.

The 'barrow' Group 261
There were 24 deposits associated with the 'barrow', Group 261. An additional five deposits were part of this group, but have not been included in the group analysis as some only had less than 1g of bone, and others were redeposited cremated bone recovered from non-burial features (Table 5.2). The remaining cremation deposits are detailed in Table 5.3.

Group 261 had five non-adult burials, 18 adult burials and one indeterminate. Of the adult burials, five were

Table 5.1   Deposits with burnt bone of less than 1g

Cut number	Fill number	Sample number	Total weight (g)	Comment
260005	260077, 260078	26018, 26019	<1	Not a cremation burial, redeposited
260009	260010	26108	<0.1	Not a cremation burial, redeposited
260033	260034, 260088, 260089	26034, 26035, 26036	<0.1	Not a cremation burial, redeposited
260244	260245	26174	<0.1	Not a cremation burial, redeposited
260252	260075, 260096	26050, 26057	<0.1	Not a cremation burial, redeposited
260388	260390	26270	<0.1	Not a cremation burial, redeposited
260395	260396	26275	<0.1	Not a cremation burial, redeposited
260436	260432	26295	<0.1	Accessory vessel 16 – Not a cremation burial, redeposited
260462	260463	260305	<0.1	Not a cremation burial, redeposited
260469	260470	260316	<0.1	Not a cremation burial, redeposited
180203	180204	1834	<0.1	Not a cremation burial, redeposited
–	260349	–	0.9	Mound material layer, redeposited cremated bone
260382	–	–	0.5	Posthole, redeposited cremated bone
260587	–	–	0.2	Posthole, redeposited cremated bone
–	260653	–	0.7	Fill of broken accessory vessel within unurned cremation burial, redeposited

Table 5.2   Redeposited human bone in features within Group 261

Cut number	Total weight (g)	Largest fragment size (mm)	Comments	Notes
260333	52.2	27 × 21	Adult ?male	Redeposited cremated bone from burial 260339
260451	1	4 × 4	Unidentified	Redeposited
260037	0.7	11 × 4	From base of truncated urn	Residual cremated bone
260366	1.5		Unidentified	Redeposited
260307	19.5	16 × 13	?Non-adult	Cranial fragments. Redeposited in later cut within 260323. Probably the same individual

estimated to be male and two female. All the burials were of single individuals, no repeated elements were observed. The total weight of the adult burials varied, ranging from 4.6g to 1650.5g, averaging 378g. The greater weights were from the urned or protected (stone capping) burials. These six urned burials averaged 705g, compared to the 18 unurned, which averaged 276g.

Four of the adult burials were tentatively aged mature-older adult and older adult. Burial 260439, for example, displayed joint degeneration on unidentified fragments in the form of osteophytic lipping. This is a common feature, and is age-related (Roberts and Manchester 2005), thereby allowing a tentative suggestion that this individual is an older adult. One individual, burial 260099, was estimated to be between 18 and 20 years old at the time of death, due to identification of a recently fused humeral head. The shale stone covering of this burial infers protection from truncation, so the

low weight of 77.6g was an intentional 'token' deposit. The non-adult burials varied in weight between 31.7g and 386.5g, three were unurned and two were urned. The highest weight was from the unurned burial 260160, which was estimated to be between 4 and 12 years at the time of death. The weight of bone deposited represents 77.2% of the expected weight (Trotter and Hixon 1973). Non-adult burial 260323 was cut by 260307, which contained non-adult human bone (see Table 5.3). This redeposited bone is thought to be from 260323 and would add a further 19.5g to total weight of the burial.

The weights of cremation burials 260339, 260439, 260025, 260035 and 260239 are all around or above 1000g, which suggests these represent a large proportion of the individual (based on whole-person cremated bone weights from modern crematoria of between 1000–3000g (McKinley 2000, 404)). The other cremated bone deposits are likely to be a token amount.

Fragmentation was recorded using largest fragment size and distribution throughout sieve fractions. The largest average fragment size (46mm) was the same as the average of 45mm for other recorded Bronze Age cremation burials (McKinley 1994a, 341). Table 5.4 presents the distribution of bone through the fraction sizes. The bone in all the burials (except where it came from a completely sealed container) was worn and chalky in appearance. This is suggestive of an acidic soil environment for the buried remains, which will have weakened the bone and thereby increased fragmentation.

High fragmentation of the bone appeared to be generally associated with the absence of an urn (or other protection), but also low weight. The unurned burials tended to have more weight in the 5–10mm fraction or 5–2mm fraction, although this was not a clear division: for example cremation burial 260025 had 64% in the <10mm fraction and was unurned. A high weight of cremated bone did appear to correlate with over 50%

Table 5.3   Group 261 cremated bone deposits summary

Cut number	Total weight (g)	Urn number	Notes	Largest fragment size (mm)	Age	Sex	Pathology
260323	144.9	None	Cranial & phalanges.	30 × 15	?Non-adult		
260326	343.3	None	Cranial, tooth root, vert, fem, tib.	44 × 31	Mature–older adult	?Male	
260339	1650.5	Stone capping	All areas represented.	73 × 17	Adult	Male	
260439	986.5	P26.4, Ra.17	All areas represented.	119 × 20	Older adult	Female	Joint degeneration
260449	4.6	None	Cranial fragments.	31 × 7	?Adult		
260019	31.7	None	Cranial, rib, petrous portion, tooth root.	24 × 7	Child over 1 year		
260134	463.5	None	Cranial, tooth root, phalanges, long bone, rib.	46 × 11	Adult	?Male	
260178	73.2	P26.6, Ra.7	Cranial, mandible, hum, vert.	24 × 8	?Non-adult		
260183	670.6	Limestone capping 260174	All areas represented.	50 × 18	Adult		
260254	165.6	Unurned, with accessory vessel P26.20, Ra.3	Cranial, vert, pubis, carpal, metacarpal.	32 × 11	Adult		
260295	6.2	None	Unidentified.	14 × 5	Indeterminate		
260342	344.5	None	Most areas represented.	48 × 37	Adult		
260015	189.2	None	Cranial, rib, vert.	36 × 8	Adult		
260017	82.9	Unurned with accessory vessel P26.24	Tooth roots, cranial, tib.	36 × 15	Adult		
260021	264.4	P26.3, Ra.1	All areas represented.	48 × 21	Non-adult		
260023	23.2	None	Cranial, tooth root.	25 × 11	Adult		
260025	944.1	None	All areas present.	75 × 16	Older adult	Male?	
260035	1183.4	P26.5, Ra.5	All areas present.	92 × 20	Older adult	Female?	
260039	23.6	None	Unidentified.	27 × 8	?Adult		
260099	77.6	Shale stone covering	Cranial, rib, lower limb.	65 × 8	18–20y		
260160	386.5	None	All areas represented.	35 × 35	4–12y		
260239	936.7	None	All areas present.	69 × 23	Adult	Male?	Patella enthesophyte
260242	17.5	None	Unidentified.	28 × 10	Adult		
260261	202.4	None	Upper limb, cranial.	42 × 12	Adult		

Table 5.4   Group 261 cremated bone weight distribution by sieve fraction size

Cut number	<10 mm (g)	<10 %	5–10 mm (g)	5–10 %	5–2 mm (g)	5–2 %	Total (g)
260323	28.9	19.9	49.4	34	66.7	45.9	**144.9**
260326	152.5	44.4	132.6	38.6	58.2	16.9	**343.3**
260339	916.7	55.5	648.3	39.3	84.1	5.09	**1650.5**
260439	682.7	69.2	226.7	22.9	77.1	7.8	**986.5**
260449	1.7	36.9	1.5	32.6	1.4	30.4	**4.6**
260019	3.2	10.09	6.9	21.7	21.6	68.1	**31.7**
260134	204.5	44.1	168.8	36.4	90.2	19.4	**463.5**
260178	21.1	28.8	32.4	44.2	19.7	26.9	**73.2**
260183	304.7	45.4	248.3	37	117.6	17.44	**670.6**
260254	36.2	21.85	94.9	57.3	34.5	20.83	**165.6**
260295	0	0	0	0	6.2	100	**6.2**
260342	157.7	45.7	130.3	37.8	56.5	16.4	**344.5**
260015	1.4	0.7	104.4	55.2	83.4	44.1	**189.2**
260017	33.4	40.2	28.5	34.4	21.0	25.3	**82.9**
260021	99.4	37.6	82.7	31.2	82.3	31.1	**264.4**
260023	0.0	0.0	11.5	50.0	11.7	50.0	**23.2**
260025	623.8	64.8	278.0	29.4	42.3	4.5	**944.1**
260035	810.8	68.5	267.1	22.5	105.5	8.9	**1183.4**
260039	0.0	0.0	14.1	59.7	9.5	40.3	**23.6**
260099	23	29.6	28.1	36.2	26.5	34.1	**77.6**
260160	94.7	24.5	117.0	30.3	174.8	45.2	**386.5**
260239	484.0	51.7	369.2	39.4	83.5	8.9	**936.7**
260242	0.0	0.0	10.2	58.3	7.3	41.7	**17.5**
260261	55.8	27.5	84.5	41.7	67.9	33.5	**202.4**

in the <10mm fraction. The non-adult burials were the most fragmented, with the majority of the bone in the smaller fraction sizes, even where they were urned burials. Fragmentation level affects the identification of elements and estimation of age and sex.

The elements identified for each deposit were divided by skeletal area (Table 5.5). As cranial fragments are more readily identifiable (McKinley 1998), these were the most identified elements for the non-adult and low weight deposits. The largest weighted deposits had about 50% of the bone identified to area of the skeleton. This corresponds with the larger fragment sizes seen in these burials. The least fragmented and highest weighted burials allowed bone to be identified to element in each of the areas, although none were the expected proportions, especially in the axial skeleton area.

Where the burial was recovered in spits and quadrants there did not appear to be a deposition bias in the ordering within the feature or urn. Small bones, such as phalanges and tooth roots were present alongside larger fragments. There was a single instance of a possible animal tooth root observed in cremation burial 260239.

Bronze Age cremation burials contain animal bone in about 16% of cases (McKinley 1997, 132). These were usually small animals such as sheep/goat, pig or bird.

All the cremated bone was completely white in colour. This has been observed at temperatures over 645°C (McKinley 2000, 405), over 750°C (Lyman 1994) and greater than 800°C (Schmidt and Symes 2008). The consistent white colour throughout all the body areas indicates the whole of the individual was within the hottest area. Therefore, the pyre achieved a very high heat for enough time to completely calcine the bone. Only burial 260178 had a hint of grey and a few others had very rare hints on the interior aspect.

Discussion of the 'barrow' (Group 261)

Individuals identified as non-adult to older adult, male and female were present in the burial assemblage. It has been observed from previously studied assemblages that 'primary' Bronze Age barrow burials consistently produce the highest weight of bone (McKinley 1997, 142). The weights of 18 such burials varied between 902.3g and 2747g with an average of 1525.7g (ibid.).

Table 5.5   Group 261 weight of cremated bone by skeletal area. Unid - Unidentified

Cut number	Skull (g)	Skull %	Axial (g)	Axial %	Upper limb (g)	Upper limb %	Lower limb (g)	Lower limb %	Unid limb (g)	Unid limb %	Unid (g)	Unid %	Total weight
260323	3.2	2.21	0	0.00	0	0.00	0	0.00	12.2	8.42	129.5	89.37	144.9
260326	72.4	21.09	1.3	0.38	0	0.00	9.9	2.88	37.3	10.87	222.4	64.78	343.3
260339	295	17.87	42.2	2.56	118	7.15	129.6	7.85	5.1	0.31	1060.6	64.26	1650.5
260439	162.2	16.44	24.3	2.46	79.8	8.09	166.9	16.92	59.5	6.03	493.8	50.06	986.5
260449	0.9	19.57	0	0.00	0	0.00	0	0.00	0.8	17.39	2.9	63.04	4.6
260019	5.7	17.98	0	0.00	0	0.00	0	0.00	2	6.31	23.8	75.08	31.7
260134	100.5	21.68	4.3	0.93	0.8	0.17	32.2	6.95	23.3	5.03	302.4	65.24	463.5
260178	2.9	3.96	0.8	1.09	2.1	2.87	1.3	1.78	10.9	14.89	55.2	75.41	73.2
260183	92.7	13.82	19.9	2.97	14.8	2.21	8.6	1.28	113.6	16.94	421	62.78	670.6
260254	9.8	5.92	2.2	1.33	0.8	0.48	0	0.00	18.3	11.05	134.5	81.22	165.6
260295	0	0.00	0	0.00	0	0.00	0	0.00	0	0.00	6.2	100.00	6.2
260342	23.7	6.95	3	0.90	1.7	0.51	22.2	6.65	121.6	35.18	172.3	49.82	344.5
260015	0.8	0.42	1.7	0.90	0	0.00	0	0.00	0	0.00	186.7	98.68	189.2
260017	15	18.09	0	0.00	0	0.00	4.1	4.95	6.5	7.84	57.3	69.12	82.9
260021	54.5	20.61	2.6	0.98	0.5	0.19	11.2	4.24	20.9	7.90	174.7	66.07	264.4
260023	1.4	6.03	0	0.00	0	0.00	0	0.00	0	0.00	21.8	93.97	23.2
260025	151.7	16.07	54.3	5.75	73.5	7.79	70	7.41	122.6	12.99	472	49.99	944.1
260035	135.8	11.48	30.9	2.61	74.7	6.31	290.1	24.51	62.2	5.26	589.7	49.83	1183.4
260039	0	0.00	0	0.00	0	0.00	0	0.00	0	0.00	23.6	100.00	23.6
260099	1.9	2.45	4	5.15	0	0.00	12.8	16.49	0	0.00	58.9	75.90	77.6
260160	38.7	10.01	3.7	0.96	3.4	0.88	9 7	2.51	13.2	3.42	317.8	82.23	386.5
260239	75.1	8.02	17.9	1.91	37	3.95	83.3	8.89	177.9	18.99	545.5	58.24	936.7
260242	0	0.00	0	0.00	0	0.00	0	0.00	0	0.00	17.5	100.00	17.5
260261	26.2	12.94	0.1	0.05	2.7	1.33	6.4	3.16	19.6	9.68	147.4	72.83	202.4

With a weight of 1650.5g, cist burial 260339 could have fulfilled this role. It is probable that the human remains from burial 260339 comprise the majority of the individual (whole-person cremated bone weights from modern crematoria vary from 1000–3000g, McKinley 2000, 404). However, the deposition of this burial in a stone cist protected it from some of the taphonomic factors, which clearly affected other less well-protected burials, for which lower weights and higher fragmentation levels were recorded. However, the lower weights of some of the urned and unurned burials cannot be explained entirely by taphonomy and must therefore be selected deposits.

The cremated bone was abraded and chalky in appearance, which is characteristic of an acidic burial environment. This would contribute to loss of trabecular bone (spongy bone of the vertebral bodies for example), which is reflected in the low levels of axial

skeleton in the identified bone. The white colour of the bone demonstrates a high temperature pyre of sufficient time to completely calcine the bone.

The 'pyre hollow' Group 268
This group comprised five burials of cremated bone. Burial 260402 came from a broken accessory vessel (260401) and weighed 0.1g. Such a small quantity of cremated bone is likely to be an incidental inclusion, and this deposit is not included in further discussion. Table 5.6 includes further features which contained very small quantities of cremated bone. These are considered to be intrusive redeposited bone.

Of the four cremation burials (Table 5.7), two were unurned and the remainder were either urned or had capping stone. The highest weighted burials corresponded with the greater level of protection. Cremation burial 260397 had a very low weight, 5g, and very small

Table 5.6   Group 268 features with cremated bone

Cut number	Total weight (g)	Size of fragment	Comment	Notes
260489	3.6	35 × 2	Small pit same as 260596	Redeposited cremated bone
260596	8.8	22 × 12	Small pit same as 260489	Redeposited cremated bone
260492	0.9	–	2 tiny pieces of cranial fragment, ?non-adult	Redeposited cremated bone

Table 5.7   Group 268 cremated bone summary

Cut number	Total weight (g)	Urn	Notes	Max fragment size (mm)	Age	Sex	Pathology
260397	5	None	None identified	5 × 5	Adult	–	–
260407	739.7	Capping	Skull, long bone, axial	61 × 16	Older adult	–	Spinal degenerative joint disease & osteophytosis Mandibular tooth PM2 lost antemortem
260424	361	None, accessory vessel P26.11	Cranial, vert, lower limb	61 × 29	Adult	?Male	–
260474	1795.2	P26.8, Ra.18	Nearly all skeleton present	144 × 23	?Older adult	?Male	Osteophytosis lumbar spine

Table 5.8   Group 268 cremated bone weight distribution by sieve fraction size

Cut number	<10 mm	<10 %	5–10 mm	5–10 %	5–2 mm	5–2 %	Total weight
260397	0	0	2.7	54	2.3	46	5
260407	338.7	45.7	269	36.4	132	17.8	739.7
260424	164.6	45.6	141.2	39.1	55.2	15.2	361
260474	1652.5	92	82.2	4.6	60.5	3.4	1795.2

Table 5.9   Group 268 weight of cremated bone by skeletal area

Cut number	Skull (g)	Skull %	Axial (g)	Axial %	Upper limb (g)	Upper limb %	Lower limb (g)	Lower limb %	Unid limb (g)	Unid limb %	Unid (g)	Unid %	Total weight
260397	0	0	0	0	0	0	0	0	0	0	5	100	5
260407	61	8.25	20.7	2.8	8.1	1.1	62.5	8.4	15.5	2.1	571.9	77.32	739.7
260424	36.2	10	10	2.7	3.1	0.8	56.2	15.5	9.4	2.6	246.1	68.2	361
260474	230.2	12.82	146.9	8.18	264.4	14.73	641.9	35.76	0	0	511.8	28.51	1795.2

fragment size, 5mm, and had no identifiable elements. This feature is therefore probably redeposited cremated bone or a heavily truncated burial. The bone in all cases was white, with the very rare hint of grey. The bone within the unurned burials was abraded around the edges. Cremation burial 260474 was exceptional; the inverted urn had protected the cremated bone from soil intrusion. The cremated bone was therefore not subjected to the taphonomic effects afforded to all the other burials. Removal of the bone from urn was simply a matter of carefully lifting it, as there was no soil matrix (Fig. 5.1). The high weight reflects the completeness of the burial and it is very likely that this was the entire individual as collected from the pyre.

The age of all the burials in this group was adult, of which three were very likely to be in the older age range.

Fig. 5.1   Burial 260474, laboratory excavation. 100mm scale

Two of the burials were tentatively identified to male. Pathologies were observed on some of the cremated bone. These mostly relate to degeneration of the joints and a single instance of tooth loss during the lifetime of the individual.

As expected the burial 260474 had over 90% of fragments in the greater than 10mm fraction. The other burials were more evenly distributed with 260407 and 260424 having 45% in the <10mm fraction and 260397 had none (Table 5.8). It is interesting to note that despite the protection of the capping burial 260407 had the same level of fragmentation as the unurned burial 260424. The distribution of identified elements for this group of burials demonstrates that all areas of the skeleton were selected for burial from the pyre (Table 5.9). In particular, it is noticeable from burial 260474 that the quantities are very close to the 'ideal' percentage for each area. The skull should be 18.2%: for burial 260474 it was 13%; the upper limb should be 23.1% and it was 15%; the lower limb should be 38.1% and it was 36%. The axial, however, should be 20.6%, but burial 260474 only had 8%. So, despite the cushioning effect of the inverted urn, the spongy bone found in the axial skeleton did not survive complete enough to be identified. It is possible that the high temperature of the pyre, which fully calcined the bone, made it very brittle and prone to fragmentation. The post-pyre handling and weight of other bone inside the urn crushed spongy bone beyond identification. There was only 25% of the bone unidentified. It was possible to lay out the bone in anatomical position, as you would an unburnt skeleton, as the fragments were so large and easily identified. There were no repeated elements in this burial, of what is likely to be an older adult male. There was osteophytosis up to 3–4mm on the lumbar 4 and 5 vertebrae and the first sacral body. This additional bone growth can be age-related. The elements were distributed throughout the urn, with all areas present in each spit. It is concluded that there was no ordering to the deposition. Burial 260474 with a weight of 1795.2g is slightly above the

average weight that has been calculated for 'primary' Bronze Age barrow burials. It was considered that time spent collecting bone from the pyre and deposition in a container reflected 'status' of the individual (McKinley 1997, 142). Burial 260474 displayed a fine example of the effect of the pyre in the severe warping of the right radial bone. This bone was completely U-shaped when it should have been straight. This would only have been possible if the individual was burnt on a very hot pyre which reached high temperatures very quickly, forcing out the moisture from the bone causing it to warp. Long bones are more prone to deformation and it indicates a fresh cremation and extreme temperatures as high as 1600°C, transforming the bone salts (Ubelaker and Rife 2007, 50). Other areas of the skeleton, such as the cranium, also demonstrated severe warping.

The western group: Group 2610
This group lay some distance west of the other groups. There were ten deposits, six of which were contained within an urn. Three were identified as male and three were female. Nine were adult burials and one indeterminate (Table 5.10). The total weights averaged 331g and ranged from 4.7g–746.3g. The largest deposit was 746.3g (cremation burial 260276) from an urn. The smallest weight was burial 260288 at only 4.7g and had heavily abraded edges. This deposit may or may not be an intentional interment or it could be a heavily truncated burial. There were no identifiable elements.

The identifications of male or female for the burials were based on a single element of either cranial or pelvic morphology and are therefore tentative. The presence of degenerative changes on joint surfaces implied an older age range (Roberts and Manchester 2005). Cremation burial 260303 had the auricular surface present allowing a more precise age to be estimated. There were no non-adults identified in this group.

Pathology was confined to degenerative changes of the spinal column, except for arachnoid granulations on the endocranial surface of cremation burial 260276. These (asymptomatic, aetiology unknown) endocranial lesions are usually found on the frontal bone in older females (Mann and Murphy 1990).

Table 5.11 shows that there appeared to be no correlation between urned burials and a high percentage of large fragment sizes. Most fragments were in the 5–10mm fraction, which implies a large degree of fragmentation. This prevented identification of elements and most likely occurred after deposition (McKinley 1994a).

Due to the high fragmentation level the quantity of identified elements was quite low (Table 5.12). Limb and skull elements were the most frequently identified which corresponds with how much more easily they are recognised. The distribution of elements within the urn or pit did not appear to be selective. All areas of the skeleton were represented throughout the spits and

Table 5.10   Summary of cremation burials from Group 2610

Cut number	Total weight (g)	Urn number	Notes	Largest fragment size (mm)	Age	Sex	Pathology
180172	176.2	Ra. 18.01 accessory vessel P18.1 (inverted)	Most areas represented.	65 × 15	Adult	–	
180184	162.9	none	Cranial, tooth root, unid long bone, phalanx.	29 × 8	Adult	–	
260207	141.3	P26.7, Ra.9	Cranial, vert, unid long bone.	44 × 9	Adult	?Female	
260210	725.8	P26.9, Ra.8	Most areas present.	80 × 19	Adult	?Male	
260229	355.3	P26.12, Ra.11 (broken)	Most areas represented.	56 × 10	Adult	?Male	
260231	442.1	P26.18, Ra.10	Cranial, vert, pelvis, long bone, rib, tooth root.	53 × 12	Adult	?Female	
260236	71.6	none	Cranial, tooth root, vert, long bone.	54 × 15	Mature–older adult	–	Vertebral joint Degeneration.
260276	746.3	P26.15, Ra.13	Cranial, long bone, vert, hand phalanx, rib, pelvis, tooth root.	70 × 18	Older adult	?Female	Arachnoid granulations, osteophytosis vertebral bodies.
260288	4.7	none	Unidentified.	13 × 5	Indeterminate	–	
260303	493.2	none	Cranial, vert, rib, upper limb, lower limb, tooth root, phalanx.	54 x 18	20–40 years	?Male	

Table 5.11   Group 2610 cremated bone weight distribution by sieve fraction size

Cut number	<10 mm	<10 %	5–10 mm	5–10 %	5–2 mm	5–2 %	Total weight
180172	24.3	13.8	85.3	48.4	48.2	27.3	176.2
180184	17.4	10.6	65.9	40.4	78	47.8	162.9
260207	44.1	31.7	89.9	64.6	7.3	5.2	141.3
260210	395.2	54.4	290.6	40	40	5.5	725.8
260229	136	38.2	151.4	42.6	67.9	19.1	355.3
260231	141.7	32.1	186	42.1	114.4	25.8	442.1
260236	15.4	21.5	36.7	51.2	19.5	27.2	71.6
260276	272.7	36.5	257.8	34.5	215.8	28.9	746.3
260288	0	0	0	0	4.7	100	4.7
260303	244.4	49.5	220	44.6	28.8	5.8	493.2

quadrants. All the bone was white in colour, with very rare hints of grey. The edges of the cremated bone were abraded, more so in the unurned burials or where the bone was in the backfill. This group represents possibly ten adult burials of which none are the complete quantity of skeleton available after the pyre. An average of 331g and largest weight 746.3g is significantly less than a full adult weight (McKinley 2000, 404). This is not unusual as it is frequently found that 50% or less of the bone available after cremation is included in the burial (McKinley 2000). As found in the other groups, bone was abraded, trabecular bone was frequently absent and there were high fragmentation levels. The cremated bone was consistently white in colour indicating a high pyre temperature was achieved for a substantial period of time.

All the burials were of single individuals and there was no evidence of animal bone. It was possible to tentatively assign sex to six burials, three male and three female. A more precise age was estimated for three burials and places them in the mature-older age categories. Pathology was confined to joint degeneration, which is a very frequent finding in all time periods (Roberts and Manchester 2005).

Table 5.12   Group 2610 weight of cremated bone by skeletal area. Unid = unidentifiable

Cut number	Skull (g)	Skull %	Axial (g)	Axial %	Upper limb (g)	Upper limb %	Lower limb (g)	Lower limb %	Unid limb (g)	Unid limb %	Unid (g)	Unid %	Total weight
180172	14.7	8.34	1.2	0.68	3.4	1.93	0	0.00	24.8	14.07	132.1	74.97	**176.2**
180184	14.6	8.96	0	0.00	0	0.00	0	0.00	12.3	7.55	136	83.49	**162.9**
260207	13.1	9.27	0.5	0.35	0	0.00	0	0.00	17.7	12.53	110	77.85	**141.3**
260210	122.9	17.10	7.5	1.13	36.7	5.52	90.7	13.64	48.2	6.39	419.8	56.22	**725.8**
260229	50.1	15.08	7.2	2.47	14	4.37	25.5	9.32	5.9	2.28	252.6	66.47	**355.3**
260231	20.8	5.01	4.1	0.99	1.8	0.43	1.2	0.29	104.2	25.09	310	74.64	**442.1**
260236	1	1.40	0.5	0.70	0	0.00	0	0.00	13.1	18.30	57	79.61	**71.6**
260276	50.6	8.00	19	3.00	10.1	1.60	47.8	7.56	116.5	18.42	502.3	79.44	**746.3**
260288	0	0.00	0	0.00	0	0.00	0	0.00	0	0.00	4.7	100.00	**4.7**
260303	62.9	12.75	47.4	9.61	18.3	3.71	47.5	9.63	4.3	0.87	312.8	63.42	**493.2**

Discussion

There were three groups representing different areas of burial. The total number of cremated bone deposits fully discussed was 38. These were unevenly distributed amongst the groups with 24 in the barrow area (Group 261), four in the 'pyre hollow' (Group 268) and ten in the western group (Group 2610).

Age range

Of the cremation burials, 31 were adult and five were non-adult (two were undetermined). Precise adult ages were not generally possible and where identified were often reliant on a single factor. Adults from all the age groups were identified from across the groups. Only older adults were identified from the barrow area (the very low weighted burial 260397 was identified to adult only). The five non-adults represented 13% of the aged individuals. The number of non-adults to adults varies considerably throughout populations and history. Where there is a high infant death rate, it would be expected to have a high birth rate (Chamberlain 2006), so amongst the living population there would be a high number of children. As the death rate in this period is not known, then it cannot be stated whether 13% represents the correct amount of children or not. The pattern of distribution of non-adults amongst the groups shows they were present in the barrow area only. They are completely absent from the pyre hollow and the group to the west. Sites 18 and 26 (St Clears road scheme) and Site 513 Land North-West of Steynton, Milford Haven, Pembrokeshire had a similar range of adult age groups represented (Fotaki and Holst 2014a), although Site 513 did have an unusually large quantity of non-adults. At Site 513 there were 15 deposits with bone, of which five were double burials, so a total of 20 individuals. Three other features were identified as burials although they did not yield bone. This is a similar number to Site 26 with 24 burials in the barrow area.

Sex distribution

Of the adults represented, eleven were male and five were female. The identification of double the number of males may be partially due to the osteological methods which rely on the presence of enlarged features on the male skull and pelvis making them more likely to be identified (Weiss 1972). However, a similar finding by Walsh (2013) from Bronze Age inhumations (156 inhumations from the north of England for comparison, as these are more accurately aged and sexed) was 60% males to 31% females. Interestingly Brück (2009) found that of Early Bronze Age inhumation and cremation burial, 'the female dead were more likely to be cremated than their male counterparts' (Brück 2009, 4). At Site 513 Land North-West of Steynton, Milford Haven, Pembrokeshire none of the burials were sexed (Fotaki and Holst, 2014a), so it is not possible to compare results.

With such a small number of sexed adults any apparent patterning across the groups is likely to be inflated. The groups are also very uneven in size. There does not appear to a sex bias in the location of burial.

Of the older adults identified there were three female and one male from the St Clears road scheme cremation burials. It is interesting to note that Walsh (2013) found that more females than males lived into the older age group in the Bronze Age inhumations.

Pathological conditions

Pathology identified from the cremated bone was limited. It was mostly age-related joint degeneration (commonly called arthritis, although this needs particular diagnostic criteria in dry bone), particularly the spine. In a modern population one third of adults over 65 years suffer from joint disease. Stress on the joints increased in the Bronze Age from the Neolithic, which may tie in with the intensification of farming. It rose from 10.2% to 16.8% of individuals with joint disease (Roberts and Cox 2003). There was a single instance of tooth loss which had occurred before death (ante-mortem), this is usually caused by caries. Ante-mortem tooth loss has been calculated at 13.2% for the Bronze Age (ibid.) an increase from the Neolithic and possibly due to the intensification of agriculture and increase in cereal crop consumption. A single instance of arachnoid granulations was observed; these are small indentations usually inside the frontal bone of the cranium. They have no apparent health implications and are commonly seen in older adults. These are similar findings to other sites. Walsh (2013) found dental disease, degenerative joint disease, trauma and scurvy occurred amongst the 332 Early Bronze Age individuals examined from the north of England. Site 513, Land North-West of Steynton, Milford Haven, Pembrokeshire, also observed mostly age-related degenerative changes amongst the adult cremation burials (Fotaki and Holst, 2014a).

Total weight of cremated bone

Weight ranged at Sites 18 and 26 from 3.6g–1795.2g; the average was 304g. The majority of the weights are far below the expected amount for a full adult (McKinley 2000, 404) or child (Mann and Murphy 1990). An average of 327g–466g has been calculated for this period (McKinley 2005, 14). Complete recovery of the entire cremated remains was not important or desired in the Bronze Age (Rebay-Salisbury 2010). Interment of a few body parts appeared to suffice for the funerary rites. The remainder of the cremated bone may have been left on the pyre, scattered in the landscape (or watercourse) or given to the mourners (ibid.).

Sites 18 and 26 cremation burials appeared to have no correlation between weight of bone and age or sex. No patterns in bone weights have emerged from other sites either (McKinley 1997, 139).

In comparison of weight recovered, Site 513 Land North-West of Steynton, Milford Haven Pembrokeshire had an average of 645g (Fotaki and Holst, 2014a). The higher average weight can be explained by the number of multiple burials recovered from Site 513. All the burials at Sites 18 and 26 were single. Multiple burials are seen less often than single in the Bronze Age period. For example, out of 109 cremation burials, 19 were multiple (17%) from the Bronze Age cremation burials examined in the north-west of England (Walsh 2013). Of the four burials with over 1000g weight from Site 513, Land North-West of Steynton, Milford Haven, Pembrokeshire, all were multiple burials. This site appears to be unusual in the quantity of multiple burials at 40%. In contrast Sites 18 and 26 have none,

it would be expected that at least 5% were multiple (as found from a sample of *c.* 4000 multi-period burials, McKinley 1997, 130). Sites 37.17 Land North of Llwyn-Meurig, Trecastle, Powys and Site 47 Land North-West of Cwm-Camlais-Isaf, Trallong, Penpont and Llanfihangel, Powys also produced Bronze Age cremation burials (Fotaki and Holst 2014b and 2014c). There were only eight cremated bone deposits from Site 38.17 and 12 from Site 47. The bone weights were very low from Site 38.17 at 16–111g, and ranged from 8–1754g at Site 47. Again the higher weighted burials were from multiple individuals (Site 47) (Fotaki and Holst 2014b and 2014c).

Pyre technology

The practice of cremation accelerates the transformation of the corpse (Rebay-Salisbury 2010). This is most easily seen in the final colour of the cremated bone. There was a very consistent white colour observed amongst the bone from Sites 18 and 26. White is the result of a high pyre temperature for a sustained period (several hours). It is the final colour from the range that bone goes through in the process of cremation. To achieve a consistent white colour to all body parts (the high-fat areas burn better than, for example, hands and feet) the pyre would have to be maintained to keep an even temperature across the area where the corpse lay. In contrast, the colour range of bone from Site 47 Land North-West of Cwm-Camlais-Isaf, Trallong, Penpont and Llanfihangel, Powys was quite varied from brown to white (Fotaki and Holst 2014c). This indicates that fully calcined bone, completely white, was important to the mourners at Sites 18 and 26.

Fragmentation levels of cremated bone

It was observed that fragmentation was the same across all groups and was higher than average. This is likely to be because of post-depositional disturbance. Other factors could have been the high temperature and rapid dehydration as seen in the very white bone observed, which resulted in a very brittle bone. Fragmentation occurs during the cremation process and may be increased if movement occurs at this point. Little is known about methods of recovery from the pyre. It was probably left to cool overnight and then the remaining wood ash was raked or poked in order to collect the bones, resulting in further fragmentation. Cultural practices can impact to a degree on fragmentation, such as extinguishing the pyre with water or wine and deliberate crushing (Rebay-Salisbury 2010). However, there is no evidence to support these actions. Post-deposition processes and inclusion in an urn, or not, will also affect the level of fragmentation. It was frequently observed across all the groups that the unurned cremated bone was abraded to the edges and chalky white, which indicated erosion by the soil matrix. The urned burials were also affected where the soil had become included in the urn. It has also been noted that during post-excavation the resulting fragments are not always the same size as when they lay in the urn, having broken up during lifting along fissure lines. Urned burial 260474 demonstrated how complete fragments could be, when not affected by soil and post-excavation.

When compared to Site 513 Land North-West of Steynton, Milford Haven, Pembrokeshire which had 12 Early Bronze Age cremation burials (Fotaki and Holst 2014a), it can be seen fragmentation is quite different at Sites 18 and 26. On average 59% of the bone fragments from Site 513 were identifiable, whereas only an average of 40% were at Sites 18 and 26. It was also observed at Site 513 that all burials had fragments in the <10mm fraction and most were in this or the 5–10mm. At Sites 18 and 26 this was not the case. It can be suggested that perhaps the burial environment here contributed to the higher fragmentation levels.

Burial 260474
Burial 260474 from Site 26 was a particularly interesting deposit with the very high level of preservation and low disturbance. The highest weights at Site 513 Land North-West of Steynton, Milford Haven, Pembrokeshire were 1200g and these were multiple individuals (Fotaki and Holst 2014a). The 1700g from burial 260474 of a single individual really highlights its importance. It also demonstrated the effect of post-depositional factors on cremated bone, if we assume that all the other cremated bone was picked out from the pyre in the same way. Further, it clearly demonstrates that full collection of bone could be achieved and deposits of less than this were clearly intentional. The severe deformation of the cremated bone in 260474 gives clear insight into the pyre technology available in the Early Bronze Age, which must have created temperatures up to 1600°C (which is extremely high; half of that is normally sufficient).

Burial 260339
Burial 260339 was also of very high weight for a single individual, at 1650.5g, especially considering it was protected only by a stone capping. This again is a higher weight than that of three intermingled individuals at Site 513 Land North-West of Steynton, Milford Haven, Pembrokeshire (1200g) (Fotaki and Holst 2014a). It is suggested that perhaps since it is in a different group to burial 260474 they are both 'primary burials'. Further high weights were seen in three burials in the barrow area, all *c.* 1000g. These are perhaps other high-status individuals.

The large assemblage of Early Bronze Age cremation burials from Sites 18 and 26 contribute to the increasing information available about cremation practice and burial at this time in South Wales. This group possibly reflects the living population who chose to bury their dead in this way, at this place.

5.2 Animal bone
Andy Clarke

Period 2 Early Neolithic

Site 25
A single fragment of bone (1g) was recovered from deposit 250165, the fill of pit feature 250164 (Table 5.13). The bone was unidentifiable but its calcined state clearly indicates prolonged heating to temperatures in excess of 800°C (Lyman 1994, 386).

Period 3 Bronze Age

Sites 18 and 25
A total of nine fragments (28g) of bone were recovered (Table 5.13). The only identifiable fragments were a partial cattle (*Bos taurus*) radius identified from deposit 180472, a fill of the possible drying oven 180304, and a fragment of sheep/goat (*Ovis aries/Capra hircus*) metapodial from the fill of pit 250079. These types of bones are typical inclusions in assemblages consisting of the waste from secondary butchery. However, such an inference cannot be made from single fragments and it is more than likely that the bones are residual in nature. The remaining seven fragments (7g) were all unidentifiable to species and too fragmentary to ascertain either a human or animal origin but displayed colouration ranging from blue/black through to bright white indicating heating from between 400 to 800°C (Lyman 1994, 386).

5.3 Plant macrofossils and charcoal
Sarah Cobain

A total of 538 bulk soil samples were processed and assessed for plant macrofossil and charcoal remains. Of these, 474 samples were taken from contexts dating to the Early Neolithic and Bronze Age periods. The remainder are reported on in detail separately. Following post-excavation assessment, 23 of these samples were deemed suitable for plant macrofossil analysis and 159 for charcoal analysis. The samples were from Early Neolithic pits and postholes at Sites 25 and 37, Bronze Age cremation burials and associated pits, postholes and tree throws at Sites 18/26, Bronze Age pits at Sites 25, 35 and 37 and a Bronze Age burnt mound at Site 32. The aim of full analysis was to identify and record all plant remains and charcoal and to provide additional information regarding the function of features sampled, socio-economic activities and to infer the composition of the local woodlands and flora (Cobain 2014a).

Methodology

Plant macrofossil and charcoal remains were retrieved by standard flotation procedures by Cotswold Archaeology using a 250-micron sieve to collect the flot and 1mm mesh to retain the residue. The residue was dried and sorted by eye and the floated material scanned and seeds

Table 5.13   Identified animal species by fragment count (NISP) and weight and context

Context number	Feature number	Sample number	BOS	O/C	Burnt and unidentifiable	Total	Weight (g)
			Period 2 Early Neolithic				
			Site 25				
250165	250164	N/A			1	1	1
Subtotal					1	1	1
			Period 3 Bronze Age				
			Site 18				
180173	180172	1822			1	1	1
180472	180304	N/A	1			1	19
180524	180304	1860			4	4	5
180533	180304	1867			1	1	1
			Site 25				
250080	250079	N/A		1	1	2	2
Subtotal			1	1	7	9	28
Grand total			1	1	8	10	29
Weight (g)			19	2	10		

BOS = cattle; O/C = sheep/goat

identified using a low power stereo-microscope (Brunel MX1) (×10–×40). Identifications were carried out with reference to images and descriptions by Cappers *et al.* (2006), Neef *et al.* (2012), Berggren (1981) and Anderberg (1994). Up to 100 charcoal fragments of the >2mm sieve fraction were fractured by hand to reveal the wood anatomy on radial, tangential and transverse planes and identified using an epi-illuminating microscope (Brunel SP400) (x40–x400). Identifications were carried out with reference to images and descriptions by Gale and Cutler (2000), Schoch *et al.* (2004) and Wheeler *et al.* (1989). Nomenclature and habitat description follows Stace (1997).

Results

The plant macrofossil and charcoal remains were generally well preserved with 17 individual plant and 11 tree/shrub species identified. The detailed results of analysis are presented in Tables 5.14–5.23. Where the taxa are not sufficiently well preserved to observe subtle anatomical differences required for full identification, all the possibilities are listed (for example hawthorn/rowan/crab apple (C*rataegus monogyna/Sorbus/Malus sylvestris*)).

Period 2 Neolithic

Site 25
Charcoal recovered from pits 250103, 250109, 250119, 250141 and 250117 contained large amounts of oak (*Quercus*), alder (*Alnus glutinosa*), hazel (*Corylus avellana*) and alder/hazel, hawthorn/rowan/crab apple (C*rataegus monogyna/Sorbus/Malus sylvestris*), cherry species (*Prunus*) and willow/poplar (*Salix/Populus*).

Site 37
The samples from pits 370017, 370019, 370043, 370037, 370052, 370073, 370085, 370119, 370123 and 370153 revealed a large number of plant macrofossil and charcoal remains. The vast majority of the plant macrofossils were made up of hazelnut shells with smaller numbers of crab apple (*Malus sylvestris*) pips and stalks, fruit (possible crab apple) flesh and skin fragments, a cherry species stalk and bramble (*Rubus*) seeds. Cereal remains were identified as emmer (*Triticum dicoccum*) and emmer/spelt wheat (*Triticum dicoccum/Triticum spelta*), wheat (*Triticum*) species, naked barley (*Hordeum vulgare*) and oat (*Avena*) cereal grains, and cereal chaff including emmer and emmer/spelt wheat glume bases and spikelet forks, culm nodes, barley rachis and straw fragments. In addition ash (*Fraxinus excelsior*) and grass species seeds and stems were recorded. Charcoal was abundant and identified as oak, alder, hazel, alder/hazel, hawthorn/rowan/crab apple, cherry species, blackthorn (*Prunus spinosa*), willow/poplar, birch (*Betula*) and gorse/broom (*Ulex/Cytisus*).

Period 3 Bronze Age

Site 18
Pit 180174 contained a large assemblage of charcoal identified as oak, alder/hazel and hazel. Drying oven 180304 contained no plant macrofossils but a large assemblage of oak and gorse/broom charcoal was recorded.

Cremation burials and related features at Site 18 and Site 26
Plant remains recovered within the cremation burials and pits, postholes and a tree throw were generally low

Table 5.14 Plant macrofossil identifications Period 2 (Site 37)

Site				37	37	37	37	37	37
Context number				370018	370021	370042	370035	370053	370074
Feature number				370017	370019	370043	370037	370052	370073
Sample number (SS)				3706	3701	3708	3709	3710	3715
Flot volume (ml)				798	2564	655	1399	368	426
Sample volume processed (l)				20	19	18	9	9	7
Charred items per litre of soil				45.3	15.2	133.9	80.6	57.6	52.1
Period				2	2	2	2	2	2
Plant macrofossil preservation				Good	Good	Good	Good	Good	Good
Habitat Code	**Family**	**Species**	**Common Name**						
HSW	Betulaceae	*Corylus avellana* L.	Hazelnut shells (fragment >10mm)	4	–	–	–	–	–
HSW		*Corylus avellana* L.	Hazelnut shells (fragment >5mm)	50	15	71	69	101	6
HSW		*Corylus avellana* L.	Hazelnut shells (fragment >2mm)	844	25	2339	635	414	181
HSW		*Corylus avellana* L.	Hazelnut shells (fragment <2mm)	+++++	–	+++++	+++++	++++	++++
HSW	Oleaceae	*Fraxinus excelsior* L.	Ash	–	1	–	–	–	–
E	Poaceae	*Hordeum vulgare* L.	Barley grain (naked)	–	3	–	–	1	5
E		*Hordeum vulgare* L.	Barley rachis	–	–	–	–	–	3
E		*Triticum*	Wheat sp. grain	–	–	–	–	–	7
E		*Triticum dicoccum*	Emmer wheat grain	–	87	1	5	–	44
E		*Triticum dicoccum*	Emmer wheat glume base	–	3	–	–	–	69
E		*Triticum dicoccum*	Emmer wheat spikelet fork	–	2	–	–	–	17
E		*Triticum dicoccum/ Triticum spelta*	Emmer/spelt wheat grain	–	8	–	1	1	–
E		*Triticum dicoccum/ Triticum spelta*	Emmer/spelt wheat glume base	–	1	–	–	–	17
E		*Triticum dicoccum/ Triticum spelta*	Emmer/spelt wheat spikelet fork	–	–	–	–	–	9
E		*Poaceae*	Indet. cereal grain (whole)	1	17	–	4	–	2
E		*Poaceae*	Indet. cereal grain (fragment >2mm)	1	118	–	10	1	–
E		*Poaceae*	Indet. cereal grain (fragment <2mm)	–	++++	–	–	–	++
E		*Poaceae*	Straw	–	–	–	–	–	1
HSW	Rosaceae	*Malus sylvestris* (L.) Mill.	Crab apple pip	–	1	–	–	–	–
HSW		*Malus sylvestris* (L.) Mill.	Crab apple stem	1	5	–	–	–	1
HSW		*Malus sylvestris* (L.) Mill.	?Crab apple flesh (fragment)	4	2	–	1	–	–
HSW		*Prunus* L.	?Cherries stem	–	–	–	–	–	1
HSW/D		*Rubus* L.	Brambles	–	–	–	–	–	2
Total				905	288	2411	725	518	365

Table 5.15   Plant macrofossil identifications Period 2 (Site 37)

Site				37	37	37	37	37	37
Context number				370086	370087	370120	370124	370155	370156
Feature number				370085	370085	370119	370123	370153	370153
Sample number (SS)				3705	3707	3712	3711	3714	3713
Flot volume (ml)				923	1981	241	215	182	244
Sample volume processed (l)				19	13	9	8	7	9
Charred items per litre of soil				45.3	1073.2	35.7	136.6	46.3	55.7
Period				2	2	2	2	2	2
Plant macrofossil preservation				Moderate	Good	Good	Good	Good	Good
Habitat Code	Family	Species	Common Name						
HSW		*Corylus avellana* L.	Hazelnut shells (fragment >10mm)	–	3	–	5	–	–
HSW	Betulaceae	*Corylus avellana* L.	Hazelnut shells (fragment >5mm)	94	973	11	107	21	32
HSW		*Corylus avellana* L.	Hazelnut shells (fragment >2mm)	762	12937	307	977	300	458
HSW		*Corylus avellana* L.	Hazelnut shells (fragment <2mm)	++++	++++++	++++	++++++	++++	++++
E		*Avena* L.	Oats grain	–	–	–	1	–	–
E		*Hordeum vulgare* L.	Barley grain (naked)	–	–	–	1	–	–
E		*Triticum*	Wheat sp. grain	–	–	1	–	–	1
E		*Triticum dicoccum*	Emmer wheat grain	1	5	–	–	1	3
E		*Triticum dicoccum/ Triticum spelta*	Emmer/spelt wheat grain	1	6	–	–	–	–
E	Poaceae	*Poaceae*	Indet. cereal grain (whole)	–	1	–	–	–	4
E		*Poaceae*	Indet. cereal grain (fragment >2mm)	2	7	1	–	2	3
E		*Poaceae*	Culm node (whole)	–	1	1	–	–	–
E		*Poaceae*	Grass sp. seed	–	–	–	1	–	–
P		*Poaceae*	Grass sp. stem	–	1	–	1	–	–
HSW		*Malus sylvestris* (L.) Mill.	Crab apple pip	–	4	–	–	–	–
HSW		*Malus sylvestris* (L.) Mill.	Crab apple stem	–	4	–	–	–	–
HSW	Rosaceae	*Malus sylvestris* (L.) Mill.	?Crab apple flesh (fragment)	–	8	–	–	–	–
HSW		*Malus sylvestris* (L.) Mill.	?Crab apple skin (fragment)	–	1	–	–	–	–
HSW		*Prunus* L.	?Cherries stem	–	1	–	–	–	–
Total				860	13952	321	1093	324	501

in quantity and, with the exception of two features, did not warrant further analytical work (Cobain 2014a, 147). The collective remains identified included hazelnut shells, oak involucres (acorn cups), blackthorn pips, a small number of barley/possibly barley cereal grains, culm nodes, straw fragments and seeds including black-bindweed (*Fallopia convolvulus*), ribwort plantain (*Plantago lanceolata*), knotweed (*Persicaria*), bramble (possible blackberry) (*Rubus*), cleavers (*Galium aparine*), brassica-type, vetch/pea-type (*Vicia/Lathyrus*), medick/clover (*Medicago/Trifolium*) and stitchwort (*Stellaria*) (Cobain 2014a, 155–64).

Table 5.16   Plant macrofossil identifications Period 3 (Sites 18 and 26)

Site				18	18	18	18	26
Context number				180173	180173	180173	180173	260004
Feature number				180172	180172	180172	180172	260254
Sample number (SS)				1817	1822	1823	1824	26093
Flot volume (ml)				200	304	206	73	875
Sample volume processed (l)				4	8	8	7	27
Charred items per litre of soil				1.5	7.5	7	3.1	5.4
Period				3	3	3	3	3
Plant macrofossil preservation				Good	Good	Moderate	Moderate	Good
Habitat Code	Family	Species	Common Name					
D/A	Amaranthaceae	*Chenopodium* L. (*Blitum* L.)	Goosefoots	–	–	–	1	–
HSW		*Corylus avellana* L.	Hazelnut shells (fragment >5mm)	–	7	16	–	20
D	Brassicaceae	*Brassica* L.	Cabbages/Mustards	–	1	–	4	–
HSW	Fagaceae	*Quercus petraea* (Matt.) Liebl./ *Quercus robur* L.	Sessile Oak/ Pedunculate Oak involucre (whole)	–	1	–	–	–
E	Poaceae	*Poaceae*	Indet. cereal grain (fragment >2mm)	–	–	–	–	1
E		*Poaceae*	Culm node (whole)	–	–	–	–	5
P		*Poaceae*	Grass sp. stem	3	38	2	12	73
P		*Poaceae*	Grass sp. stem (fragment <2mm)	++++	++++	++++	++++	++++
P		*Poaceae*	Grass sp. root	3	10	35	5	–
E		*Poaceae*	Straw	–	–	–	–	5
HSW	Rosaceae	*Malus sylvestris* (L.) Mill.	Crab apple pip	–	–	1	–	–
HSW		*Malus sylvestris* (L.) Mill.	?Crab apple flesh (fragment)	+	++	++	+	–
HSW		*Prunus* L.	Cherries pip (fragment)	–	3	2	–	11
HSW		*Prunus spinosa* L.	Blackthorn pip	–	–	–	–	12
HSW		*Prunus spinosa* L.	Blackthorn pip (fragment)	–	–	–	–	17
A/D	Rubiaceae	*Galium aparine* L.	Cleavers	–	–	–	–	1
Total				6	60	56	22	145

The plant remains from cremation burials 180172 and 260254 were fully analysed. Cremation burial 180172 contained hazelnut shells, an oak involucre (acorn cup), a crab apple pip, cherry species pip fragments, a large number of grass stems and roots and a small amount of vitrified material which has been tentatively identified as fruit flesh. Cremation burial 260254 revealed a small assemblage of plant macrofossils identified as hazelnut shells, grass stems, culm node, straw, an indeterminate cereal grain fragment, a cleavers seed and a moderate number of whole sloe pips, and pip fragments and cherry species pip fragments.

Charcoal has been analysed from cremation burials 260449, 260323, 260326, 260339, 260183, 260254, 260342, 260025, 260035, 260160 and 260239 and posthole 260282 within Group 261 (features/burials within the barrow area); pit 260281 (outside the barrow area); cremation burials 260407, 260424 and 260474, pits 260456, 260561, 260596 and 260469, small pit/posthole 260189, accessory vessel pit 260436 and posthole 260275 within Group 268 (features/

Table 5.17   Plant macrofossil identifications Period 3 (Sites 25 and 37)

Site				25	25	25	37	37	37
Context number				250065	250074	250096	370107	370108	370110
Feature number				250063	250073	250093	370106	370106	370106
Sample number (SS)				2502	2503	2510	3702	3703	3704
Flot volume (ml)				92.5	38	38	367	106.5	109
Sample volume processed (l)				36	18	19	9	14	19
Charred items per litre of soil				71.4	6.6	4.5	41.6	35.1	8.7
Period				3	3	3	3	3	3
Plant macrofossil preservation				Good	Good	Good	Good	Good	Good
Habitat Code	**Family**	**Species**	**Common Name**						
HSW	Betulaceae	*Corylus avellana* L.	Hazelnut shells (fragment >10mm)	27	–	–	13	54	–
HSW		*Corylus avellana* L.	Hazelnut shells (fragment >5mm)	101	51	67	40	67	5
HSW		*Corylus avellana* L.	Hazelnut shells (fragment >2mm)	1111	–	–	320	355	154
HSW		*Corylus avellana* L.	Hazelnut shells (fragment <2mm)	+++	–	–	+++	+++	+++
D	Brassicaceae	*Brassica* L.	Cabbages/ Mustards	–	–	–	–	1	3
HSW/ He	Dennstaed-tiaceae	*Pteridium* Gled. Ex Scop.	Bracken frond	–	–	–	1	5	–
P/D	Poaceae	*Arrhenatherum elatius* (L.) P. Beauv. ex J. & C. Presl	False Oat-grass	–	–	–	–	–	1
E		*Hordeum vulgare* L.	Barley grain (naked)	1154	30	5	–	2	3
E		*Hordeum vulgare* L.	Barley rachis	25	–	–	–	1	–
E		*Triticum*	Wheat sp. grain	5	–	–	–	–	–
E		*Triticum dicoccum*	Emmer wheat grain	2	–	–	–	–	–
E		Poaceae	Indet. cereal grain (whole)	27	11	2	–	–	–
E		Poaceae	Indet. cereal grain (fragment >2mm)	118	26	10	–	1	–
E		Poaceae	Indet. cereal grain (fragment <2mm)	–	+++	+++	–	–	–
P		Poaceae	Grass sp. stem	–	–	–	–	2	–
E		Poaceae	Straw	–	–	–	–	1	–
HSW	Rosaceae	*Malus sylvestris* (L.) Mill.	Crab apple stem	–	–	–	–	2	–
HSW		*Malus sylvestris* (L.) Mill.	?Crab apple flesh (fragment)	–	–	–	++++++	++++++	++++
HSW		*Prunus* L.	Cherries pip (fragment)	–	–	1	–	–	–
HSW		*Prunus spinosa* L.	Blackthorn pip (half)	1	–	–	–	–	–
Total				2571	118	85	374	491	166

Table 5.18   Plant macrofossil identifications Undated (Sites 12, 13, 18, 28 and 36)

Site				12	12	13	18	28	36
Context number				110407= 110404	110404= 110407	130105	180382	280003	360026
Feature number				110405	110405	130103	180391	280004	360027
Sample number (SS)				101	102	1301	1847	2801	3601
Flot volume (ml)				60	203	166	6	30.5	156
Sample volume processed (l)				9	9	8	9	9	5
Charred items per litre of soil				31.3	24.9	12	19.4	2.1	4.6
Period				0	0	0	0	0	0
Plant macrofossil preservation				Good	Good	Good	Good	Good	Good
Habitat Code	Family	Species	Common Name						
HSW	Betulaceae	*Corylus avellana* L.	Hazelnut shells (fragment >10mm)	1	1	–	–	–	–
HSW		*Corylus avellana* L.	Hazelnut shells (fragment >5mm)	279	210	47	172	8	22
D	Brassicaceae	*Brassica* L.	Cabbages/ Mustards	2	4	48	–	8	–
HSW/ He	Dennstaed-tiaceae	*Pteridium* Gled. Ex Scop.	Bracken frond	–	–	1	–	–	1
P	Poaceae	*Poaceae*	Grass sp. stem	–	–	–	1	–	–
HSW	Rosaceae	*Malus sylvestris* (L.) Mill.	Crab apple stem	–	3	–	–	–	–
HSW		*Malus sylvestris* (L.) Mill.	?Crab apple flesh (fragment)	–	4	–	–	–	–
HSW		*Malus sylvestris* (L.) Mill.	?Crab apple skin (fragment)	–	?2	–	–	–	–
HSW		*Prunus* L.	Cherries pip (fragment)	–	–	–	–	1	–
HSW		*Prunus spinosa* L.	Blackthorn pip (half)	–	–	–	2	–	–
HSW/D		*Rubus* L.	Brambles	–	–	–	–	1	–
HSW/He/D		*Rubus idaeus* L.	Raspberry	–	–	–	–	?1	–
Total				282	224	96	175	19	23

burials within area of hollow 260391); and cremation burials 260229, 260276 and 180184 within Group 2610 (features/burials 235m to the west of barrow area). The range of species within these features was relatively narrow, consisting dominantly of oak with smaller quantities of alder/hazel, hazel, cherry species and blackthorn also recorded.

Site 25
Pit 250063 contained a large assemblage of hazelnut shells, naked barley grains and smaller numbers of wheat species and emmer wheat cereal grains. A small number of barley rachis and a sloe pip fragment were also identified. Pits 250073 and 250093 contained similar assemblages although with charred plant remains in smaller quantities with hazelnut shells, naked barley cereal grains and a cherry species pip fragment identified. Charcoal from all three pits together with pit 250061 was abundant and identified as oak, maple (*Acer campestre*), alder, hazel, alder/hazel, hawthorn/ rowan/crab apple, birch, cherry species and blackthorn.

Site 32
Charcoal from burnt mound trough 320015, pit 320008 and spread 320020 was abundant and moderate to well-preserved, and identified as oak, ash, alder, hazel, alder/hazel, hawthorn/rowan/crab apple, cherry species and blackthorn.

Site 35
Pit 350033 contained a large assemblage of charcoal recorded as oak, alder, hazel, alder/hazel, hawthorn/rowan/crab apple, cherry species and blackthorn.

Site 37
Fills 370107, 370108 and 370110 within pit 370106 contained a large assemblage of hazelnut shells and smaller quantities of naked barley cereal grains and rachis, straw fragments, a crab apple stalk, grass stems, bracken fronds (*Pteridium*), brassica-type and false oat-grass seeds and large quantities of vitrified material, tentatively identified as fruit flesh. Charcoal was abundant and identified as oak, hazel, alder/hazel, hawthorn/rowan/crab apple and cherry species.

Prehistoric
Although undated, the features described below contained plant macrofossil assemblages exhibiting characteristics consistent with features of a prehistoric date.

Site 12
Fill 110404=110407 within pit 110405 contained a large assemblage of charred hazelnut shells, along with a crab apple stalk and possible crab apple flesh/skin fragments and brassica-type seeds. Charcoal was abundant and identified as oak, hazel, alder/hazel, cherry species and blackthorn.

Site 13
Upper fill 130105 within pit 130103 contained a moderate assemblage of hazelnut shells, brassica-type seeds, a bracken frond. Charcoal was abundant and identified as oak, gorse/broom, blackthorn and hawthorn/rowan/crab apple.

Site 18
Pit 180391 contained a large assemblage of hazelnut shells, two sloe pip fragments and a grass stem. Charcoal was present in small quantities and identified as oak, hazel and alder/hazel.

Site 25
Pits 250109 and 250119 contained the same range of charcoal as the features that were analysed with Neolithic dating, largely oak, with some alder/hazel.

Site 28
Pit 280004 contained a small number of hazelnut shells, brassica-type seeds, a cherry species pip fragment, a possible raspberry (*Rubus idaeus*) and a bramble seed.

Site 36
Pit 360027 contained a small number of hazelnut shells and a bracken frond. Charcoal was moderately abundant, and identified as oak, hazel and alder/hazel.

Discussion

Period 2 Early Neolithic

Structured deposition
The Early Neolithic pits at Site 37 contained large assemblages of plant macrofossil material. Whilst the majority of the remains consisted of hazelnut shells, the highest number being just under 14,000 fragments in deposit 370087, there was an interesting assemblage of remains from other wild and cultivated foodstuffs within the fills. Wild foods are represented by crab apple (stalks, pips and possible fruit flesh and skin), cherry (stalk) and bramble/blackberry (seeds). Cultivated foodstuffs included emmer and emmer/spelt wheat (grains and glume bases and spikelet forks), wheat species (grains), naked barley (grains and rachis) and oat (grain).

Neolithic pits containing this quantity of carbonised plant remains are relatively uncommon across Britain, although occurrences are becoming more frequent with the increasing number of development-led excavations (Garrow 2012, 217). The pits from this site contain a mixture of pottery, flint (including leaf-shaped arrowheads in pits 370037 and 370019 and a scraper in pit 370153) as well as the charred plant remains and charcoal. It is possible this assemblage simply represents domestic refuse and this is an interpretation suggested by Hinton (2006, 38) when analysing remains from a Late Neolithic pit at Claypit Lane, Westhampnett. However, excavation of an increasing number of these assemblages has pointed towards an interpretation of structured deposition or closing deposits (Garrow 2012, 217). This is where a selection of material (be it artefactual, charred plant remains, charcoal and/or bone) is deliberately placed into an archaeological feature, perhaps associated with some kind of ritual event (Robinson 2000, 87). The presence of grain, apples and cherries may suggest an event connected to the ending of life cycles (Chaffey and Brook 2012, 207) and hoping for a good harvest the following year.

Many pits with large assemblages of charred foodstuffs have been recorded from the Late Neolithic period, for example Clifton Quarry, Worcestershire (Clapham pers. comm.) and Claypit Lane, Westhampnett, West Sussex (Hinton 2006, 36). However, one Early Neolithic example has been recorded at Project Dixie, Hayes Farm, Clyst Honiton, Devon which contained charred apples, acorns, hazelnut shells, emmer, emmer/spelt wheat and grain, flax, and viburnum seeds along with loomweights, pot and animal bone (Cobain 2014b, 43–4).

The pit at Hayes Farm contrasts to those excavated at Site 37 as very little charcoal was recorded and it appeared as if the charred plants had been individually selected and deposited. At Site 37 the mixture of charred plant remains and charcoal suggests these remains were deposited as scoops of midden rather than individual deposition of the charred remains. This structured

Table 5.19   Charcoal identifications Period 2 (Sites 25 and 37)

Site			25	25	25	25	25	37	37	37
Context number			250104	250110	250118	250120	250142	370018	370021	370035
Feature number			250103	250109	250117	250119	250141	370017	370019	370037
Sample number (SS)			2512	2516	2517	2514	2519	3706	3701	3709
Flot volume (ml)			33	5	44	4	3	798	2564	1399
Sample volume processed (l)			17	8	5	8	10	20	19	9
Period			2	2	2	2	2	2	2	2
Charcoal quantity (>2mm)			++++	++++	+++++	+++	+++			
Charcoal preservation			Good	Moderate	Good	Moderate	Moderate	Good	Good	Good
Family	**Species**	**Common Name**								
Betulaceae	*Alnus glutinosa* (L.) Gaertn.	Alder	–	–	–	–	–	1	–	–
	Alnus glutinosa (L.) Gaertn.	Alder r/w	3	–	–	–	–	1	–	–
	Alnus glutinosa (L.) Gaertn./ *Corylus avellana* L.	Alder/ Hazel	33	–	9	3	2	3	9	1
	Alnus glutinosa (L.) Gaertn./ *Corylus avellana* L.	Alder/ Hazel r/w	–	–	2	–	–	1	1	2
	Alnus glutinosa (L.) Gaertn./ *Corylus avellana* L.	Alder/ Hazel twig	2	–	–	–	–	–	–	–
	Corylus avellana L.	Hazel	20	–	1	–	–	11	15	2
	Corylus avellana L.	Hazel r/w	14	–	10	1	–	5	2	8
Fagaceae	*Quercus petraea* (Matt.) Liebl./ *Quercus robur* L.	Sessile Oak/ Pedunculate Oak	11	24	35	15	18	55	43	17
	Quercus petraea (Matt.) Liebl./ *Quercus robur* L.	Sessile Oak/ Pedunculate Oak h/w	3	6	–	–	–	13	18	–
	Quercus petraea (Matt.) Liebl./ *Quercus robur* L.	Sessile Oak/ Pedunculate Oak r/w	–	–	28	–	–	7	9	–
Rosaceae	*Crataegus monogyna* Jacq./ *Sorbus* L./ *Malus sylvestris* (L.) Mill.	Hawthorn/ Rowans/ Crab apple	5	–	7	–	–	1	–	–
Salicaceae	*Crataegus monogyna* Jacq./ *Sorbus* L./ *Malus sylvestris* (L.) Mill.	Hawthorn/ Rowans/ Crab apple r/w	1	–	8	–	–	1	–	–
	Prunus L.	Cherries	7	–	–	–	–	–	3	–
	Prunus spinosa L.	Blackthorn twig	–	–	–	–	–	1	–	–
	Salix L./*Populus* L.	Willows/ Poplars r/w	1	–	–	–	–	–	–	–
Number of Fragments:			100	30	100	19	20	100	100	30

Table 5.20   Charcoal identifications Period 2 (Site 37)

Site			37	37	37	37	37	37	37	37	37
Context number			370042	370053	370074	370086	370087	370120	370124	370155	370156
Feature number			370043	370052	370073	370085	370085	370119	370123	370153	370153
Sample number (SS)			3708	3710	3715	3705	3707	3712	3711	3714	3713
Flot volume (ml)			655	368	426	923	1981	241	215	182	244
Sample volume processed (l)			18	9	7	19	13	9	8	7	9
Period			2	2	2	2	2	2	2	2	2
Charcoal quantity (>2mm)			++++	++++++	++++++	++++	++++++	+++++	+++++	+++++	++++++
Charcoal preservation			Good	Good	Good	Moderate	Good	Good	Good	Moderate	Good
Family	**Species**	**Common Name**									
Betulaceae	*Alnus glutinosa* (L.) Gaertn./ *Corylus avellana* L.	Alder/Hazel	–	1	6	–	8	5	2	–	3
	Alnus glutinosa (L.) Gaertn./ *Corylus avellana* L.	Alder/Hazel r/w	–	1	1	–	–	–	3	1	–
	Alnus glutinosa (L.) Gaertn./ *Corylus avellana* L.	Alder/Hazel twig	–	–	1	–	–	3	1	–	–
	Betula L.	Birches r/w	–	–	–	–	–	–	2	–	–
	Corylus avellana L.	Hazel	9	–	5	–	15	–	–	–	–
	Corylus avellana L.	Hazel r/w	4	–	6	1	9	–	2	–	4
	Corylus avellana L.	Hazel r/w twig	–	–	–	1	–	1	2	–	–
Fabaceae	*Ulex* L./*Cytisus* Desf.	Gorses/ Brooms twig	–	1	1	–	–	–	–	–	–
Fagaceae	*Quercus petraea* (Matt.) Liebl./ *Quercus robur* L.	Sessile Oak/ Pedunculate Oak	11	18	58	21	46	14	15	26	22
	Quercus petraea (Matt.) Liebl./ *Quercus robur* L.	Sessile Oak/ Pedunculate Oak h/w	4	9	13	7	5	2	1	3	–
	Quercus petraea (Matt.) Liebl./ *Quercus robur* L.	Sessile Oak/ Pedunculate Oak r/w	2	–	3	–	17	1	–	–	–
	Quercus petraea (Matt.) Liebl./ *Quercus robur* L.	Sessile Oak/ Pedunculate Oak twig	–	–	2	–	–	3	2	–	–
Rosaceae	*Crataegus monogyna* Jacq./ *Sorbus* L./ *Malus sylvestris* (L.) Mill.	Hawthorn/ Rowans/ Crab apple twig	–	–	–	–	–	–	–	–	1
	Prunus L.	Cherries twig	–	–	–	–	–	1	–	–	–
	Prunus spinosa L.	Blackthorn twig	–	–	3	–	–	–	–	–	–
Salicaceae	*Salix* L./*Populus* L.	Willows/ Poplars	–	–	1	–	–	–	–	–	–
Number of Fragments:			30	30	100	30	100	30	30	30	30

Table 5.21   Charcoal identifications Period 3 (Sites 18 and 25)

Site			18	18	18	25	25	25	25
Context number			180175	180175	180473	250062	250065	250074	250096
Feature number			180174	180174	180304	250061	250063	250073	250093
Sample number (SS)			1829	1830	1856	2511	2502	2503	2510
Flot volume (ml)			38	56	1960	22	92.5	38	38
Sample volume processed (l)			1	2	47	1	36	18	19
Period			3	3	3	3	3	3	3
Charcoal quantity (>2mm)			++	+++++	++++++	+++	+++++	+++	++++
Charcoal preservation			Good	Good	Good	Good	Good	Good	Good
Family	**Species**	**Common Name**							
Aceraceae	*Acer campestre* L.	Field maple	–	–	–	–	–	1	2
	Acer campestre L.	Field maple r/w	–	–	–	–	–	–	1
Betulaceae	*Alnus glutinosa* (L.) Gaertn.	Alder	–	–	–	–	3	–	–
	Alnus glutinosa (L.) Gaertn.	Alder r/w	–	–	–	1	–	–	–
	Alnus glutinosa (L.) Gaertn./*Corylus avellana* L.	Alder/Hazel	–	5	–	16	29	28	17
	Alnus glutinosa (L.) Gaertn./*Corylus avellana* L.	Alder/Hazel r/w	–	–	–	5	–	1	26
	Alnus glutinosa (L.) Gaertn./*Corylus avellana* L.	Alder/Hazel twig	–	–	–	–	1	–	–
	Betula L.	Birches r/w	–	–	–	–	1	–	–
	Corylus avellana L.	Hazel	3	1	–	4	5	11	8
	Corylus avellana L.	Hazel r/w	–	–	–	4	8	3	32
	Corylus avellana L.	Hazel r/w twig	–	–	–	–	2	–	–
Fabaceae	*Ulex* L./*Cytisus* Dcsf.	Gorses/Brooms twig	–	–	45	–	–	–	–
Fagaceae	*Quercus petraea* (Matt.) Liebl./*Quercus robur* L.	Sessile Oak/Pedunculate Oak	39	38	23	–	21	31	3
	Quercus petraea (Matt.) Liebl./*Quercus robur* L.	Sessile Oak/Pedunculate Oak h/w	8	6	–	–	4	9	–
	Quercus petraea (Matt.) Liebl./*Quercus robur* L.	Sessile Oak/Pedunculate Oak r/w	–	–	32	–	–	1	1
Rosaceae	*Crataegus monogyna* Jacq./*Sorbus* L./*Malus sylvestris* (L.) Mill.	Hawthorn/Rowans/Crab apple	–	–	–	–	6	6	1
	Prunus L.	Cherries	–	–	–	–	13	3	5
	Prunus L.	Cherries r/w	–	–	–	–	5	–	4
	Prunus L.	Cherries twig	–	–	–	–	1	–	–
	Prunus spinosa L.	Blackthorn	–	–	–	–	–	6	–
	Prunus spinosa L.	Blackthorn twig	–	–	–	–	1	–	–
Number of Fragments:			**50**	**50**	**100**	**30**	**100**	**100**	**100**

Table 5.22   Charcoal identifications Period 3 (Sites 32, 35 and 37)

Site			32	32	32	35	37	37	37
Context number			320020	320009	320016	350034	370107	370108	370110
Feature number			–	320008	320015	350033	370106	370106	370106
Sample number (SS)			32003	32002	32001	35001	3702	3703	3704
Flot volume (ml)			159	313	646	298	367	106.5	109
Sample volume processed (l)			9	10	8	9	9	14	19
Period			3	3	3	3	3	3	3
Charcoal quantity (>2mm)			+++++	++++	++++++	+++++	++++++	+++	+++
Charcoal preservation			Good	Moderate	Good	Good	Good	Good	Good
Family	**Species**	**Common Name**							
Betulaceae	*Alnus glutinosa* (L.) Gaertn.	Alder	9	–	–	7	–	–	–
	Alnus glutinosa (L.) Gaertn.	Alder r/w	–	–	6	3	–	–	–
	Alnus glutinosa (L.) Gaertn./*Corylus avellana* L.	Alder/Hazel	–	5	7	28	16	–	3
	Alnus glutinosa (L.) Gaertn./*Corylus avellana* L.	Alder/Hazel r/w	3	–	1	2	7	9	1
	Corylus avellana L.	Hazel	2	–	5	25	9	2	5
	Corylus avellana L.	Hazel r/w	4	–	4	–	31	15	11
	Corylus avellana L.	Hazel r/w twig					6	–	1
Fagaceae	*Quercus petraea* (Matt.) Liebl./*Quercus robur* L.	Sessile Oak/ Pedunculate Oak	57	22	65	19	20	4	6
	Quercus petraea (Matt.) Liebl./*Quercus robur* L.	Sessile Oak/ Pedunculate Oak h/w	–	–	5	4	7	–	2
	Quercus petraea (Matt.) Liebl./*Quercus robur* L.	Sessile Oak/ Pedunculate Oak r/w	5	–	–	–	–	–	1
	Quercus petraea (Matt.) Liebl./*Quercus robur* L.	Sessile Oak/ Pedunculate Oak twig	–	–	7	–	2	–	–
Oleaceae	*Fraxinus excelsior* L.	Ash	–	1	–	–	–	–	–
Rosaceae	*Crataegus monogyna* Jacq./*Sorbus* L./ *Malus sylvestris* (L.) Mill.	Hawthorn/ Rowans/Crab apple	8	2	–	6	–	–	–
	Crataegus monogyna Jacq./*Sorbus* L./ *Malus sylvestris* (L.) Mill.	Hawthorn/ Rowans/Crab apple r/w	1	–	–	1	1	–	–
	Prunus L.	Cherries	4	–	–	3	–	–	–
	Prunus L.	Cherries twig	–	–	–	–	1	–	–
	Prunus spinosa L.	Blackthorn	–	–	–	2	–	–	–
	Prunus spinosa L.	Blackthorn r/w	7	–	–	–	–	–	–
Number of Fragments:			100	30	100	100	100	30	30

Table 5.23   Charcoal identifications Undated (Sites 12, 13, 18 and 36)

Site			12	13	18	36
Context number			110404 =110407	130105	180382	360026
Feature number			110405	130103	180391	360027
Sample number (SS)			101 and 102	1301	1847	3601
Flot volume (ml)			203	166	6	156
Sample volume processed (l)			9	8	9	5
Period			0	0	0	0
Charcoal quantity (>2mm)			+++++	+++++	+++	++++
Charcoal preservation			Good	Moderate	Moderate	Good
Family	Species	Common Name				
Betulaceae	*Alnus glutinosa* (L.) Gaertn./*Corylus avellana* L.	Alder/Hazel	7	–	3	4
	Alnus glutinosa (L.) Gaertn./*Corylus avellana* L.	Alder/Hazel r/w	2	–	15	–
	Alnus glutinosa (L.) Gaertn./*Corylus avellana* L.	Alder/Hazel twig	3	–	4	–
	Corylus avellana L.	Hazel	16	–	–	18
	Corylus avellana L.	Hazel r/w	9	–	6	1
	Corylus avellana L.	Hazel r/w twig	1	–	1	–
Fabaceae	*Ulex* L./*Cytisus* Desf.	Gorses/Brooms r/w	–	2	–	–
Fagaceae	*Quercus petraea* (Matt.) Liebl./*Quercus robur* L.	Sessile Oak/Pedunculate Oak	56	66	1	52
	Quercus petraea (Matt.) Liebl./*Quercus robur* L.	Sessile Oak/Pedunculate Oak h/w	3	29	–	23
	Quercus petraea (Matt.) Liebl./*Quercus robur* L.	Sessile Oak/Pedunculate Oak r/w	1	–	–	2
Rosaceae	*Crataegus monogyna* Jacq./*Sorbus* L./*Malus sylvestris* (L.) Mill.	Hawthorn/Rowans/Crab apple twig	–	1	–	–
	Prunus L.	Cherries	1	–	–	–
	Prunus spinosa L.	Blackthorn	1	1	–	–
	Prunus spinosa L.	Blackthorn r/w	–	1	–	–
Number of Fragments:			100	100	30	100

Key- + = 1–4 items; ++ = 5–20 items; +++ = 21–40 items; ++++ = 40–99 items; +++++ = 100–500 items; ++++++ = >500 items
A = arable weeds; D= opportunistic species; P = grassland species (possible pasture); He = heathland species; HSW = hedgerow/shrub/woodland plant;
E = economic plant
? = morphology of seed/charcoal similar to this species
r/w = roundwood branch
h/w = heartwood (tyloses present)
indet. = indeterminate

deposition of midden has been recorded more locally within Early to Late Neolithic pits at Site 21.02, Land East of Cilsan, Llangathen, Carmarthenshire (Hart *et al.* 2013, 8) and Early Neolithic pits at Site 26.05 Land West of Cwmifor, Manordeilo and Salem, Carmarthenshire (Barber and Hart 2014a, 10) where deliberately broken or burnt flint tools may indicate curated objects, and have been deposited alongside pottery and deposits of midden, forming structured deposits.

Wild and cultivated foodstuffs
Hazelnuts, crab apple and cherries would all have been sourced from local areas of shrubby woodland. Hazelnuts would have been roasted and eaten, added to stews, or processed into a type of biscuit for long-term storage. Crab apples and cherries may have been eaten raw, although they can be very sour, and were likely processed for consumption. There is little direct evidence for processing techniques; however, many

'recipes' have been proposed such as juices, ciders and sauces (Zohary *et al.* 2013, 135; Wood 2001).

Cereals were dominated by emmer and emmer/spelt wheat, with smaller amounts of naked barley identified (Fig. 5.2). A single oat grain was recovered although the absence of any floret bases means it is not possible to identify this as cultivated or wild. Given only a single grain was recovered, it is most likely to be a wild weed intrusion.

Whilst emmer wheat appears to be the dominant crop, this may be a product of the different processing techniques required for glume wheats (emmer/spelt) and free-threshing cereals (barley).

Once harvested and threshed, the bulk emmer/spelt wheat spikelets would have been parched (over a hearth) and pounded to separate the grain from its component chaff, producing glume bases and spikelet forks. The grain would then have undergone second winnowing and second sieving stages to separate out the glume bases/spikelet forks and any remaining weed seeds and the clean grain would then be ready to use (Hillman 1981, 132–3). After harvesting and threshing barley ears require hummeling (similar to pounding) to remove the basal part of the awns from the grain (ibid., 134–5). As parching is not required, barley is less likely to be exposed to fire, thereby accidently burnt, and as such may be under-represented within the charred crop assemblage.

The presence of a number of emmer and emmer/spelt wheat glume bases/spikelet forks and barley rachis suggests part of the deposited midden waste originated from the parching (emmer/spelt wheat) and hummeling (barley) stages of crop processing. The clean grain produced would have been used to produce breads, possibly ale and utilised as fodder.

There are debates in the literature regarding the relative importance of crops and wild foods during the Neolithic (Stevens and Fuller 2012, 707; Moffett *et al.* 1989, 247; Robinson 2000, 89). The large number of wild food remains from the Early Neolithic pits (98.6% of the assemblage; 148.1 charred items per litre of soil) compared to cereal waste (1.4% of the assemblage; 2.1 charred items per litre of soil) (Fig. 5.3) does appear to back up assertions that arable agriculture was not as widespread or developed as rapidly as initially thought, and that wild foods played a more important part in Early Neolithic diet. However, it has also been suggested that the recovery of relatively small numbers of charred cereal remains may be because cereals/crop-processing waste was simply not exposed to fire as readily as, say, hazelnut shells (which have no other use other than as fuel), whereas spoilt cereals and chaff can be used as fodder. In addition cereal production is a time-consuming task; care would be taken to avoid accidental loss of valuable crops (Jones 2000, 80). The cereal assemblages from pits at Site 37 consisting of emmer and emmer/spelt wheat and barley are typical of those found within other Early Neolithic pits in South Wales such as those excavated at Site 26.05, Land West of Cwmifor, Manordeilo and Salem, Carmarthenshire (Carruthers 2014, 37–42) and Site 51.07 Land North-West of Pen-y-Crug, Yscir, Powys (Giorgi 2014, 45).

Fuel for domestic use
The charcoal from Early Neolithic pits at Site 37, whilst forming part of structured deposits, appears to have originated from burnt domestic refuse. The charcoal from Early Neolithic pits and postholes at Site 25 is also likely derived from burnt domestic waste. The range of species utilised as fuel was narrow and dominated by

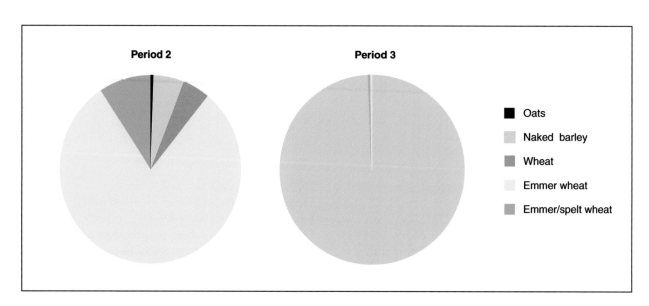

Fig. 5.2   Percentage of emmer wheat, emmer/spelt wheat, naked wheat, barley and oat in Periods 2 and 3

oak, hazel and alder/hazel with smaller quantities of alder, cherry species, blackthorn, willow/poplar, birch and hawthorn/rowan/crab apple recorded (Fig. 5.4). A total of 21% of the assemblage exhibited curved growth rings, identifying fuel derived from small twigs or small branches which indicates the use of brushwood bundles alongside large timbers from mature wood for fuel. The presence of fuelwood from species which are also sources of food (hazel, blackthorn, crab apple) may indicate the two were being gathered at the same time.

Local woodland and flora

Evidence for herbaceous taxa was rare, with grass stems as the only identifiable remains. This may be a reflection of the deliberate deposition of specific material within the pits, or simply because the lighter, smaller weed seeds turned to ash more quickly than denser remains such as hazelnut shells. As a result, it is not possible to reconstruct local flora.

The charred wild/cultivated food remains and charcoal suggests the local area was oak-hazel woodland with cleared areas utilised for settlement, arable cultivation and possibly pasture. On the woodland margins, shrubby species such as cherry species, blackthorn, birch and hawthorn/rowan/crab apple would have established. A single ash seed indicates the presence of ash trees within the oak-hazel woodland, although its absence from the fuelwood assemblage suggests ash did not form a dominant component of woodland in this period. The identification of a small amount of alder and willow/poplar indicates some areas of wet ground or a stream close to both sites. Additionally gorse/broom may indicate heathland development nearby.

Period 3 Bronze Age

Structured deposition

Pit 370106 was one of two pits at Site 37 which have been dated to the Early Bronze Age/Beaker period. Pit 370068 was not sampled, but pit 370106 contained large deposits of charred material including hazelnuts (shells), crab apple (stalk), fruit (charred flesh) and barley (grains). Taken together with other artefactual finds within the pit, including 14 sherds of pottery from a single Beaker vessel and a broken flint scraper, this suggested the material has been deliberately placed as some form of structured deposition. Given the location of this pit, in the same area as other Early Neolithic pits containing structured deposits, it is possible that this area held some kind of significance and had been revisited. Evidence for returning to an area for this type of ritual activity has been seen at other sites such as Site 26.05 Land West of Cwmifor, Manordeilo and Salem, Carmarthenshire (Barber and Hart 2014a, 10–11) and at Hayes Farm Quarry, Clyst Honiton, in Devon (Hart *et al.* 2014c, 50–1) where an interpretation of revisiting an area as part of a 'continued memory' has been proposed.

Cremation burials

Plant macrofossil remains within the cremation burials were generally low in quantity and mostly appeared to be associated with herbaceous taxa utilised as tinder or growing on the ground (grass stems, ribwort plantain, knotweed, clover/medick) where the cremation pyres were constructed. The hazelnut shells, acorn cups and cherry pip fragments may have originated from items attached to branches/poles used to construct the pyres. Despite these being low in quantity, the variety of remains recorded is much wider than that observed within cremation burials at Site 222/233 Land North-East of Vaynor Farm, Llanddowror, Carmarthenshire where only a small number of hazelnut shells, indeterminate fruit stone and grain were identified (Rackham 2013, 22–8).

Of particular interest was the relatively large assemblage of charred sloe pips (12 whole, 17 fragments) and hazelnut shells (20 fragments) from cremation burial 260254 at Site 26. Cremation burial 180172 (Site 18) also contained a 23 hazelnut shells, an acorn cup, an apple pip and five cherry species pip fragments, which may represent offerings burnt alongside the human remains.

Wild and cultivated foodstuffs

When considering the combined plant macrofossil assemblage from pits at Site 37 and at Site 25, it appears that cereal crops were becoming a more important component of diet, with their representation increasing from 1.4% in the Early Neolithic to 34% in the Early Bronze Age (Fig. 5.3). However, when looking individually at the plant remains from both sites, Site 37 suggests a continued dominance in the exploitation of wild foods (98.1% wild food; 0.7% cereal waste) and Site 25 reveals in addition to a large number of wild food remains (52.7% of the assemblage), a large cereal waste component (47.3% of the assemblage). The reason for these differences may be a result of differing site functions with the pit at Site 37 having a ritual function and the pits at Site 25 possibly associated with domestic activity. This being the case, it is not possible to deduce any firm conclusions regarding the relative importance of crops and wild foods during this period based on the information from these sites.

Similar to the Early Neolithic, hazelnuts, crab apple and cherries would all have been sourced locally and either eaten raw, or processed for consumption. The most numerous cereal identified was naked barley, a switch from emmer wheat which dominated in the Early Neolithic period (Fig. 5.2). However, the limited number of samples means it is not possible to deduce whether this represents a change in cereal preference. The mechanism by which this large assemblage of barley became charred and deposited in this pit is of interest as, as discussed above, barley (unlike glume wheats) does not require exposure to fire for processing.

It is possible therefore that this assemblage represents grain which had spoilt and was subsequently used as fuel. Alternatively it may have become accidently burnt during food production. Barley would have been utilised for producing bread, possibly for ale production and for fodder.

Fuel within cremation burials

The range of species identified within the cremation burials and associated pits, postholes and tree throw at Sites 18 and 26 was narrow and consisted of dominantly of oak with hazel, alder/hazel, cherry species and black-thorn also recorded (Fig. 5.5). This does however correlate with cremations from nearby Sites 222/233 Land North-East of Vaynor Farm (Challinor 2013a, 29) and Site 513 Land North-West of Steynton, Milford Haven, Pembrokeshire (Challinor 2014a, 61) where only a narrow range of species was observed.

Only 12.5% of the identifiable fragments within the cremation burials/associated features at Sites 18 and 26 displayed evidence of curved growth rings, compared to 29.9% within the domestic/industrial fuelwood assemblage. The low percentage of roundwood elements may be a reflection of large timbers being used within the pyre construction, although it may also be a result of the selection process during the collection of cremated bone for burial. If the bone is preferentially selected, the charcoal element will be biased towards smaller more fragmented pieces which are accidently incorporated with the cremated bone. Despite this, cremation burials 260035 and 260254 did reveal larger roundwood oak charcoal fragments providing evidence for the use of oak branches, averaging 10–15cm (uncharred) diameter. There was also evidence for small hazel branches (uncharred diameter approximately 5–10cm) within cremations 260436 and 260064. Taken together this evidence suggests the cremation pyres were constructed from larger oak timbers with smaller oak and hazel poles.

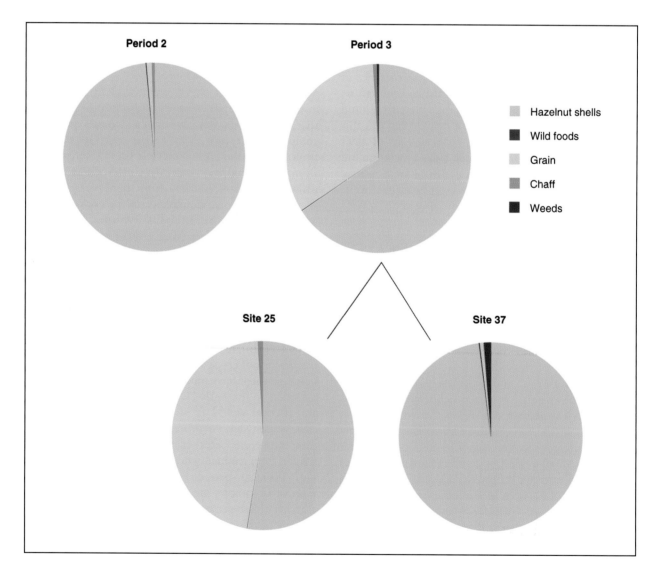

Fig. 5.3   Percentage of grain, chaff, wild foods, weeds and hedgerow/scrub/woodland species in Periods 2 and 3

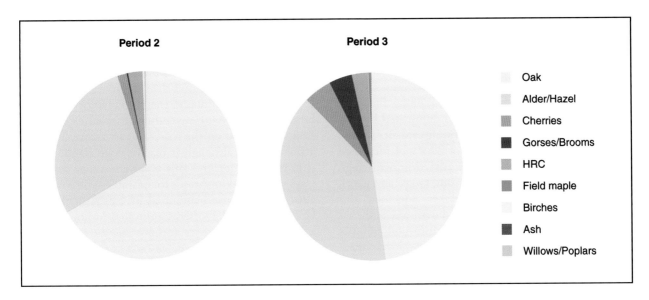

Fig. 5.4   Percentage of species utilised as fuel (for domestic activities) in Periods 2 and 3

Given that oak is one of the densest and most calorific fuels (Gale and Cutler 2000, 205) it would be the most efficient choice of fuel within cremation pyres. The presence of a small number of cherry species, black-thorn, hazel and alder/hazel fragments exhibiting tightly curving growth rings are indicative of fragments from twigs, which were likely used (alongside grass) as tinder.

There has been some discussion as to whether choice of species correlates with age/gender of the individual; however, no strong evidence of a link has yet been found (Smith 2002, 22). The majority of the cremation burials containing sufficient charcoal for analysis were identified as adult and male (Chapter 5.1) with only cremation burial 260035 being identified as an adult female, cremation burial 260323 as a subadult and 260160 as an infant. For this reason, together with the very narrow species assemblage, it was not possible to assess any correlation between age, gender and fuel choice within these cremation burials.

The charcoal assemblage provides few observable changes in the use of fuel within funerary activities throughout the life of the cremation cemetery. The amount of oak is recorded as 94% and 94.5% of the identifiable charcoal within burials and features 235m to the west of barrow area (Group 2610) and features/burials within the barrow area (Group 261) (respectively), compared with 88.4% within features/burials within the area of hollow 260391 (Group 268) and decreases further to 76.5% within the features outside the barrow area.

This trend may simply reflect availability of fuel within the local woodlands. Cremating human remains uses a large quantity of wood – up to 500kg (McKinley 1994b, 80), which would have a visible impact on local woodlands. Where trees had been cleared, faster

growing species such as hazel would regenerate and, as discussed above, it appears these are being utilised perhaps as smaller poles, alongside larger oak timbers, as part of the pyre structure.

Fuel for domestic use
Fuel exploited for domestic use/burnt mound activities during the Early Bronze Age is similar in composition to that during the Early Neolithic, although the overall percentages differ. There is a decrease in the amount of oak from 66.8% in the Early Neolithic assemblage to 47.8% in the Early Bronze Age with associated increases

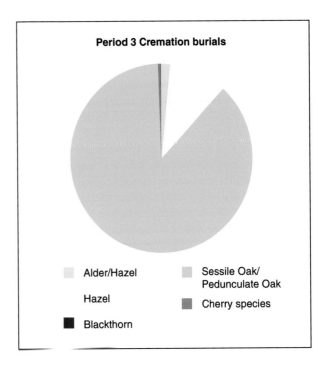

Fig. 5.5   Fuel utilised within Period 3 cremation pyres

in the use of alder/hazel (from 28.3% to 39.9%), cherry species (from 1.7% to 4.9%) and gorse/brooms (from 0.2% to 4%) along with the first presence of maple (0.4%) and ash (0.1%) (Fig. 5.4).

The majority of the charcoal from Sites 18, 25, 35 and 37 originates from pits containing fuel of a domestic origin. The assemblage is dominated by oak, with identification of tyloses providing evidence for the use of mature timbers. A total of 29.9% of identified fragments exhibited evidence of curved growth rings, mostly fragments originating from twigs and small diameter branches (2–3cm). Taken together, this suggests domestic fires were fuelled with oak branches and mature timbers along with brushwood bundles (deadwood twigs/branches) including alder, hazel, birch, hawthorn/rowan/crab apple, cherry species and blackthorn.

The percentage of fragments identified as roundwood/twigs (29.9%) is slightly higher than recorded within the Neolithic assemblage (21%). This together with the decrease in the amount of oak recorded in the Early Bronze Age assemblage could reflect the increasing pressure on woodland resources, with oak being reserved for specific activities requiring high temperatures and for building construction, with good, but slightly less efficient fuels being used for small domestic fires.

Of interest was the drying oven 180304 at Site 18 which contained no plant macrofossils but did include a large assemblage of charcoal, some of which had been heated to such a high temperature it had turned shiny and vitrified, similar to coal. The charcoal assemblage was identified as oak (55%) and gorse/broom (45%). Drying ovens would have been used either to parch the bulk spikelets to facilitate the release of grain or to dry clean grain in preparation for milling. Despite the absence of grain, this feature has been interpreted as a cereal drier based on its shape/form which is consistent with other cereal driers of this period.

It is however unusual not to find any charred grains or cereal chaff within the burnt ash/residue of a cereal drier. The bulk spikelets/grain would be dried on some form of mesh/woven platform above the fire and given the small size and slender shape of grain, some element of spillage would be expected. Whilst it is possible that any spilt grain/cereal chaff completely burnt to ash, there are several other explanations that may account for the absence of burnt cereal remains.

One explanation could be that because the heating of cereal grains/bulk spikelets requires relatively low heat, a fire would be lit and allowed to die down before the grain was added. In this case, it is possible the cereal drier was lit, but then for some reason never used to dry grain, A second reason could be that the grain, rather than being dried on a woven mesh platform, was dried within mesh bags suspended from a superstructure covering the drier. This would be an efficient use of space, allowing several bags of grain to be dried at once, or even allow a multifunctional use for the cereal drier, drying grain and smoking strips of meat or fish at the same time.

A third possibility is that the cereal drier was being used to bake bread, rather than to process cereals. This has been suggested due to the high quantity of gorse/broom compared to any other charcoal assemblages from this period on the road scheme. Gorse/broom is a poor fuel as although it reaches high temperatures, it burns very quickly. This is advantageous for some tasks such as baking bread; for example Grigson (1987, 126) records gorse being used by bakers in the West Country (Devon, Dorset, Cornwall). Although this is a documentary reference, it is possible the properties of gorse were being exploited as early as the Bronze Age, and this feature was being used to bake bread.

Fuel for use in burnt mounds
Charcoal from Site 32 was retrieved from the fills of pit 320008 and trough 320015 and burnt mound deposit 320020. The charcoal identified consisted dominantly of oak, with small amounts of alder, hazel, alder/hazel, ash, cherry species, blackthorn and hawthorn/rowan/crab apple. The majority of the charcoal was highly fragmented (particularly in comparison to that from other sites along the road scheme). It was possible to identify the use of roundwood, twigs and mature oak timbers; however, identifiable fragments (exhibited curved growth rings or tyloses) were only present in small numbers and there were insufficient to deduce what types of timber were dominantly used.

The charcoal assemblage from these features is relatively wide although the majority of the fragments were identified as oak and alder/hazel. This is a theme repeated across many other burnt mound sites excavated on the Welsh Pipelines and has been attributed to the ease with which you can manage oak and hazel woodlands, providing readily available fuel (Hart *et al.* 2013, 150). The additional species identified vary from site to site and seem simply to reflect local fuel availability. At Site 32 these include ash, cherry species, blackthorn and hawthorn/rowan/crab apple whereas at Site 25.06 Land North of Rhosmaen House, Manordeilo and Salem only alder/hazel, oak and hawthorn/rowan/crab apple was additionally identified (Challinor 2013b, 10–11). These contrast with Site 506 Land East of Glan-rhŷd Bridge, Lampeter Velfrey, Pembrokeshire where, in addition to oak and alder/hazel, birch, holly, ivy and willow/poplar were identified (Challinor 2014b, 27–8).

Local woodland and flora
Herbaceous taxa were again relatively rare, with the largest assemblage within cremation burials deposits at Sites 18 and 26. These included grassland species (ribwort plantain, medick/clover, vetch/peas and grass stems/roots), opportunistic (knotweed, brassica-type and stitchworts) and arable weeds (cleavers, black-

bindweed). This suggests the area surrounding Sites 18 and 26 was open grassland with opportunistic weeds colonising newly disturbed ground. The presence of cereal crops at Sites 25 and 37 may suggest arable fields are located in the vicinity of these sites and the identification of bracken at Site 37 may indicate heathland development nearby.

The charcoal and the wild food plant remains from these sites suggest a mature oak-hazel woodland landscape with the periphery of open areas (settlement/ fields) colonised by scrub woodland including cherry species, blackthorn and hawthorn/rowan/crab apple. In addition maple and birch were recorded at Site 25 and ash at Site 32 and may form a minor component within the local woodland. The presence of alder at Sites 32 and 35 suggests the presence of wet ground or a stream nearby.

5.4 Geoarchaeological monolith samples
Phil Stastney with monolith descriptions by Nick Watson

This document reports on the stratigraphy and bioarchaeology of one monolith sample taken from Site 26. The work comprised a geoarchaeological assessment of Monolith 260306 taken through the fills of Bronze Age funerary pit 260391 to determine the stratigraphic sequence and duration of backfill within this feature, which has been interpreted as a hollow in which there was burial-related activity, including cremation pyres. This report discusses the geographic, geological and methodological background to the geoarchaeological works and the stratigraphy of the monolith is described in detail.

Previous geoarchaeological works carried out as part of the archaeological mitigation measures in advance of the construction of the new section of the A477 road have taken the form of litho-, magneto-, chrono-, and biostratigraphic assessment and analysis of boreholes drilled through the floodplain of the River Taf. These works were undertaken initially in order to characterise the sediments and accompanying biological assemblages, and latterly to reconstruct environments associated with late prehistoric human activity (Wilkinson and Batchelor 2012; Wilkinson and Watson 2012; Stastney and Batchelor 2014).

Methodology
Monolith 260306, 0.5m in length, was collected by Cotswold Archaeology staff and sent to ARCA's Winchester laboratory for examination. In the laboratory monoliths were photographed and described to standard geological criteria (Tucker 1982; Jones *et al.* 1999; Munsell Color 2000). The archive of the geoarchaeological works consists of one monolith sample retained by ARCA at the University of Winchester and digital records (comprising photographs of the monoliths and lithological records) retained on the University of Winchester server.

Results and discussion

Geology
The monolith was taken from funerary pit 260391 at Site 26 at NGR: 224770 214510 (monolith 260306) (Barber *et al.* 2014). The British Geological Survey (BGS) map the bedrock lying beneath Site 26, Vaynor Farm as Robeston Wathen Limestone and Sholeshook Limestone (undifferentiated), which is also of Ordovician age. No superficial deposits are mapped in the vicinity of Site 26 (BGS 2014).

Lithostratigraphy

Monolith 260306
The lithology of monolith 260306 taken from funerary pit 260391 is shown in Table 5.24. The base of the monolith consists of 0.07m of light olive brown (2.5Y 5/3) clast-supported gravel of angular pebble-sized sandstone/quartzite clasts in a silt/clay matrix (contexts 260393 and 260413). This unit was unconformably overlain by a 0.21m-thick unit of brown (10YR 5/3) diamict (i.e. poorly sorted sediment) consisting of sub-angular granular to cobble-sized quartzite clasts in a silt/clay matrix with rare granular-sized charcoal fragments (context 260364).

The unconformity (i.e. sharp, undulating boundary) between the two sedimentary units in monolith 260306 may be indicative of a hiatus in deposition. The generally coarse-grained and poorly sorted nature of both units is not suggestive of gradual, low-energy sediment accumulation. Rather the material in this monolith appears to have either been deliberately backfilled or to have accumulated rapidly as a result of the erosion of the

Table 5.24   Lithology of monolith 260306 from funerary pit 260391

Sample	Contexts	Top	Base	Lithology	Description
260306		0.00	0.22	No recover	Void.
	260364	0.22	0.43	Diamict	10 YR 5/3 Brown diamict of angular to sub-angular granular to cobble-sized quartzite/clasts in a silt/ clay matrix. Rare granular-sized fragments of charcoal. Sharp boundary to:
	260393 260413	0.43	0.50	Diamict	2.5 Y 5/3 Light olive brown diamict of angular pebble-sized sandstone/ quartzite? clasts in a silt/clay matrix.

sides of the Bronze Age pyre pit 260391 (e.g. small-scale debris flow).

5.5 Bronze Age cremation burials: radiocarbon dating and chronological modelling
Frances Healy, Sarah Cobain and Elaine Dunbar

Introduction and methodology

Scientific dating
Sixteen radiocarbon results, 13 for cremated human bone and 3 for charcoal or charred plant material, have been obtained for samples from this complex. These were selected based on the quantity of bone/charred material available and the spatial and stratigraphic positions of the features in order to chronologically model the complex. They account for: 9 of the 23 cremation deposits in Group 261, the main concentration of burials surrounded by the vestigial ditch; the 4 cremation deposits in Group 268 in hollow 260391 immediately to the north-east, as well as one from a pit cut by the hollow; and 2 of the 9 cremation deposits in Group 2610, the group of cremation burials 230m to the west (Table 5.25).

Charcoal and charred plant samples were pretreated as described by Mook and Waterbolk (1985) and cremated bone samples were prepared as described by Lanting *et al.* (2001). All samples were combusted to carbon dioxide as described by Vandeputte *et al.* (1996), graphitised as described by Slota *et al.* (1987), and dated by Accelerator Mass Spectrometry (AMS) as described by Freeman *et al.* (2010). The $\delta^{13}C$ values were produced by Isotope Ratio Mass Spectrometry (IRMS) on subsamples of the carbon dioxide that had been combusted for dating. The laboratory maintains continuous programs of internal quality control. It also takes part in international intercomparisons (Scott 2003; Scott *et al.* 2007; 2010a–b).

Chronological modelling
The methods employed here have been fully described by Bronk Ramsey (1995; 2001; 2009a), Bronk Ramsey and Lee (2013), and Bayliss *et al.* (2011). The results from the complex are analysed within a Bayesian framework (Buck *et al.* 1996; Bayliss 2009). The principle behind the Bayesian approach to the interpretation of data is encapsulated by Bayes' theorem (Bayes 1763). In essence, new data collected about a problem ('the standardised likelihoods' – in this case calibrated radiocarbon dates) are analysed in the context of existing experience and knowledge of that problem ('prior beliefs' – in this case the archaeology) by expressing both as probability density functions. The combination of the two permits a new understanding of the problem ('posterior beliefs'). Such estimates will vary with the model(s) employed, and several different

models may be constructed based on varying interpretations of the same data (Bayliss *et al.* 2007). The purpose of modelling is to progress beyond the dates at which individual samples left the carbon cycle to the dates of the archaeological events associated with those samples.

Prior beliefs fall into two main categories: informative and uninformative. Informative prior beliefs employed in modelling dates from archaeological contexts often derive from the stratigraphic relations between the contexts of samples. In Fig. 5.6, for example, the dates from cremation burials in Group 268 are constrained by the prior information that pit 260561, the context of radiocarbon date *SUERC-61280*, was earlier than hollow 260391 which contained the cremation burials in the group. An uninformative prior belief employed here, based on burial rite, pottery styles and spatial organisation, is that the samples dated are representative of a more-or-less continuous episode of activity, the creation and use of the cremation cemetery, without necessarily including the earliest or the latest material generated by it (Buck *et al.* 1992). This assumption is necessary to constrain the scatter inherent in radiocarbon dates, which would otherwise make episodes of activity appear to start earlier, continue longer, and end later than they actually did (Steier and Rom 2000). In this sense, 'phase' simply means a group of related dates without internal sequence.

The model is defined in OxCal, detailing the radiocarbon results and specifying the known relative ages of the samples. Once the calibrated probability distributions of individual radiocarbon ages have been calculated, the program attempts to reconcile these distributions with the prior information by repeatedly sampling each distribution to build up a set of solutions consistent with the model structure. This is done using a random sampling technique (Markov Chain Monte Carlo or MCMC) which generates a representative set of possible dates. This process produces a posterior density distribution for each sample's calendar age, which occupies only a part of the calibrated probability distribution. Posterior distributions are also calculated for events that do not map directly onto particular radiocarbon dates. They include estimates for the starts and ends of episodes of activity (e.g. Fig. 5.6: *start cremation cemetery*). By taking the difference between parameters, estimates for the durations of episodes of activity (i.e. the difference between its start and its end (e.g. Fig. 5.7: *duration Collared Urns*) and estimates of the intervals between certain events (e.g. Fig. 5.7: *end Collared Urns/ end cremation cemetery*) can be made. These estimates can be partly negative if the two parameters overlap.

Highest posterior density intervals, the date ranges describing the posterior distributions at a given level of probability, are conventionally printed in italics (e.g. *'1935–1815 cal BC'*) to distinguish them clearly from simple calibrated radiocarbon dates. Each posterior distribution has a parameter name which is also printed

Table 5.25   Radiocarbon dates and calibrations from Bronze Age cremation burials (Fig. 5.6)

Lab No.	Material	Feature	Radiocarbon Age BP	δ $^{13}C_{IRMS}$ ‰	Calibrated date range BC (2σ)	Highest posterior density interval cal BC (95% probability)
Barrow (Group 261)						
SUERC-50367	Cremated human bone	Context 260446 Cremation 260439, with Collared Urn P26.4	3580±25	−23.9	2020–1880	*1975–1875 (94%); 1840–1825 (1%)*
SUERC-61118	Cremated human bone	Context 260345 Cremation 260342	3571±27	−24.1	2020–1830	*1965–1875 (88%); 1845–1815 (5%); 1800–1780 (2%)*
SUERC-61276	Cremated human bone	Context 260614 Cremation 260035, with Collared Urn P26.5	3555±30	−23.0	2010–1770	*1955–1865 (70%); 1850–1770 (25%)*
SUERC-61274	Cremated human bone	Context 260238 Cremation 260239	3530±30	−21.2	1950–1750	*1940–1765*
SUERC-61119	Cremated human bone	Context 260004 Cremation 260254	3479±29	−23.2	1890–1690	*1890–1735 (92%); 1715–1695 (3%)*
SUERC-61273	Cremated human bone	Context 260320 Cremation 260323	3414±30	−25.2	1870–1630	*1875–1840 (5%); 1815–1800 (1%); 1780–1645 (89%)*
SUERC-61282	Single fragment of indeterminate fruit flesh	Context 260030 Cremation 260029, with accessory vessel P26.21	3403±30	−23.8	1770–1620	*1865–1845 (2%); 1775–1640 (93%)*
SUERC-61272	Cremated human bone	Context 260337 Cremation 260339	3390±30	−25.7	1760–1620	*1770–1635*
SUERC-61275	Cremated human bone	Context 260640 Cremation 260021, with plain biconical pot P26.3	3363±30	−26.9	1750–1560	*1750–1630*
Pyre hollow (Group 268)						
SUERC-61280	Single fragment of hazel (*Corylus avellana*) charcoal	Context 260553 Pit 260561, cut by hollow 260391	3522±30	−26.0	1940–1750	*1955–1855 (93%); 1850–1830 (2%)*
SUERC-61120	Cremated human bone	Context 260420 Cremation 260424	3563±29	−24.3	2020–1780	*1935–1865 (57%); 1850–1770 (38%)*
SUERC-61121	Cremated human bone	Context 260510 Cremation 260474, with Collared Urn P26.8	3538±27	−24.9	1950–1770	*1925–1765*
SUERC-50368	Cremated human bone	Context 260409 Cremation 260407	3537±27	−26.1	1950–1770	*1925–1765*
SUERC-61281	Single fragment of hazel (*Corylus avellana*) charcoal	Context 260490 Cremation 260489	3450±30	−28.5	1890–1680	*1880–1835 (20%); 1830–1685 (75%)*
Western group (Group 2610)						
SUERC-61122	Cremated human bone	Context 260213 Cremation 260210, with Collared Urn P26.9	3567±29	−23.1	2020–1780	*1965–1870 (83%); 1845–1810 (7%) 1805–1775 (5%)*
SUERC-61255	Cremated human bone	Context 180173 Cremation 180172, with accessory vessel P18.1	3534±30	−24.0	1950–1760	*1940–1765*

The calibrations in the 'calibrated date range BC (2σ)' column are calculated by the maximum intercept method (Stuiver and Reimer 1986), and are cited as recommended by Mook (1986): rounded outwards by 10, since all the standard deviations are 25 or more. They thus differ slightly from the calibrations shown in Table 2.1 which were calculated by the probability method. The calibrations in the '*Highest posterior density interval cal BC*' column are derived from model shown in Figure 5.6 and are rounded outwards by 5.

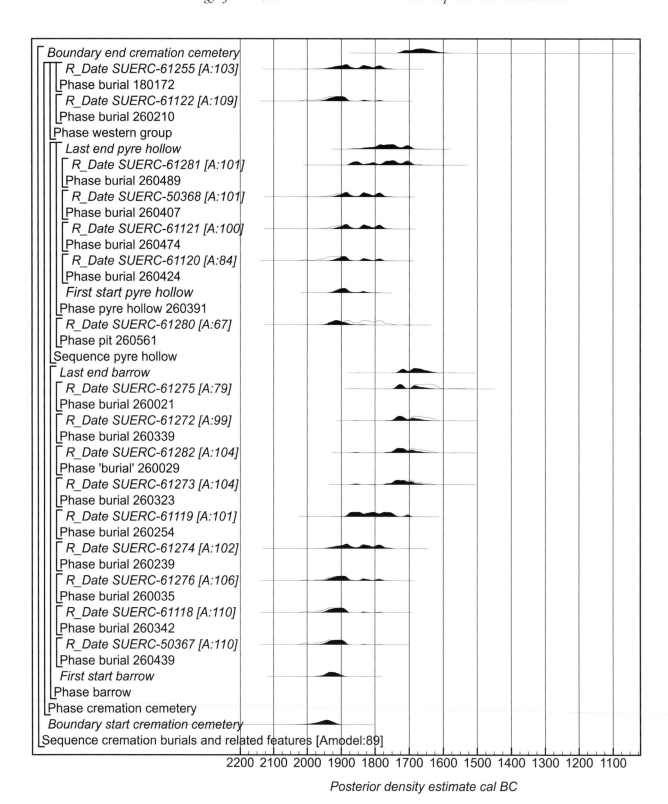

Fig. 5.6   The preferred chronological model for radiocarbon dates from the cremation cemetery, defined by the square brackets at the left-hand side and by the OxCal keywords (Bronk Ramsey 2009a). For each date, the total distribution represents the simple radiocarbon date and the solid distribution is derived from and constrained by the model.

in italics; in some cases (e.g. *start cremation cemetery*) these are unique identifiers, but in others the italicisation distinguishes between the posterior distribution of a particular radiocarbon sample (e.g. *SUERC-*

61274) and the simple calibrated radiocarbon date of that sample (i.e. SUERC-61274).

Statistics calculated by OxCal provide a guide to the reliability of a model. One is the individual index

Table 5.26   Durations and intervals derived from the model shown in Figure 5.6 (Fig. 5.7)

Parameter	Highest posterior density interval (95% probability)	Highest posterior density interval (68% probability)
duration cremation cemetery	*180–320 years*	*210–290 years*
duration barrow	*175–315 years*	*205–285 years*
duration pyre hollow	*30–220 years*	*60–170 years*
duration Collared Urns	*15–175 years*	*40–50 years (3%); 70–160 years (65%)*
start barrow/start western group	*−35 to +140 years*	*−15 to +50 years*
start barrow/start pyre hollow	*−10 to +125 years*	*0 to 65 years*
end pyre hollow/end barrow	*−10 to +175 years*	*20 to 125 years*
end Collared Urns/ end cremation cemetery	*55 to 270 years*	*95 to 210 years*

of agreement which expresses the compatibility of the prior and posterior distributions (e.g. Fig. 5.6: *SUERC-61255 [A: 103]*). If the posterior distribution is situated in a high-probability region of the prior distribution, the index of agreement is high. If the index of agreement falls below 60 (a threshold value analogous to the 95% significance level in a χ^2 test), the place of the radiocarbon date in the model requires further assessment. Another index of agreement, Amodel, is calculated from the individual agreement indices, and indicates whether the model as a whole is likely, given the data. In most circumstances, it too has a threshold value of 60.

Sample selection

Samples were selected to ensure as far as possible that they were contemporary with their contexts, in other words that they had only recently left the carbon cycle when buried and were in their original contexts rather than redeposited in later ones. Thirteen were fragments of cremated bone from coherent cremation deposits. They should thus, on the face of it, date the deaths of the buried individuals. Enthusiasm for the dating of apatite from cremated bone has been modified by the progressive realisation that carbon can be exchanged between bone apatite carbonate and other sources, notably fuel and the corpse itself, during the cremation process (Hüls *et al.* 2010). Its effects should be insignificant if the fuel consisted of short-lived taxa or of branchwood from longer-lived taxa, but could be substantial if fuels with a considerable inbuilt age were used. The relationship between fuel type and the final composition of a cremated bone sample is not, however, straightforward, since the nature and extent of such exchanges can vary with the particular circumstances of individual cremations, experimental results being highly variable (Snoeck *et al.* 2014). The pyres for the cremation burials at Sites 18 and 26 seem to have consisted mainly of larger oak timbers with smaller oak and hazel poles (Chapter 5.3). It is thus possible

that older carbon may have been incorporated into the samples to varying and unknown extents. This question is explored further in 'An alternative model' below. The remaining three samples were single fragments of short-lived material from contexts with no or very little cremated bone: hazel charcoal from pit 260561, charred fruit flesh from pit 260029, which contained an accessory vessel but no human remains, and hazel charcoal from pit 260489, which contained only a minimal amount of human bone. The single fragments eliminate the risk of combining material of different ages in the same sample (Ashmore 1999).

Results, calibration and discussion

The radiocarbon results and associated measurements are listed in Table 5.25. All are conventional radiocarbon ages that have been corrected for fractionation (Stuiver and Polach 1977). In the 'Calibrated date range BC (2σ)' column of Table 5.25, the radiocarbon results have been calibrated by the maximum intercept method (Stuiver and Reimer 1986); in the '*Highest posterior density interval cal BC (95% probability)*' column, the illustrations, and the Bayesian modelling calibration has been undertaken using the probability method (Stuiver and Reimer 1993). All calibrations, as well as the Bayesian chronological modelling described below, have been undertaken using OxCal v4.3 (http://c14.arch.ox.ac.uk/) and the IntCal13 calibration curve (Reimer *et al.* 2013). Wiggles in the calibration curve are the cause of some multimodal probability distributions. Highest posterior density intervals have been rounded outwards to five years.

The preferred model

The chronological model is shown in Fig. 5.6. Durations and intervals derived from it are shown in Figure 5.7 and listed in Table 5.26. This model treats all the sampled contexts as belonging to a single more-or-less continuous phase of activity, within which there is no independently demonstrated stratigraphic relationship between the cremations in the area of the barrow, within the vestigial ring ditch (Group 261), and those in the adjacent pyre hollow (Group 268). It incorporates a single stratigraphic relationship, between pit 260561 and pyre hollow 260391, which cut the pit. On the grounds that there is as yet no reliable way of assessing the extent of exchange with other carbon sources, dates for cremated bone are treated as contemporary with the burials from which they came. The model has good overall agreement (Amodel 89).

Overall chronology
According to this model, the complex began to develop in *2015–1900 cal BC (95% probability)*, probably *1970–1920 cal BC (68% probability*; Fig. 5.6: *start cremation cemetery)*, the earliest burials being in the area of the barrow (Group 261). Burials in the pyre hollow (Group 268) to the north-east began later, in *1935–1815 cal BC (95% probability)*, probably *1925–1875 cal BC (67% probability*; Fig. 5.6: *start pyre hollow)*. This would have been *−10 to +125 years (95% probability)*, probably *0 to 65 years (68% probability)* after the start of burial in the barrow area (Fig. 5.7: *start barrow/start pyre hollow)*. The earlier of the two dated burials in the western group (Group 2610), was deposited in *1965–1870 cal BC (83% probability)*, probably *1940–1885 cal BC (68% probability*; Fig. 5.6: *SUERC-61122)*, *−35 to +140 years (95% probability)*, probably *−15 to +50 years (68% probability)* after the start of burial in the barrow area (Fig. 5.7: *start barrow/ start western group)*. The second of the two dated burials

here was made in *1940–1765 cal BC (95% probability)*, probably *1920–1870 cal BC (35% probability)* or *1845–1915 cal BC (19% probability)* or *1800–1775 cal BC (14% probability*; Fig. 5.6: *SUERC-61255)*, but two dates provide an insufficient basis on which to estimate the span of the ten burials in the group.

Burials were placed in hollow 260391 for *30 to 220 years (95% probability)*, probably *60 to 170 years (68% probability*; Fig. 5.7: *duration pyre hollow)*, until *1850–1685 cal BC (95% probability)*, probably *1800–1735 cal BC (56% probability)* or *1720–1695 cal BC (12% probability*; Fig. 5.6: *end pyre hollow)*. Burials in the barrow area continued for *−10 to +175 years (95% probability)*, probably *20 to 125 years (68% probability)* after the end of burial in the pyre hollow (Fig. 5.7: *end pyre hollow/end pyre barrow)* and spanned the entire use of the cemetery, over a total period of *180 to 320 years (95% probability)*, probably *210–290 years (68% probability*; Fig. 5.7: *duration cremation cemetery)*, until *1730–1595 cal BC (95% probability)* probably *1715–1700 cal BC (9% probability)* or *1695–1630 cal BC (59% probability*; Fig. 5.6: *end cremation cemetery)*.

Individual burials and pottery chronology
Fig. 5.8 and Table 5.27 show an ordering of all the dated burials, regardless of location. The distributions are extracted, already constrained, from the model shown in Fig. 5.6. The results are compatible with the provisional interpretation of burial 260439 as primary to the barrow, although this would be by a narrow margin, since it is only *57% probable* that 260439 was earlier than 260342, 25m to the south-east.

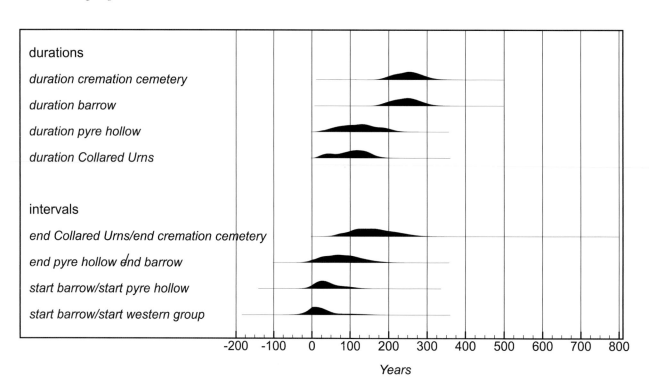

Fig. 5.7   Selected durations and intervals derived from the model shown in Figure 5.6 (Table 5.26)

The ordering shows that, while pottery was included in some burial deposits throughout the duration of the cemetery, Collared Urns were confined to its earlier use. It is possible to calculate a start date for their deposition of *1970–1890 cal BC (95% probability)*, probably *1945–1905 cal BC (68% probability*; Fig. 5.8: *start Collared Urns*); an end date of *1910–1860 cal BC (23% probability)* or *1855–1765 cal BC (72% probability)*, probably *1895–1875 cal BC (11% probability)* or *1845–1815 cal BC (26% probability)* or *1805–1775 cal BC (31% probability*; Fig. 5.8: *end Collared Urns*); and a duration of *15–175 years (95% probability)*, probably *70–160 years (65% probability*; Fig. 5.7: *duration Collared Urns)*. Accessory vessel P18.1 in the western group was buried within this period, in *1940–1765 cal BC (95% probability)*, probably *1920–1870 cal BC (35% probability)* or *1845–1815 cal BC (19% probability)* or *1800–1775 cal BC (14% probability*; Fig. 5.8: *SUERC-61255)*. Other styles of pot were buried later: accessory vessel P26.21 in the barrow in *1775–1640 cal BC (93% probability)*, probably *1750–1680 cal BC (68% probability*; Fig. 5.8: *SUERC-61282)*; and plain biconical vessel P26.3 in the barrow in *1750–1630 cal BC (95% probability)*, probably *1740–1710 cal BC (38% probability)* or *1695–1665 cal BC (30% probability*; Fig. 5.8: *SUERC-61275)*.

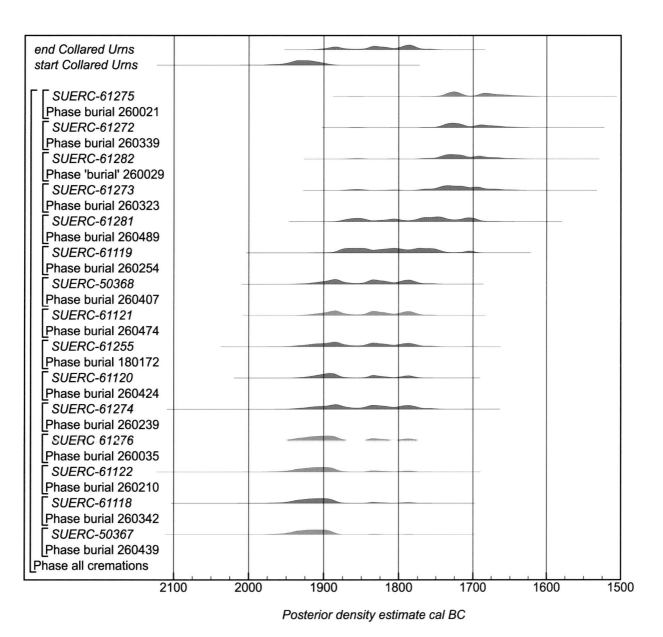

Fig. 5.8   An ordering of all dates for cremation burials, extracted, already constrained, from the model shown in Figure 5.6, together with estimates for the start and end of Collared Urn use at the site (Table 5.27). Burials with Collared Urns are shown in red, those with accessory vessels in blue, and one with a plain biconical vessel in purple.

Table 5.27   An ordering of dates for cremation burials (Fig. 5.8).

	260439 SUERC-50367	260342 SUERC-61118	260210 SUERC-61122	260035 SUERC-61276	260239 SUERC-61274	260424 SUERC-61120	180172 SUERC-61255	260474 SUERC-61121	260407 SUERC-50368	260254 SUERC-61119	260489 SUERC-61281	260323 SUERC-61273	260029 SUERC-61282	260339 SUERC-61272	260021 SUERC-61275
260439 SUERC-50367	-	57	62	72	88	85	86	92	92	98	99	100	100	100	100
260342 SUERC-61118		-	55	65	83	79	81	87	88	95	97	99	100	100	100
260210 SUERC-61122			-	60	79	74	77	83	84	92	96	99	99	100	100
260035 SUERC-61276				-	70	63	67	74	74	86	92	98	99	99	100
260239 SUERC-61274					-	41	47	53	53	71	83	95	97	99	100
260424 SUERC-61120						-	56	64	64	80	89	97	98	99	100
180172 SUERC-61255							-	56	56	73	84	96	98	99	100
260474 SUERC-61121								-	51	70	82	95	97	99	100
260407 SUERC-50368									-	69	82	95	97	99	100
260254 SUERC-61119										-	67	89	92	95	97
260489 SUERC-61281											-	75	81	85	90
260323 SUERC-61273												-	57	63	73
260029 SUERC-61282													-	57	67
260339 SUERC-61272														-	61
260021 SUERC-61275															-

Each cell shows the % probability that the date in the left-hand column is earlier than the date in the top row. It is, for example, 57% probable that SUERC-50367 is earlier than SUERC-61118.

The 20th/19th to 19th/18th-century cal BC currency of dated Collared Urns at the site falls in the earlier part of the span for the style in Wales calculated by Wilkin (2014), which extends into the 17th century cal BC (2014, table 2.6, 392, 399). His estimate of *2140–1910 to 1735–1510 cal BC (95% probability)*, probably *2055–1950 to 1690–1580 cal BC (68% probability)* is based on 13 AMS dates on cremated bone. It is furthermore comparable with an estimate for the currency of Collared Urn in Ireland, based on 14 AMS dates on cremated bone of *2075–1880 cal BC (95% probability)* to *1865–1780 (19% probability)* or *1775–1565 cal BC (76% probability)*, probably *1995–1895 cal BC (68% probability)* to *1855–1835 cal BC (8% probability)* or *1730–1610 cal BC (60% probability*; Bayliss and O'Sullivan 2013).

The lack of 17th or 16th-century cal BC dates associated with Collared Urns at Site 26 may stem from the forms of the urns dated. All four (Fig. 4.6, P26.4–5; Fig. 4.7, P26.8–9) are relatively large, of Law's types B or C (Law 2016; Garrow *et al.* 2014, fig. 8). Smaller Collared Urns, of Law's type A, are however present (Fig. 4.7, P26.10–11). If an observation made in East Anglia has any relevance in south-west Wales, then the smaller urns could be later. At Low Ground, Over, Cambridgeshire, they appeared only in the second phase of the latest of three barrows, although larger forms had been placed in earlier contexts (Garrow *et al.* 2014, 231, figs 11, 18). If a preference for depositing smaller forms later in the currency of the style extended across Britain, then P26.10–11 might post-date the dated urns from the complex.

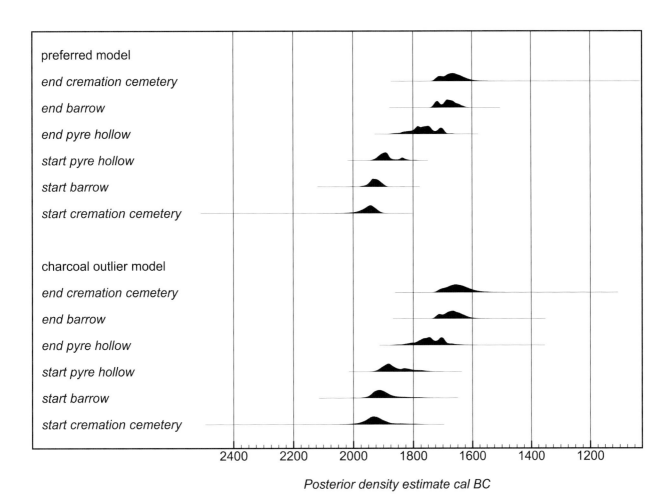

Fig. 5.9   A comparison of key parameters extracted from the preferred model (Figure 5.6) and from a second model in which dates measured on cremated bone are offset by relating them to a distribution for the proportions of wood of different ages available in a typical woodland (Bronk Ramsey 2009b, 1023)

Table 5.28   Parameters shown in Figure 5.9

	Preferred model		Alternative model	
Parameter	*Highest posterior density interval cal BC (95% probability)*	*Highest posterior density interval cal BC (68% probability)*	Highest posterior density interval cal BC (95% probability)	Highest posterior density interval cal BC (68% probability)
start cremation cemetery	2015–1900	1970–1920	2015–1795	1970–1890
start barrow	1970–1890	1945–1905	1970–1785	1945–1875
start pyre hollow	1935–1815	1925–1875 (67%) 1840–1835 (1%)	1930–1760	1915–1850 (59%) 1840–1820 (9%)
end pyre hollow	1850–1685	1800–1735 (56%) 1715–1695 (12%)	1840–1645	1785–1690
end barrow	1735–1630	1730–1705 (18%) 1700–1655 (50%)	1730–1605	1715–1705 (5%) 1700–1635 (63%)
end cremation cemetery	1730–1595	1715–1700 (9%) 1695–1630 (59%)	1725–1565	1695–1615

The plain biconical pot P26.3 is the latest dated vessel from the complex, and is tentatively attributed to the Biconical Urn tradition (Chapter 4.2). Its 18th/17th-century cal BC date is compatible with the apparent emergence of Biconical Urns towards the end of the Early Bronze Age (Healy 1996, 112).

An alternative model

The possibility of already-old fuel having contributed to the carbonate in cremated bone samples, noted above, prompts an alternative model. Here the dates for cremated bone are offset by relating them to a distribution for the proportions of wood of different ages available in a typical woodland, based on the hypothesis that the fuel constitutes a representative sample of a forest in which trees are more than one and less than 1000 years old (Bronk Ramsey 2009b, 1023: Outlier_Model ("Charcoal", Exp(1,10,0),U(0,3), "t")). This is not entirely appropriate, since the wood for the pyres was clearly selected (Chapter 5.3). It should nonetheless provide an indication of the kind of difference that mature fuel might make to the results. Apart from the use of the charcoal outlier for cremated bone (although not for the three short-life charcoal and charred plant samples), the structure of the model is identical to that shown in Fig. 5.6. It too has good overall agreement (Amodel 97). The results of both are compared in Fig. 5.9 and Table 5.28. While all the modelled dates for cremated bone, and consequently all the estimated parameters, become slightly more recent, the differences are slight. The medians of the estimated parameters shown in Fig. 5.9 vary by 14 to 22 years; those for individual dates by 5 to 47 years, most of them by around 20 years. Durations are effectively unchanged, with differences of between 3 and 11 years between the medians of the spans estimated by the two models. The effect of mature pyre wood on the results would probably be slight, especially given the variable extents to which older carbon might have been incorporated into the samples, as discussed above.

Chapter 6
Discussion
Andrew Mudd

6.1 Mesolithic/Early Neolithic visitations

Site 25 in the Taf valley yielded the largest number of worked lithics on the project (203) with around 28 (14%) diagnostically Mesolithic or Mesolithic/early Neolithic (Chapter 4.1). These were all redeposited or unstratified. Little can be said about the Mesolithic occupation here but the marked concentration of lithics in this location, with just occasional finds from elsewhere, suggests that this location in the lower Taf close to its confluence with the River Coran, a tributary flowing in from the south, was a significant venue for Mesolithic hunter-gatherers (Fig. 6.1). A single late Mesolithic radiocarbon date (5762–5648 cal BC) on charcoal from an apparently isolated posthole or small pit (250117) indicates some kind of presence at this time, but it lacks clear context. While the activities carried out are not apparent from this limited evidence, it can be suggested that this was the location of temporary camps visited on repeated occasions on a route that early hunters took following or anticipating the movements of game. Generally for South Wales, a model of seasonal movement between the coast and inland camps has been proposed, and it is thought that the river valleys offered natural routeways through a predominantly wooded landscape, providing both relatively easy passage and clear visibility (Barton *et al.* 1995, 110–11). The question of territoriality, particularly in the later Mesolithic, is however a pertinent one, and it is not clear that the same groups visited coastal and inland sites (Aldhouse-Green 2000, 39–40). In either case, the local landscape at the time may have offered other opportunities such as clearings favoured by grazing deer and wild cattle, fish from the river or wildfowl on valley lakes.

In view of evidence of Early Neolithic occupation at this site, it may be suggested that it became a location of persistent visitation, inviting suggestions of a degree of continuity in the ways of living and habits of movement of the local population after *c.* 4000 BC. Features of confirmed Early Neolithic date here are quite sparse comprising just two pits (250176 and 250103) with pottery although there was a diffuse scatter of similar looking features (Fig. 2.1). The level and nature of Early Neolithic activity here is therefore uncertain, and economic indicators are lacking, but it is of interest that charcoal from pit 250103 derives from a wide range of tree species, including oak, alder, hazel, hawthorn-type, cherry and willow. This suggests that primary woodland had been cleared by this time, perhaps an indication of the intensity of land-use before any real evidence of arable farming.

6.2 Early Neolithic occupation

There is firmer evidence for Early Neolithic occupation at Site 37 on higher land below the crest of Brandy Hill (Fig. 2.3). This took the form of two clusters of pits, some containing concentrations of pottery, flints and charred plants, including cereals. Radiocarbon dates from each of the clusters overlap between *c.* 3700 and 3600 BC so they may have been contemporaneous, but not necessarily so. The pottery, some of which is decorated, accords with this dating, although slight variations such as the decorated vessels with thickened rims being limited to the western cluster may indicate a chronological distinction. Overall, the styles are considered to be of the 'secondary' or 'post-inception' phase of the Welsh Early Neolithic ceramic tradition, which suits a date after 3700 BC (Chapter 4.2, this report). The large groups of material, which include pottery, food remains, tools and hearth debris in various combinations suggest the site of a habitation. There the tentative suggestion of the footprint of at least part of a small rectangular structure, about 3–4m square, from the arrangement of five postholes (370038, 370045, 370061, 370083, 370117). The evidence is inconclusive but domestic architecture in the Early Neolithic, while still rare, is now known to have been varied (Darvill 2010, 84 and table D). House 1 at Clegyr Boia, Pembrokeshire, showed irregular lines of four or five postholes about 2m apart, although the hollow into which the building had been cut was slightly larger. Even so, at 7m long by 3.5m wide, the building is among the smaller examples included in Darvill's synthesis (ibid., table D) and this may have been a regional trait. House 2 at Clegyr Boia also showed irregular wall lines about 3m apart, although it may have been larger than the surviving 5m in length (Lynch *et al.* 2000, 49–51, fig. 2.2). Another possible example comes from near Cwmifor in the Towy valley in Carmarthenshire above its confluence with the River Dulais where three lines of pits/postholes defined a possible Early Neolithic house about 6m wide and perhaps 10m long (Barber and Hart 2014a; see also Pannett 2012). Again the evidence is equivocal, but even with large and relatively clear ground plans, such as the 'halls' at Llandegai, Gwynedd (Lynch and Musson 2001, fig. 8; Kenney 2008, fig. 7), walls lines can appear irregular, with 'missing' postholes including corner posts, a situation probably attributable to the effects of later truncation on features of varied size and depth (Kenney 2008, 19). The character of these Early Neolithic buildings and associated features suggests quite small settlements with just one or two houses, small groups of pits and sometimes external hearths or fire pits (Lynch *et al.* 2000, 49–51). At Site 37 a possible working hollow, lying north of the possible house may have been associated with the Early Neolithic occupation.

The Early Neolithic features at Site 37 are of particular interest in showing evidence for depositions that appear to have been non-utilitarian, or 'structured' in a premeditated manner. The lack of a clear pattern to these deposits makes the rationale behind them difficult to elucidate. None of the pots were complete and even where sherds were from a single vessel, as in pit 370119, they were well fragmented. It is possible, however, that this pot had been deliberately broken. This pit also contained two artefacts of the same volcanic tuff used to make Group VIII axeheads and it is possible they were made from axehead flakes. A fragment of an axehead of this material came from pit 370049 inside the putative house. The recognition of deliberately placed deposits in early Neolithic domestic contexts does not appear to be common, particularly when compared with the later Neolithic when deposits incorporating Peterborough ware and Grooved ware seem far more structured (see Kenney 2008, 50–5 for a discussion of the Llandegai Neolithic pits and comparisons, and Pannett 2012 for a recent review of South Wales). At Llandegai, Lynch and Musson (Llandegai I) and Kenney (Llandegai II) consider the posthole fills of

the early Neolithic houses in detail and argue against deliberately placed deposits (Lynch and Musson 2001, 29; Kenney 2008, 29–30). Although pottery was found in a number of the postholes within the buildings, the small and abraded nature of the sherds, often from several different vessels, support their interpretation as more fortuitous collections of domestic rubbish. There is a strong suggestion, however, that the houses were burnt down or dismantled at the end of their lives, so it is possible that closure rituals may have been undertaken and that debris may have been deliberately used (if not carefully selected) to fill the vacant postholes (Kenney 2008, 21–2). There is also some suggestion of the deliberate placement of an exceptional arrowhead, made from imported flint, in the packing of one of the main postholes in the Llandegai II house (ibid., 25). This would support the proposition that selected material could also be deposited as a foundation deposit for a Neolithic house. In cases where soil disturbances had mixed post-packing and postpipe fills, it is possible that both foundation and abandonment depositions could be present without the prospect of being able to distinguish between them. The material from the postholes and pits of the putative house at Site 37 (Cluster 2), and the pits in the western cluster (Cluster 1) show some of the ambiguous evidence of those at Llandegai. The material may have deliberately selected, although it is not possible to say whether this related to foundation or closure rituals, or something else.

Across the site as whole the pottery appears to show a restricted selection but represents a variety of different vessels apparently not selected on the basis of form or decoration (Chapter 4.2). Attention can be drawn to parts of three decorated vessels from pits 370119, 370123 and 370153 in the western cluster which may be seen as a more significant group, while sherds from pit 370054 on the eastern extremity of the site were unusual in having been burnt. In a similar manner, the lithics did not seem to be random collections of waste material. While not common (just 24 pieces) and spread between several features, they comprised a high proportion of tools (Chapter 4.1) and for that reason appear to have been selected from the wider range of available material. Leaf-shaped arrowheads came from pits 370037, 370054 and 370019. This pattern resonates with the lithics assemblage from the Llandegai II house where a large proportion of the flints were retouched pieces, despite the sieving undertaken to recover knapping debitage (Smith 2008, 23). This need not, however, imply deliberate deposition, but perhaps instead a restricted range of material on the site, with knapping presumably having been undertaken elsewhere.

The pottery and lithics do not give a clear indication of the range of contacts of the local inhabitants. The source of clay and tempering for the pots is thought to be local although the material is not distinctive

(Ixer, Chapter 4.2). The source of the 'acid tuff' for the axehead fragment and other stone items is likely to have been the Preseli Hills to the north-west (Chapter 4.5) and thus also relatively local. The flint is not local to the immediate area, but without the presence of cortex it is not clear whether it derived from primary sources – such as the Chalklands of southern England – or from beaches nearer to hand (Chapter 4.1).

The botanical remains from Site 37 are significant, establishing that cultivation of emmer wheat and naked barley were undertaken, alongside the selection of wild foods – indicated particularly by hazelnut shells, but including also crab apple, cherry and bramble seeds. It is the range of material that marks this assemblage out as unusual and it is possible that burnt food waste was deliberately buried. The remains do not seem to have been separated from hearth waste, however, because charcoal was also present and so there may have been token handfuls of burnt remains or midden material deposited.

The botanical remains also indicate that the land here supported a mixed vegetation, with the wood species present including gorse/broom, blackthorn, cherry, birch, hawthorn-type and willow/poplar and alder, as well as oak and hazel, unless it can be supposed that wood for burning was collected from a very wide catchment of mobility. This shows that extensive clearance of primary 'wildwood' had taken place and that farming probably took place in a mosaic of woodland, scrub and small cultivated fields. As a point of interest, this appears to contrast with the possible domestic site near Cwmifor in the Towy valley with similar or slightly earlier radiocarbon dates, where along with the evidence of hazelnuts, emmer wheat and barley, the charcoal was dominated by oak, with some alder/hazel also present (Rackham 2014). It is possible that this shows a slightly different pattern of agricultural colonisation in this area.

6.3 Beaker/Early Bronze Age revisitations

The absence of evidence for activity between about 3300 and 2500 BC is noteworthy but difficult to account for. It is possible that some of the undated features are Middle or Late Neolithic in date, but without the evidence of pottery have gone undetected. Given the presence of Peterborough ware and Grooved ware in pits in other parts of South Wales (Pannett 2012) this seems unlikely, and their absence would seem to indicate different patterns of settlement in this area in the later part of the Neolithic. This may have related to a change to more mobile pastoral groups (ibid.). The henge at Vaynor may have been a determining influence in this respect, the impression being that it created something of an 'exclusion zone' for other activity at this time.

Early Bronze Age activity is attested in the same general areas as the Early Neolithic occupations (Sites 25 and 37) where the presence of shallow pits containing small quantities of pottery and charred hazelnuts are notably similar to the Early Neolithic remains. The Beaker pits at Site 25 also contained wheat and barley. A slightly later Early Bronze Age radiocarbon date came from fire pit 250061 a little way to the south of this group and there may have been more widespread occupation in the Early Bronze Age here. Some of the pits appear to have been suitable for storage and this may suggest a settlement of some form. In this connection the presence of a curving ditch (250028) in the south-eastern corner of the site can be noted. This has the appearance of a penannular drainage gully, or part of a circular ring-groove house, of about 11m diameter with the ditch terminal indicating an entrance facing west. While undated and close to the group of Early Neolithic pits, it seems more likely to belong with the Bronze Age occupation, or even a later one here, as circular Early Neolithic buildings are without precedent. Early Bronze Age buildings are also rare in Wales and most, such as that at Stackpole Warren, were post-built and without encircling gullies (Benson *et al.* 1990; Lynch *et al.* 2000, 87, fig. 3.3). There is a possible example of a plank-built or partly plank-built Early Bronze Age roundhouse of this size from Atlantic Trading Estate, Barry (Sell 1998), but unfortunately the dating evidence is very weak. Middle Bronze Age house constructions are not well defined in Wales either, and post, or post-and-stone walls may have been most common (Lynch *et al.* 2000, 91–5). A Middle Bronze Age house at Brean Down, Somerset, was partly defined by a wall-slot as well as a 'stormwater gully' (Structure 95, Bell 1990) and there are examples of slot-trench construction from Ireland at this time. Of the 78 Irish Bronze Age houses reviewed by Doody (2000), 17 incorporated slot-trenches of circular or near-circular form (ibid., 139). There are several from Carrigatogher, Co. Tipperary (Hackett 2009, 15–16), presumably representing roundhouse walls constructed of split timbers. It is considered possible therefore, if without strong supporting evidence, that Site 25 contained a roundhouse of Early Bronze Age date contemporary with some of the pits here.

6.4 Bronze Age cremations

The excavations have revealed evidence of Bronze Age cremation-related activity over a distance of *c.* 300m across the width of the road easement (*c.* 40–60m) between Pentrehowell and Vaynor Farm (Site 26) (Fig. 6.1). The remains, including burials and possible pyre sites, as well as other features, are for the most part scattered but include 38 intentional deposits of cremated bone. Twenty-four of these are associated with a possible barrow (Group 261) and a further five with the 'pyre hollow' (Group 268) making a close group of 29 in an area covering *c.* 20m by 20m. Here, pits, hollows, postholes and a setting of stones suggest a range of

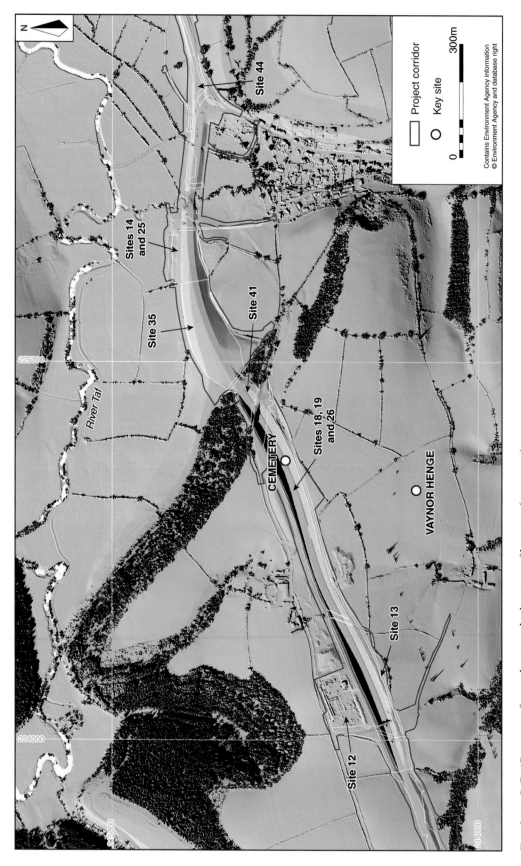

Fig. 6.1   LiDAR image of area showing the location of key sites (1:10,000)

associated features. Many contained charcoal and small amounts of cremated bone and they would appear to represent a variety of funerary structures and activities. The 'barrow' here remains somewhat conjectural as the area was truncated to a level below the contemporary ground surface. The burials belonging to this group may instead have been in a flat cemetery enclosed by a ditch. Ring ditches without any form of interior mound are known or suspected from various sites, including some in Wales (Garwood 2007, fig. 4.2). A small ring ditch near Trecastle (Powys) formed part of a linear barrow cemetery, which included standing cairns, along the ridge of Mynydd Bach (Darvill forthcoming). Here the ring ditch showed no evidence of a central mound and the burial site is assumed to have been marked by the ditch alone (ibid.). Ring ditches can be seen as part of a continuum of 'open-area funerary-ceremonial sites', including ring cairns, which sometimes became places of burial later in their existence (Garwood 2007, 34). At the 'barrow' site here the peripheral burials are interpretable as respecting or having been cut through a central mound (below), but the evidence is far from conclusive.

The cremation deposits themselves were varied. Some had bones contained within vessels (variously decorated and positioned inverted or upright) or were associated with empty vessels within the same grave pit. Other bones were simply placed in grave pits or cists within pits, sometimes capped with a stone slab. Where bone was identifiable, men, women and juveniles were present, although juveniles were relatively rare and most individuals were unsexed because of the fragmentary and partial nature of the remains.

The diversity of funerary practices in the Bronze Age has long been recognised – even as far back as 1890:

'so varied are the circumstances attending interments that it would be scarcely wrong to say that no two burials are in every respect alike'
(Greenwell 1890, 64).

This absence of a clear pattern to how the dead were treated, and the ubiquity of the phenomenon across the British Isles, has led to the discouraging view of a 'complexity, even idiosyncrasy, perceived to be analytically challenging to the point of unpatterned intractability' (Garwood and Barclay 2011, 419). Recent excavations and interpretations of earlier excavations have drawn attention to not only the variety of material evidence for burial customs, but also the range and sequence of practices for which there is evidence within and around burial sites. The approach focuses on the site as an arena for ritual performance where the burial of the deceased was just one aspect (and one that was not invariably present), and on the ways in which these actions and depositions developed over the course of time. It has been suggested that a focus on agency and the logic of development offers a more productive alter-

native way of classifying burial sites than the traditional concern with outward forms of earthworks, burials and artefacts (Garwood 2007; Last 2007b, 156).

Examining the sequence and interpreting the meaning of the remains from Site 26 suffers from the plough-truncated nature of the site and the consequent lack of stratigraphy. However, the availability of 16 radiocarbon dates from this complex, which have been the subject of Bayesian modelling, provides a framework for proposing a chronological sequence. Allied to this, comparisons with information from upland sites, where mounds or cairns allow the better preservation of stratigraphy, allows some comparable appreciation of the ways many of these sites were constructed and used over time.

It can be assumed that there was a reason to choose this particular site for burial. It may have been a significant place in the Neolithic period. In the wider landscape the Vaynor Farm Henge, 350m to the south, constructed between 2700 and 2400 BC and still present as an earthwork in the Roman period, appears likely to have influenced the location of burial in early Bronze Age in a general sense, perhaps as part of a sacred landscape. There is, however, no clear origin to the site of the 'barrow'. The earliest dated feature is cremation burial 260439 (2022–1882 cal BC) towards the centre of the barrow as defined by the remnant ring ditch. It is not precisely central, nor is the ring ditch demonstrably a primary feature, but within ring ditches or barrows central burials are commonly the earliest and sometimes the only ones present. 'Cemetery mounds', where several individuals were placed in the same barrow or cairn, often without a recognisable 'primary' burial, are particularly characteristic of Bronze Age Wales (Lynch *et al.* 2000, 126) but primary burials may be recognisable as well. At Brenig 45 a central burial was surrounded by several peripheral burials which were mostly demonstrably later as they had been cut through the turf mound (Lynch 1993, 74–5). At Fan Foel, Mynydd Ddu, a burial cist was constructed on the original ground surface, probably centrally to an original mound constructed around it. There was evidence of a primary stone kerb to the mound and of burning and trampling before barrow construction. A later stone kerb, stratigraphically above the mound material, contained at least one secondary cremation (Hughes and Murphy 2013). On the plough-flattened site of Fan Round Barrow, Ceredigion, the radiocarbon dates alone suggest a sequence with a possible pair of cremations (7 and 36) at the centre of the mapped mound and later cremations slightly further out (Schlee 2013). The caveat here is that the radiocarbon dates have enough statistical overlap to make them potentially all part of the same event (ibid., 100).

There are therefore grounds for suggesting that cremation 260439 at Site 26 was a 'primary' burial by reason of its location and date, although the burial itself may have been preceded by preparatory activities, including perhaps the cremation ceremony. Cremation 260439 (2022–1882 cal BC) was that of a mature woman contained within an inverted Collared Urn. Because the vessel had been inverted in a pit it contained all the bone and other material collected from the pyre, but despite the relatively large quantity of bone (986g) this would only have represented part of the skeleton, implying that a process of selection had been carried out. This may have been undertaken adjacent to the grave pit where a group of small pits lay precisely central to the ring ditch, perhaps implying their primacy. The pits contained charcoal and some human bone, so it is clear that their infilling was contemporary with some of the cremation-related activity. The groups of postholes inserted through their fills and nearby indicate small structures whose purpose (and date) remains unclear. They may have been for drying or smoking material connected with the funerary ritual, or have been related to the selection of material for burial. Stake structures are not uncommonly found under barrows, in Wales and elsewhere, sometimes in the centre and associated with burnt timbers when the term 'mortuary structure' may be appropriate. However, this burning is often not associated with pyre material and the wooden structure need not have provided a framework for a pyre (see examples discussed by Lynch 1993, 78–80).

Cremation 260342 may have been buried at the same time as cremation 260439 as its date is very similar (with a 57% chance of being later; Table 5.27). This was not associated with a vessel and comprised a relatively small quantity of bone, perhaps because of truncation, and identified only as an adult. This appears to have been paired with nearby cremation 260183, sealed in a pit covered by a limestone slab without a vessel. A relatively large quantity of bone of an adult (670g) would still have represented a selection of that originally present. Also within the central area and perhaps positioned with respect to cremation 260439 was cremation 260099, the 'token' burial (77g) of young adult without a vessel in a pit capped by a shale slab. Cremation 260449 comprised fragments of skull only (4.9g) and it is not clear that this was a deliberate deposit. Another burial (cremation 260035) would seem to have been part of the early group in this area. Its date (2011–1774 cal BC) was slightly later than that of 260439 (72% probability) and 260342 (65% probability; Table 5.27). Like cremation 260439, cremation 260035 was of an adult woman contained in an inverted Collared Urn.

There therefore may have been a group of primary cremation burials towards the centre of a ring ditch around an area where manipulation of the cremated bone was undertaken before burial. The radiocarbon modelling suggests that, although the dates of the bones were quite similar, these five burials probably took place over a few generations. This would seem to imply that there was no barrow mound raised at this time. The shallowness of the surrounding ditch indicates that it could not have provided material for a mound to cover the interior to any depth, although material may have been acquired more widely for this purpose. Lowland barrows in south-west Wales were typically constructed of soil and turf (Murphy 1990). The lack of intercutting makes it probable that the grave positions were marked, perhaps by posts, for which there is evidence of several despite no provable relationships with the burials, although stone cairns may also have been present as well or instead.

The barrow ditch was presumably dug to demarcate the area used for funerary activity, but it was only visible as a slight soil stain and its interpretation, and even existence, are open to question. Ditchless barrows are a common phenomenon in upland areas. At Pant y Butler, Ceredigion, ditchless Barrow 2 showed evidence of a ring of turf apparently added outside a stone kerb bounding the barrow mound creating an alternative form of boundary marker (Murphy and Murphy 2013).

At the same time as the barrow area was in use, cremation burial was also taking place at the 'pyre hollow' (260391) on the north-eastern margin of the 'barrow'. The relationship of the pyre hollow activity to the ditch is uncertain and it is possible that the ditch (if it extended this far) was either slighted or perhaps somehow integrated with activity in and around the pyre. The origin of the hollow is not clear but it may have been a quarry for material for a mound for the barrow. Stratigraphically, however, the earliest features were a group of pits on the north-west side of the hollow, interpreted as a probable tree throw. A fragment of hazel charcoal from the upper fill of the deepest pit (260561) yielded a date of 1930–1755 cal BC, which however modelled is rather late in the overall sequence and seems likely to have been intrusive from the burnt material within the hollow. It is possible therefore that a tree, or perhaps more than one, was the focus of ritual activity here leading to its use as a burial ground. Natural features, especially trees, have sometimes been identified as the probable original object of ritual attention on barrow sites (Healy and Harding 2007, 60–5). At Pant y Butler Barrow 2 a dolerite boulder (perhaps an erratic or brought to site and erected as a standing stone) is thought to have formed the focus of the primary burial (Murphy and Murphy 2013, 41–3). Here, it is interesting to note the presence of a burnt oak plank or branch lying on the buried turf line next to the stone and grave, seemingly in a deliberate alignment with the grave, showing an aspect of burial ritual that had taken place immediately before the mound was raised.

The earliest-dated event at the pyre site was cremation 260424 (2017–1777 cal BC), a possible mature male placed in a pit without an urn. This is modelled as being probably earlier than 260474 and 260407 in the same area, and later than 260035, one of the primary group in the barrow area, but the dates are very close

(Table 5.27). Cremation 260474 was of a mature probable male in an inverted vessel which had retained all the buried remains of a nearly complete skeleton. Cremation 260407, which yielded a virtually identical date (1946–1771 cal BC), was of a mature adult without a vessel, but the pit had been capped suggesting that all the bone that had been selected for burial (740g) was present, with the implication that the rest had been disposed of elsewhere. These three groups of cremated bone on the periphery of the pyre hollow were the only ones identified as cremation burials. Other cremated bone came from pits 260397, 260489, 260492 and 260596, but in such small quantities it is likely to have been redeposited. A radiocarbon measurement on hazel charcoal associated with the bone group 260489 is calibrated to 1880–1688 cal BC, and this would seem to reflect the later phases of cremation perhaps related to the more peripheral burials at the barrow site. It is not clear at what stage the 'pyre hollow' was created but it perhaps followed the cremation burials here and may have related to the creation of the barrow mound, or the uprooting of the tree or trees that may have existed in the earlier phase.

In the barrow area burials lay in more peripheral areas, particularly on the eastern side. These included unurned cremation 260323, possibly a juvenile, dated to 1869–1628 cal BC. Nearby, cremation 260037 was in an upright vessel but this had been largely lost to truncation probably because it had been in a shallower grave, or perhaps one cut through a mound. To the north-east was cremation 260015, an unurned adult, and cremation 260326, another unurned adult. Cremation 260326 appears to have been marked by a post. In the south-east was the burial of an adult male in a cist that had been filled with stone (cremation 260339). The date 1751–1619 cal BC on the bone shows that this was one of the later burials here and it is possible that the grave pit had been cut through a cairn, or that a cairn was constructed over it. The burials in an arc on the south-eastern periphery also appear likely to be late ones. Cremation 260021, a juvenile buried with a plain biconical pot was dated to 1744–1560 cal BC, making it substantially later than the central burials. The others here comprised 260023 and 260025, both adults, 260017, an adult with fragments of a vessel, and 260019, an infant. South-west of these were the truncated remains of a possible burial 260029 in a very shallow pit containing sherds of a vessel and charcoal. Its shallowness perhaps suggests that this had been cut through a mound. A radiocarbon date on charred fruit came out at 1771–1623 cal BC. In the absence of bone it is possible that this was an offering or cenotaph deposit rather than a burial. It is possible that the peripheral burials respected a mound over the central area, or may have been buried in, or cut through, the mound itself with potentially many therefore lost to the plough. They may themselves have been constricted in an outward direction in some manner. The peripheral postholes lack regularity but they may be similar to the more irregular outer rings of stakeholes at Brenig 40, Brenig 41, and Brenig 42, which are thought to have been early demarcation features, although at Brenig 45 the outer circle was shown to have been relatively late (Lynch 1993, 51, 82). At Site 26 the peripheral postholes are perhaps too irregular and discontinuous to suggest a fence-like boundary and there may have been other structures or marker posts here.

It may be significant that the cremations in the pyre area were sealed by stone slabs (260347). While the date of this construction is not known, it is possible that this was the remains of a stone kerb (lost from the higher part of the site) which had been added to the margin of the mound. There is some evidence that stone kerbs can be late features. At Fan Foel, Mynydd Ddu, a 'secondary' stone kerb was added on the mound surface and this contained a secondary cremation of an adult and child (Hughes and Murphy 2013). At Pant y Butler Barrow 2 a stone kerb was recorded in a similar stratigraphic position after mound construction (Murphy and Murphy 2013).

The dating and disposition of the burials at Site 26 perhaps therefore suggest two main phases of use, with an early phase of burial at the core of what became the barrow and at the margin of the 'pyre hollow'. Any patterns are somewhat conjectural, but one or two points can be highlighted. In this early phase, of the six or seven burials in the barrow area, at least two were women. The other four or five were of unknown sex. In the pyre hollow area two of the three burials are thought to have been of men. Children seem to have been absent at this time from both areas. Burial 260178 in the barrow area may be an exception, although it was stratigraphically later than burial 260183 here and may have been a later insertion. At a very similar time at Fan Round Barrow, Ceredigion, four of the five individuals identified to sex were women while the sex of the fifth was undetermined (Schlee 2013). It appears possible therefore that men were buried elsewhere. The radiocarbon dating from both Site 26 and Fan suggest a short first phase of burial, perhaps of a single family group buried in sequence over a few generations. At Fan it is probable that the mound (originally recorded as a cairn 1.5m high) was constructed after this phase of burials and it is suggested that this may have been the case at Site 26. The peripheral pits at Fan dated to the Middle and Later Bronze Age and these clearly represent a later phase. The later phase at Site 26 would seem to have involved the burial of a wider range of individuals, including men and juveniles, on the periphery of the barrow but within its boundary, which may have been marked by a stone kerb. The pyre hollow does not seem to have a place of burial any longer – perhaps only where the cremation was undertaken, and there may have been other pyre sites whose remains have been entirely lost.

The interpretation of the burials towards the centre of the barrow as primary, and activity towards the perimeter as later is given further weight from the pottery. The urns found with burials 260439, 260035 and 260178 towards the central area of the 'barrow' manifest characteristics of Burgess's early Collared Urn scheme, supported by radiocarbon dating, as discussed above. The suggestion has been made, based on style and supporting radiocarbon dating, for the Biconical Urn and accessory vessels to belong to a later, or a longer-lived practice than the use of the Collared Urns (Chapter 4.2). Other than burial 260254, the remaining distribution of the Biconical Urn and accessory vessels (the latter found with or without surviving burial remains) are distributed towards the periphery of the 'barrow' arc (260017, 260029, 260007, 260029 and 260021), and beyond (260244 and 260044). The burial of miniature vessels without cremated bone may represent other types of funerary rituals.

Not only were there foci of cremation burials in the barrow and on the edge of the pyre hollow; others were found to the south-west in a more dispersed pattern, without a clear focus (Group 2610). The earliest dated one, cremation 260210 lay about 230m from the barrow and was of a man contained within an urn. The date of 2020–1779 cal BC is almost identical to the date of cremation 260424, the first burial at the pyre hollow site (although duplicated bones show that they were not from the same individual – Clough pers. comm.). Nearby were three pairs of cremation burials. Cremations 260207 and 260231 were both within vessels, one upright and one inverted, and both were possibly female. Cremations 260229 (within a vessel) and 260236 (without a vessel), and 260303 (older possible female in a vessel) with 260276 (possible male without a vessel) lay not far away. Although it is possible that the burials in the barrow area were frequently paired, the pairings were far clearer in Group 2610. There are no clear patterns of burial and the link between the paired individuals is not apparent although a close familial relationship is an obvious possibility. It seems likely that, for burials to have been made precisely next to existing ones, the burial places must have been marked, although there is no indication of this. Alternatively, it is perhaps possible that cremated remains were curated for a while, or retained in another grave, until other individuals died and their remains could be buried together. There are also peripheral single burials here: 260288 (with very little bone), 180172, an adult, returning a date of 1948–1766 cal BC and cremation 260474, an older male on the edge of the pyre hollow (but again a different individual – Clough, pers. comm.). Burial 180184 was a single burial between the barrow and Group 2610 that may have referenced another feature that has since been lost.

The dating makes it clear that burials were being made in Group 2610 at the same time as at the barrow and pyre site, although it cannot be known whether or in what fashion the different groups were related, or why the Group 2610 were buried where they were. At Coity Link Road, Bridgend, a broken and recumbent stone prompted a suggestion that a standing stone may have been the focus of one of the small groups of cremations found there (Richmond *et al.* 2015). Burials appear to have been focused on standing stones at Ystrad-Hynod, Powys (ApSimon 1973), and at Stackpole Warren, Pembrokeshire (Benson *et al.* 1990) while at Pant y Butler the primary burial was at the foot of a large stone that may originally have been upright (Murphy and Murphy 2013). There is no indication of a stone or other natural feature for the group at Site 2610, and neither is it clear that cremation burial 260210 can be considered to be a 'founder' burial for the group, and so the origins of this group of burials remains obscure.

Despite the difficulty of understanding the Bronze Age burials in this stretch of landscape, it is apparent that groups of people were being commemorated in different places, more or less at the same time, according to a variety of individual rites. The rites would appear to emphasise both distinctiveness and relatedness, probably drawing on the individual biographies of kin and gender groups. The associated pottery reflects some of this individuality, not only through form and decoration, but also through the material from which the cremation vessels were made. The grog tempering in three of the vessels (from cremations 260210, 260035 and 260439) was itself grog-tempered (Ixer, this report), so the pots themselves would have represented the third generation of vessels – a lineage of pottery perhaps reflecting the genealogy of the people buried with them. Similar 'pottery lineages' have been recognised in the Collared Urns from Coity Link Road, Bridgend, and elsewhere where it has been suggested that grog-in-grog-tempered pots may have been used to symbolise ancestors (Morris 2015, 29–30).

6.5 Bronze Age 'drying oven'

Consideration of the form of feature 180304 (Site 18) suggests that it was a type of corn-drying oven (sometimes called a kiln) where heat from a fire was channelled into a drying chamber, avoiding direct contact between the fire and the material to be heated. This separation makes it distinct from other kinds of ovens or kilns, such as pottery-firing clamps (e.g. Best and Woodward 2012) which have fire-settings or pits with heat-discoloured bases. The remains from the feature 180304 show that it was a 'figure-of-eight form', and it is apparent that the fire was lit in the central channel from where most of the charcoal was concentrated and the substrate lightly scorched (although the channel stones themselves were not fire-reddened). Charcoal in the basal fill of the north-eastern chamber suggests that the fire was fed, and the ashes raked out, from this side. This suggests that the stokehole was to some extent intentionally protected from the prevailing wind, although this would appear to counter assertions that an orientation with the prevailing wind could have helped the fire to draw (e.g. Crane 2004, 17–18; Monk and Kelleher 2005, 93). The drying chamber at the south-western end presumably acted to allow hot air to rise into some form of enclosed superstructure although the form this took has been lost.

The possible functions of corn dryers and their variants have been discussed over the years (Goodchild 1943; Reynolds and Langley 1979; van der Veen 1989; Monk and Kelleher 2005). Despite the range of dates and therefore cultural contexts for this type of structure, there are characteristics that suggest that they were a common solution to the problem of drying a crop for storage or processing. It is likely that the dryer was principally used to dry cereals before they were stored, although other possibilities include hardening the grain prior to milling, or for parching grain in the process of malting (van der Veen 1989). The absence of any charred grain at all makes any interpretation somewhat conjectural. However, the historically attested practice of drying grain by fire in western parts of the British Isles suggests that this may have been a long-standing farming tradition (Kelly 1997; Fenton 1978; Monk and Power 2014). It has been proposed that, in general, the grain in the drying chamber was placed on wickerwork trays allowing the essential circulation of hot air (Kelly 1997, 241) and this provides an explanation for why grain could become charred by falling through the floor. Early medieval Irish sources indicate that drying grain without burning it was a skilled art (ibid.). Containment in bags or baskets may also have been undertaken, although in practice drying has been found difficult to achieve if the grain is not spread thinly (Reynolds and Langley 1979, 38–9). Experiments have demonstrated the difficulty of drying cereals successfully, and the care needed with grain for breadmaking, malting, or sowing, since over-drying renders it useless for these purposes (Monk and Kelleher 2005, 95–6). The absence of charred grain at Site 18 may be a consequence of the success of the drying process, despite the shortness of the channel which gives the fire a close proximity to the drying chamber. The identification of 'vitrified' charcoal from the channel, indicating a very high temperature is a detail of the evidence that is difficult to account for, but it is possible that there was a somewhat solid floor to the dryer that perhaps retained the grain effectively but modified the effect of the fire, or that the chamber was heated briefly and intensely before being allowed to fade and the grain added to the chamber. Another explanation of the feature is that it was a baking oven rather than, or as well as, a dryer.

While corn dryers are found in Wales from the Roman period onwards, this particular shape is unusual, and the Middle Bronze Age date would make the structure unique. There are, however, comparable examples of form and date from Ireland. A figure-of-eight-shaped corn dryer from Carrigatogher, Co. Tipperary, associated with a Bronze Age circular structure and an external hearth, has three radiocarbon dates collectively ranging between *c.* 1660 and 1435 BC (Hackett 2009). A very similar structure from Knockgraffon, also in Co. Tipperary, returned a date of 1667–1496 cal BC (McQuade *et al.* 2009). Other possible Bronze Age corn dryers have also been reported, including one from Kames, Argyll (Ellis 2013), but the evidence is controversial. A recent review of Irish corn dryers shows that there are now significant numbers falling in the Irish Iron Age (*c.* 400 BC to AD 600) and within that period a peak between AD 200 to 400 and most of these are of figure-of-eight-shaped (Monk and Power 2014). There is therefore a suggestion that corn-drying kilns, and especially the figure-of-eight-shaped varieties, were an indigenous part of the Iron Age farming tradition in Ireland. There are still, however, difficulties with accepting dates in the mid second millennium BC when there are no other examples bridging the intervening 1000 years. It has been pointed out that outlying 'rogue' measurements may be expected in any collection of dates for a number of reasons, including residual charcoal, intrusive material and contamination (Monk and Power 2014, 40). Medieval corn dryers are relatively better attested both in Ireland and Wales, although in Wales their forms are often more distinctively pit-like (e.g. Welshpool – Blockley and Taverner 2002, and review by Crane 2004). At Site 18 a medieval date would perhaps be more in keeping with expectations despite the unusual shape. While it is problematic accounting for a medieval corn dryer in the absence of associated settlement, the group at Sarn-y-bryn-caled, Welshpool, dated to between the 5th and 7th centuries AD appeared to have been located at some distance from settlement (Blockley and Taverner 2002, 67), and the same is true of the corn dryers at Llandegai (Kenney 2008, 108–11) and it is possible that this was a deliberate choice of site. According to interpretations of Irish documentary sources, drying ovens may have been located preferentially close to places of threshing and storage (Monk and Kelleher 2005, 107). It is possible to envisage that they were located above a valley settlement both to achieve a suitable aspect in relation to wind direction and for reasons of proximity to where the crop was threshed, which may have been between the fields and the settlement.

6.6 Bronze Age burnt mound, Red Roses, Site 32

The burnt mound at Coldwell, Red Roses, was the only feature of this nature found. It is typical of those found in Wales and elsewhere, both in its form and the almost complete lack of any associated finds other than wood charcoal. The distinguishing features were: the remains of troughs for heating water by the addition of hot stones, a location of a nearby fire, and the mound of discarded, heat-shattered stone. The fact that the mound concealed the site of the fire and the later of the two troughs shows that it was not in its original form, but had spread down the slope over time towards the stream. Originally, the mound would presumably have formed a crescent around the eastern side of the fire. Radiocarbon dating indicates that the smaller trough (320008) was the earlier (1878–1661 cal BC: SUERC-61264) although this was actually west of the surviving mound and for this reason might be supposed to have been later. There are no other grounds for questioning the dating sequence however. The second trough (320015), with a date of 1634–1503 cal BC (SUERC-50322), shows that the use of the site covered a considerable span of time, but it is possible that usage was not continuous. The mound itself showed three layers, with two burnt stone deposits separated by a layer of redeposited clay, perhaps an indication of disuse although it is not clear for how long.

Recent archaeological work in Wales, particularly linear projects, has revealed an extremely high density of burnt mounds in lowland areas (see Schlee 2009 for the A40 Penblewin to Slebech Park Improvement Scheme, Pembrokeshire; Maynard 2011 for the A55 trunk road in Anglesey, referenced in Kenney 2012; and Hart *et al.* 2014a for the Milford Haven to Brecon gas pipeline). Of these, the closest example to the Coldwell site is from the A40 Penblewin to Slebech Park Improvement Scheme at Robeston Wathen, approximately 14km to the north-west. In its surviving condition it was comparable in size to the Coldwell mound, and may also have been crescentric in its original form, but was much altered by later disturbance. A single trough was associated with the mound, which was next to an active watercourse. A series of radiocarbon dates suggest the Robeston Wathen mound was used over an even greater span of time than the example at Coldwell (Schlee 2009).

Burnt mounds are closely associated with streams, and Hart and Rackham observe that they are probably even more common than is appreciated because linear schemes usually cross watercourses at right angles and will tend to miss adjacent sites up and down stream (Hart and Rackham 2014, 150–1). The density of sites found at Glan-rŷd Bridge, Pembrokeshire, where the pipeline briefly ran parallel to a watercourse and revealed eight mounds over a distance of 300m, illustrates that burnt mounds can form large dense groups that developed sequentially over a long period (ibid., 151, fig. 7). Similar long-lived groups have been recorded elsewhere, such as at Parc Bryn Cegin, Llandegai (near Bangor), an upland site (Kenney 2008). Kenney has also drawn attention to the problem of defining the full currency of burnt mounds from limited radiocarbon

dating, and it is possible that individual mounds were in use for longer than is assumed (Kenney 2012, 265). It is possible, therefore, that the Coldwell area was habitually visited over a longer period than this single mound and the two radiocarbon dates at present indicate.

The Coldwell site has little to add to the discussion of the function of burnt mounds, a subject debated for a considerable time with little consensus of opinion. The various views have been summarised recently from the Welsh evidence by Kenney (2012) and Hart *et al.* (2014a). What may perhaps be emphasised from the results of the present project is that, while not closely associated with settlement, burnt mounds form part of a densely occupied Bronze Age landscape and must be viewed as an integral part of the cultural traditions of the inhabitants over a considerable period of time. The Coldwell burnt mound was clearly part of the landscape and culture of the people who used other areas for settlement and burial for several hundred years during the Middle Bronze Age, if not longer. The assessment by Kenney of north-west Wales indicates a general currency of burnt mounds between 2500 BC and 800 BC, and those modelled on the Milford Haven to Brecon pipeline show dates between 2400 BC and 1400 BC (Kenney 2012, 266; Hart and Rackham 2014, 151). This persistence is a remarkable aspect of a culture that underwent changes in many other aspects, as pottery, metalwork, settlement and burial customs show.

6.7 Bronze Age settlement and landscape

There were a large number of pits and postholes of Bronze and probable Bronze Age date. Relatively few were dated by pottery and a number of others yielded radiocarbon dates from botanical remains. Others were judged to be of similar date because of the nature of their fills, particularly the presence of hazelnut shells and heat-affected soil and stones, and also by proximity to similar features that had been dated with more-or-less certainty. The 30 or so postholes formed no patterns to suggest structures of recognisable form, and they were not associated with ditched enclosures or other linear features. The nature of this 'occupation' is therefore difficult to evaluate. It is apparent, however, that the distribution was not even along the 9.5 kilometres of the road corridor but formed a more-or-less definable swathe between Llanddowror (Site 25) and Redgate/Cil-fynydd (Site 12) and were mostly dispersed along the plateau between the two (Sites 25, 35, 26, 18, 19 and 13), a linear spread of about 2km. The only exceptions to this distribution are the four 'prehistoric-like' pits at Cnwce (Site 36) and the Beaker group of three pits near Brandy Hill (Site 37) further west.

Most of the dated material makes these pits and postholes contemporary with the cremation burials at Sites 26 and 18, and so the occupation clearly related in some manner to the barrow and funeral pyre, and to the more dispersed cemetery to the west to which some of the pits are very proximal, if not actually scattered among. The corn dryer (if it is indeed Middle Bronze Age as the radiocarbon date indicates) is among the 'domestic' features on Site 18, although apparently located at a discrete distance from any other features, whether domestic or cremation-related. The absence of any radiocarbon dates falling within the first millennium BC suggests a lack of occupation anywhere on the site at this time, notwithstanding the probability of an aceramic period in the earlier part of this range (Lynch *et al.* 2000, 199) which would make features of this period difficult to identify through material remains. More generally in Wales (and elsewhere) climatic deterioration is shown through palaeoenvironmental evidence, and is suggested to have contributed to changes in land-use and depopulation from perhaps as early as 1250 BC (ibid., 140–2).

The one feature that potentially indicates a definable structure is the semicircular gully on the eastern side of Site 25 in the valley north of Llanddowror, perhaps a ring-groove forming the northern side of a roundhouse about 11m in diameter (discussed above). The feature is undated, but nearby relatively early dates come from pit 250063 (2456–2201 cal BC) and fire pit 250061 (1948–1766 cal BC). These valley features may be part of a slightly earlier cluster to those on the plateau to the west. It is probable that they related in some way to the group of standing stones to the north of Llanddowror where three have been recorded in fields to the east of Site 25 at the bottom of the valley. It is possible that others once lay even closer. No stone socket-holes were recorded within Site 25, nor on any of the other sites, although given the potentially wide variability in their form they would be difficult to recognise. Socket-hole fills would reflect the time and manner of stone removal, which may have been at any time since their erection. Standing stones are a relatively common feature of the western British Isles. While notoriously difficult to date intrinsically, and susceptible to being moved around, they are generally often associated with Bronze Age activity, sometimes marking burials (examples cited above) but at other times perhaps boundary, way, or commemorative markers (Lynch *et al.* 2000, 136–7). At Site 501 of the South Wales Pipeline project, near Llangain, Carmarthenshire, a standing stone was found to have been surrounded by groups of small pits and postholes, some with Beaker/Early Bronze Age dates, located beyond an apparent 'exclusion zone' of 20m or more (Hart and Leonard 2013a). Here, radiocarbon dates from each of the three defined groups indicate activity between about 2100 BC and 1700 BC. There is no specific evidence for what these features represent but the association with the stone is assumed to have been deliberate. They have a similarity to the groups of Beaker and Bronze Age pits uncovered 200m east

of Vaynor Henge (Site 222 of that project; Hart and Leonard 2013b), which suggest that mundane activities took place at a discreet distance from the monument.

In the absence of any clear indication of settlement in the form of buildings or constrained activity, it can be suggested that the landscape here contained, among the ceremonial and burial monuments (the henge, a barrow, standing stones and perhaps natural features such as trees) a distinctive form of temporary encampment associated with the ceremonies conducted among the features of attention. These 'domestic' features typically contain few material remains, but small quantities of burnt bone, charcoal and charred plants were perhaps the remains of feasts or offerings that accompanied the ceremonies. This suggestion can only be tentative, but the archaeological evidence demands some form of explanation. There is of course a difficulty in trying to understand the Bronze Age landscape from a relatively narrow transect, which is in effect a two-dimensional view and may not be typical of the wider area. As yet undiscovered features over the rest of this block of land may reveal other patterns. It is also possible that the Bronze Age presence is over-represented because of the amount of activity that involved burning, with the result that charcoal and other plant remains became extensively redeposited in later features. There may be some truth in this, but one would have to envisage a large number of non-Bronze Age features without any dating and filled by soils indistinguishable from Bronze Age ones. On the whole some over-representation of Bronze Age cannot be ruled out but the distribution is still strongly suggestive of an intensity of occupation here not matched in other periods.

The range of Bronze Age evidence is wide and perhaps reflects a people accustomed to movement, probably with domestic herds, in an annual round of cultural activities. The places of activity included the burnt mound sites of fire and water in the valleys, and the places of commemoration and burial on the plateau. The concept of residential mobility perhaps includes the possibility that drying corn for storage was a collective event and one of the 'commemorative rituals' in the seasonal calendar. The proximity of the corn dryer to the burial grounds perhaps shows some conceptual or metaphorical link between cremation and the productivity of the land, both processing using fire and both ultimately having transforming and preserving properties on the objects of attention. It is commonly observed that the deceased played a much more active role in prehistoric societies than they do today (e.g. Brück 2001). It can be noted that the process of cremation is not just an elaborate ritual relating to fire and its transforming properties, but results in remains that are easily handled, transported, stored and shared. They are able to participate in rituals and be deposited at critical stages of the lifecycle of the people with whom they were connected, and they can do this irrespective of when they died. The nature of the cremation burials themselves show something of this mutability and flexibility. As has been observed here and elsewhere, the ways in which the dead were treated do not reflect simple social categories such as rank and status, but appear to result from a complex engagement with aspects of the individual's persona and their relationship with the living. An understanding of the reasons behind different forms of burial also needs to take account of developments over time.

It is interesting, and perhaps significant, that there appear to have been three different groups of burials here more of less synchronous within the period *c.* 2000–1700 BC, and it is tempting to suggest that they were associated with different families or lineages. It can be suggested that the barrow reflected something of the domestic dwelling, its circularity conceptually linked to that of the roundhouse. The connection between roundhouses and round barrows or cairns has been made explicit at Sant-y-Nyll, outside Cardiff, a case where the barrow appears to have been sited on an abandoned roundhouse (Peterson 2007; see also Jones [2008] on the shared architectural features of houses and cairns). The apparent preponderance of women buried at the barrow, at least in the hypothetical pre-mound phase, may have been linked to a female-centric view of the household. It may have been considered appropriate for men to have been buried elsewhere at this time, and it has been suggested that the pyre area may have been the location of a natural feature such as a tree. The western group of burials, with the observable pattern of pairings may relate to a different group and reflected, or was designed to emphasise, different social categories – the juxtapositions between groups can be seen as a means of articulating inter-group relationships. It is perhaps also significant that these different groups shared the landscape which the henge at Vaynor had made significant to the various inhabitants of the wider region.

References

Aldhouse-Green, S. 2000 'Palaeolithic and Mesolithic Wales. Part II: the Mesolithic period', in Lynch *et al.* 2000, 23–41

Anderberg, A.L. 1994 *Atlas of seeds: Part 4* Stockholm, Uddevalla, Swedish Museum of Natural History

Anderson-Whymark, H. and Thomas, J. (eds) 2012 *Regional perspectives on Neolithic pit deposition: Beyond the mundane,* Neolithic Studies Group Seminar Papers **12** Oxford, Oxbow Books

ApSimon, A. M. 1973 'The excavation of a Bronze Age barrow and menhir at Ystrad-hynod, Llanidloes (Mont.) 1965–66', *Archaeol. Cambrensis* **122**, 35–54

ARCA 2012a *Geoarchaeological borehole sampling of the Cilfynydd Farm and on the River Taf floodplain. Specification* Unpublished Report

ARCA 2012b *A477 St Clears to Red Roses, Carmarthenshire: Geoarchaeological, bioarchaeological and chronomatic analysis* Unpublished Report **1314–16**

ARCA 2012c *A477 St Clears to Red Roses, Carmarthenshire: Geoarchaeological borehole survey* Unpublished Report

ARCA 2014 *A477 St Clears to Red Roses, Carmarthenshire: Geoarchaeological, bioarchaeological and chronomatic assessment* Unpublished Report

ArchaeoPhysica 2010a *Dol Garn, Carmarthenshire (A477 St Clears to Red Roses improvement)* Unpublished Geophysical Survey Report **DGC101**

ArchaeoPhysica 2010b *Castell Motte, Carmarthenshire (A477 St Clears to Red Roses improvement)* Unpublished Geophysical Survey Report **CMC101**

ArchaeoPhysica 2010c *Vaynor Farm, Carmarthenshire (A477 St Clears to Red Roses improvement)* Unpublished Geophysical Survey Report **VFC101**

Ashmore, P. 1999 'Radiocarbon dating: avoiding errors by avoiding mixed samples', *Antiquity* **73**, 124–30

Barber, A. and Hart, J. 2014a *South Wales gas pipeline project: Site 26.05 land west of Cwmifor, Manordeilo and Salem, Carmarthenshire: Archaeological excavation* Cotswold Archaeology Report **13308**

Barber, A. and Hart, J. 2014b *South Wales Gas Pipeline Project Site 509: Land West of Middle Bastleford, Rosemarket, Pembrokeshire: Archaeological excavation* Cotswold Archaeology Report **13252**

Barber, A. and Hart, J. 2014c *South Wales Gas Pipeline Project Site 511/514: Land South-East of Upper Neeston, Herbrandston, Pembrokeshire: Archaeological excavation* Cotswold Archaeology Report **13254**

Barber, A. and Pannett, A. 2006 'Archaeological excavations along the Milford Haven to Aberdulais natural gas pipeline 2006: a preliminary report', *Archaeology in Wales* **46**, 87–99

Barber, A., Alexander, M. and Powell, N. 2014 *A477 St Clears to Red Roses road improvement, Carmarthenshire: post-excavation assessment and updated project design* Cotswold Archaeology Report **14014**

Barton, R.N.E., Berridge, P.J., Walker, M.J.C. and Bevins, R.E. 1995 'Persistent places in the Mesolithic landscape: an example from the Black Mountain Uplands of South Wales', *Proc. Prehist. Soc.* **61**, 81–116

Bayes, T.R. 1763 'An essay towards solving a problem in the doctrine of chances', *Phil. Trans. Roy. Soc.* **53**, 370–418

Bayliss, A. 2009 'Rolling out revolution: using radiocarbon dating in archaeology', *Radiocarbon* **51**, 123–47

Bayliss, A. and O'Sullivan, M. **2013** 'Interpreting chronologies for the Mound of the Hostages. Tara and its contemporary contexts in Neolithic and Bronze Age Ireland', in O'Sullivan, M., Scarre, C. and Doyle, M. *(eds) Tara—from the past to the future. Towards a new research agenda* Dublin, Wordwell, 26–104

Bayliss, A., Bronk Ramsey, C., van der Plicht, J. and Whittle, A. 2007 'Bradshaw and Bayes: towards a timetable for the Neolithic', *Cambridge Archaeological Journal* **17.1**, supplement, 1–28

Bayliss, A., van der Plicht, J., Bronk Ramsey, C., McCormac, G., Healy, F. and Whittle, A. 2011

'Chapter 2. Towards generational time-scales: the quantitative interpretation of archaeological chronologies', in Whittle *et al.* 2011, 16–60

Bell, M. 1990 *Brean Down excavations 1983–87*, English Heritage Report **15** London

Benson, D.G., Evans, J.G., Williams, G.H., Darvill, T. and David, A. 1990 'Excavations at Stackpole Warren, Dyfed', *Proc. Prehist. Soc.* **56**, 179–245

Berggren, G. 1981 *Atlas of seeds: Part 3* Stockholm, Arlöv, Swedish Museum of Natural History

Best, J. and Woodward, A. 2012 'Late Bronze Age Pottery Production: Evidence from a 12th–11th century cal. BC settlement at Tinney's Lane, Sherborne, Dorset', *Proc. Prehist. Soc.* **78**, 207–61

BGS (British Geological Survey) 2013 *Geology of Britain viewer*, http://www.bgs.ac.uk/discovering-Geology/geologyOfBritain/viewer.html (accessed 9 February 2013)

BGS (British Geological Survey) 2014 *The British Geological Survey lexicon of named rock units*, http://www.bgs.ac.uk/lexicon/ (accessed 13 January 2014)

Blockley, K. and Taverner, N. 2002 'Excavations at Sarn-y-bryn-caled, Welshpool, Powys, in 1998–99', *Montgomeryshire Collect.* **90**, 41–68

Brickley, M. and McKinley, J. 2004 *Guidelines to the standards for recording of human remains*, IFA Paper No. 7 Reading

Bronk Ramsey, C. 1995 'Radiocarbon calibration and analysis of stratigraphy', *Radiocarbon* **36**, 425–30

Bronk Ramsey, C. 2001 'Development of the radiocarbon calibration program OxCal', *Radiocarbon* **43**, 355–63

Bronk Ramsey, C. 2009a 'Bayesian analysis of radiocarbon dates', *Radiocarbon* **51**, 337–60

Bronk Ramsey, C. 2009b 'Dealing with outliers and offsets in radiocarbon dating', *Radiocarbon* **51**, 2009, 1023–45

Bronk Ramsey, C. and Lee, S. 2013 'Recent and planned developments of the program OxCal', *Radiocarbon* **55**, 720–30

Brück, J. 2001 'Body metaphors and technologies of transformation in the English Middle and Bronze Age', in Brück, J. (ed.) *Bronze Age landscapes, tradition and transformation* Oxford, Oxbow Books, 149–60

Brück, J. 2009 'Women, death and social change in the British Bronze Age', *Norwegian Archaeological Review* **42**, 1–23

Buck, C.E., Cavanagh, W.G. and Litton, C.D. 1996 *Bayesian approach to interpreting archaeological data* Chichester, Wiley

Buck, C.E., Litton, C.D. and Smith, A.F.M. 1992 'Calibration of radiocarbon results pertaining to related archaeological events', *J. Archaeol. Sci.* **19**, 497–512

Burgess, C.B. 1986 '"Urnes of no small variety": collared urns reviewed', *Proc. Prehist. Soc.* **52**, 339–51

Burrow, S. 2003 *Catalogue of the Mesolithic and Neolithic collections in the National Museums and Galleries of Wales* Cardiff, National Museums and Galleries of Wales

CA (Cotswold Archaeology) 2012a *A477 St Clears to Red Roses road improvement archaeological specification for a programme of trial trenching on the compound site to the north of Vaynor Farm* Unpublished client report

CA (Cotswold Archaeology) 2012b *A477 St Clears to Red Roses road improvement Vaynor north archaeological evaluation (archaeological intervention 13): Summary statement* CA Commercial-in-Confidence Report

CA (Cotswold Archaeology) 2012c *A477 St Clears to Red Roses road improvement. Dol Garn: Interim report* CA Commercial-in-Confidence Report

CA (Cotswold Archaeology) 2012d *A477 St Clears to Red Roses road improvement archaeological evaluation: Summary statement* CA Commercial-in-Confidence Report

CA (Cotswold Archaeology) 2013 *A477 St Clears to Red Roses road improvement outline: Post-excavation project design* Unpublished Client Report

CA (Cotswold Archaeology) 2014a *A477 St Clears to Red Roses road improvement: Post-excavation assessment and updated project design* CA Report **14014**

CA (Cotswold Archaeology) 2014b *South Wales gas pipeline project: Site 503 land east of Vaynor Farm, Llanddowror, Carmarthenshire* CA Report **13328**

CA (Cotswold Archaeology) 2014c *South Wales gas pipeline project: Site 506 land east of Glan-rhŷd Bridge, Lampeter Velfrey, Pembrokeshire* CA Report **13249**

Cappers, R.T.J., Bekker, R.M. and Jans, J.E.A. 2006 *Digital seed atlas of The Netherlands,* Groningen Archaeological Studies **4** Eelde, Barkhuis Publishing http://dzn.eldoc.ub.rug.nl/ (accessed June–October 2015)

Carruthers, W. 2014 'Charred plant remains', in Barber and Hart 2014a, 35–44

Chaffey, G. and Brook, E. 2012 'Domesticity in the Neolithic. Excavations at Kingsmead Quarry, Horton, Berkshire', in Anderson-Whymark and Thomas (eds) 2012, 200–15

Challinor, D. 2013a 'Charcoal', in Hart and Leonard 2013b, 29

Challinor, D. 2013b 'Charcoal', in Barber and Hart 2014a, 10–11

Challinor, D. 2014a 'Charcoal', in Hart *et al.* 2014a, 61

Challinor, D. 2014b 'Charcoal', in CA 2014c *South Wales gas pipeline project: Site 506 land east of Glan-rhŷd Bridge, Lampeter Velfrey, Pembrokeshire* Unpublished CA Report **13249**, 27–8

Chamberlain, A.T. 2006 *Demography in archaeology* Cambridge, Cambridge University Press

Clark, J.G.D. 1934 'The classification of a microlithic culture: The Tardenoisian of Horsham', *Archaeol. J.* **90**, 52–77

Cleal, R. 2004 'The dating and diversity of the earliest ceramics of Wessex and South-West England', in Cleal, R. and Pollard, J. (eds) *Monuments and material culture: papers in honour of an Avebury archaeologist: Isobel Smith* Salisbury, Hobnob Press, 164–92

Clough, T.H.M. and Cummins, W.A. 1988 *Stone axe studies: Volume 2. The petrology of prehistoric stone implements from the British Isles* Council for British Archaeology Research Report **67** London

Cobain, S. 2014a 'Appendix 14: Plant macrofossil and charcoal assessment', in Barber *et al.* 2014, 138–75

Cobain, S. 2014b 'Plant macrofossils and charcoal', in Hart *et al.* 2014c, 32–45

Cook, N. 2003 'Prehistoric funerary and ritual sites in Carmarthenshire', *Carmarthenshire Antiq.* **39**, 5–21

Crane, P. 2004 'Excavations at Newton, Llanstadwell, Pembrokeshire', *Archaeology in Wales* **44**, 3–31

Darvill, T. 2010 *Prehistoric Britain* Oxford, Routledge

Darvill, T. forthcoming 'Chapter 4: Earlier Prehistoric', in Walker, K. (ed.) *The archaeology of the South Wales gas pipeline 2006–8,* Cotswold Archaeology Monograph **10** Cirencester, Cotswold Archaeology

David, A. 2007 *Palaeolithic and Mesolithic settlement in Wales with special reference to Dyfed,* Brit. Archaeol. Rep. Brit. Ser. **448** Oxford, Archaeopress

David, A. and Williams, G. 1995 'Stone axe-head manufacture: new evidence from the Preseli Hills West Wales', *Proc. Prehist. Soc.* **61**, 433–60

Doody, M. 2000 'Bronze Age houses in Ireland', in Desmond, A., Johnson, G., McCarthy, M., Sheehan, J. and Shee Twohig, E. (eds) *New agendas in Irish prehistory: Papers in commemoration of Liz Anderson* Bray, Wordwell, 135–58

EH (English Heritage) 1991 *The management of archaeological projects. Second edition (MAP2)* London, English Heritage

EH (English Heritage) 2006 *Management of research projects in the historic environment. The MoRPHE project managers' guide* Swindon, English Heritage

Ellis, C. 2013 'A Bronze Age corn-drying kiln from Argyll', *Past: newsletter of the Prehistoric Society* **75**, 3–4

Fairbairn, A.S. (ed.) 2000 'Plants in Neolithic Britain and beyond', *Neolithic Studies Group Seminar Papers* **5** Oxford, Oxbow Books

Fenton, A. 1978 *The Northern Isles: Orkney and Shetland* Edinburgh, John Donald Publishers Ltd

Fotaki, A. and Holst, M. 2014a 'Cremated bone', in Hart *et al.* 2014a, 61–6

Fotaki, A. and Holst, M. 2014b 'The human remains', in Hart, J. *South Wales gas pipeline project: Site 37.17 land north of Llwyn-Meurig, Trecastle, Powys:*

Archaeological Excavation Cotswold Archaeology Report **13315**, 28–30

Fotaki, A. and Holst, M. 2014c 'The human remains', in Hart, J. and Sausins, D. *South Wales gas pipeline project: Site 47.00 land north-west of Cwm-Camlais-Isaf, Trallong, Penpont and Llanfihangel, Powys: Archaeological excavation* Cotswold Archaeology Report **13324,** 17–24

Freeman, S.P.H.T., Cook, G.T., Dougans, A.B., Naysmith, P., Wicken, K.M. and Xu, S. 2010 'Improved SSAMS performance', *Nuclear Instruments and Methods in Physics Research B* **268**, 715–17

Gale, R. and Cutler, D.F. 2000 *Plants in archaeology. Identification manual of artefacts of plant origin from Europe and the Mediterranean* Otley, Westbury and the Royal Botanic Gardens Kew

Garrow, D. 2012 'Concluding discussion: pits and perspective', in Anderson-Whymark and Thomas (eds) 2012, 216–25

Garrow, D., Meadows, J., Evans, C. and Tabor, J. 2014 'Dating the dead: a high-resolution radiocarbon chronology of burial within an early Bronze Age barrow cemetery at Over, Cambridgeshire', *Proc. Prehist. Soc.* **80**, 207–36

Garwood, P. 1999 'Grooved ware in Southern Britain: chronology and interpretation', in Cleal, R. and MacSween, A. *Grooved Ware in Britain and Ireland,* Neolithic Studies Group Seminar Papers **3** Oxford, Oxbow Books, 145–76

Garwood, P. 2007 'Before the hills in order stood: chronology, time and history in the interpretation of Early Bronze Age round barrows', in Last (ed.) 2007a, 30–52

Garwood, P. and Barclay, A. 2011 'Making the Dead', in Morigi, T., Schreve, D., White, M. and Hey, G. (eds) *Thames Through Time Vol. 1 Early Prehistory to 1500 BC,* Oxford Archaeology Thames Valley Landscapes Monograph **32**, 383–432

Gibson, A. 1999 *The Walton Basin project: excavation and survey in a prehistoric landscape 1993–7,* CBA Research Report **118** York, Council for British Archaeology

Gibson, A. 2002 *Prehistoric pottery in Britain and Ireland* Stroud, Tempus Publishing Ltd

Gibson, A.M. 2013 'Prehistoric Pottery', in Hart *et al.* 2013, 17–19

Gibson, A.M. 2014a 'Prehistoric Pottery', in Hart *et al.* 2014a, 33–55

Gibson, A.M. 2014b 'Prehistoric Pottery', in Barber and Hart 2014a, 18–20

Gibson, A.M. 2014c 'Prehistoric Pottery', in Barber and Hart 2014b, 21–2

Gibson, A.M. 2014d 'Prehistoric Pottery', in Barber and Hart 2014c, 35–41

Gibson, A. forthcoming *Milford Haven to Aberdulais and Felindre to Brecon gas pipeline: The Neolithic and Bronze Age pottery from the archaeological investigations* in Walker, K. forthcoming

Giorgi, J. 2014, 'Charred plant remains', in Hart, J. and Leonard, C. 2014, *South Wales gas pipeline project: Site 51.07 land North-west of Pen-y-Crug, Yscir, Powys: Archaeological excavation* Cotswold Archaeology Report **13220**, 45–62

Goodchild, R.G. 1943 'T-shaped corn drying ovens in Roman Britain', *Antiquaries J.* **23**, 148–53

Green, H.S. 1980 *'The flint arrowheads of the British Isles: A detailed study of materials from England and Wales with comparanda from Scotland and Ireland'*, Part i, Brit. Archaeol. Rep. Brit. Ser. **75(i)**

Greenwell, W.G. 1890 'Recent researches in barrows in Yorkshire, Wiltshire, Berkshire etc', *Archaeologia* **5**, 1–72

Grigson, G. 1987 *The Englishman's flora* London, J.M. Dent and Sons

Hackett, L. 2009 *N7 Nenagh to Limerick high quality dual carriageway. Archaeological resolution project. Carrigatogher (Harding) site 4, E2469, Co. Tipperary,* Final excavation report Edinburgh, Headland Archaeology Ltd

Hart, J. and Alexander, M. forthcoming 'Archaeological investigations along the route of the A477 St Clears to Red Roses road improvement scheme, 2012: a summary report', *Archaeology in Wales*

Hart, J. and Leonard, C. 2013a *South Wales gas pipeline project: Site 501, Land South-West of Llwyn, Llangain, Carmarthenshire. Archaeological excavation* Cotswold Archaeology Report **13246**

Hart, J. and Leonard, C. 2013b *South Wales gas pipeline project: Sites 222 and 233, land north-east of Vaynor Farm, Llanddowror, Carmarthenshire. Archaeological Watching Brief* Cotswold Archaeology Report **13176**

Hart, J. and Rackham, J. 2014 'Discussion', in Hart *et al.* 2014a, 150–2

Hart, J., Sausins, D. and Brannlund, L. 2013 *South Wales gas pipeline project: Sites OEA11 and 21.02: Land east of Cilsan, Llangathen, Carmarthenshire: Archaeological excavation* Cotswold Archaeology Report **13338**

Hart, J., Barber, A. and Leonard, C. 2014a *South Wales gas pipeline project: Site 513: Land north-west of Steynton, Milford Haven, Pembrokeshire Archaeological Excavation* Cotswold Archaeology Report **13261**

Hart, J., Rackham, K., Griffiths, S. and Challinor, D. 2014b 'Burnt mounds along the Milford Haven to Brecon gas pipeline, 2006–2007', *Archaeol. Cambrensis* **163**, 133–72

Hart, J., Wood, I., Barber, A., Brett, M. and Hardy, A. 2014c 'Prehistoric land use in the Clyst Valley: Excavations at Hayes Farm, Clyst Honiton, 1996–2012', *Proc. Devon Archaeol. Soc.* **72**, 1–56

Healy, F. 1996 'The Fenland project number 11: The Wissey Embayment: evidence for Pre-Iron Age settlement accumulated prior to the Fenland Project', *E. Anglian Archaeol.* **78**

Healy, F. and Harding, J. 2007 'A thousand and one things to do with a round barrow', in Last (ed.) 2007a, 53–71

Hillman, G. 1981 'Reconstructing crop husbandry practices from charred remains of crops', in Mercer, R. *Farming practice in British Prehistory* Edinburgh, Edinburgh University Press, 123–62

Hinton, P. 2006 'Charred plant remains', in Chadwick, A.M. 'Bronze Age burials and settlement and an Anglo-Saxon settlement at Claypit Lane, Westhampnett, West Sussex', *Sussex Archaeol. Collect.* **144**, 7–50

Horák, J. 2014 'Petrological examination of Neolithic stone axe fragments', in Brannlund, L. *South West gas pipeline project: Sites 52.01–52.05 Land South of Llandefaelog, Yscir, Powys: Archaeological recording* Cotswold Archaeology Report **13333**, CPAT Event 102846, 17–19

Hughes, G. and Murphy, K. 2013 'Fan Foel round barrow, Mynydd Du, South Wales: archaeological excavation and palaeoenvironmental analysis, 2002–4', *Archaeol. Cambrensis* **162**, 105–46

Hüls, C.M., Erlenkeuser, H., Nadeau, M-J., Grootes, P.M. and Andersen, N. 2010 'Experimental study on the origin of cremated bone apatite carbon', *Radiocarbon* **52**, 587–99

Ixer, R.A. and Lunt, S. 1991 'Petrography of certain pre-Spanish pottery of Peru', in Middleton, A. and Freestone I. (eds) 'Recent developments in ceramic petrology', *British Museum Occasional Papers* **81**, 137–64

Jacobi, R.M. 1976 'Britain inside and outside Mesolithic Europe', *Proc. Prehist. Soc.* **42**, 67–84

Jones, A. 2008 'Houses for the dead and cairns for the living; a reconsideration of the Early to Middle Bronze Age transition in South-West England', *Oxford Journal of Archaeology* **27(2)**, 153–74

Jones, A.P., Tucker, M.E. and Hart, J.K. 1999 'Guidelines and recommendations', in Jones, A.P., Tucker, M.E. and Hart, J.K. (eds) *The description and analysis of quaternary stratigraphic field sections* Quaternary Research Association Technical Guide **7**, 27–76

Jones, G. 2000 'Evaluating the importance of cultivation and collecting in Neolithic Britain', in Fairbairn (ed.) 2000, 79–84

Kelly, F. 1997 *Early Irish farming* School of Celtic Studies, Dublin Institute for Advanced Studies

Kenney, J. 2008 'Recent excavations at Parc Bryn Cegin, Llandygai, near Bangor, North Wales', *Archaeol. Cambrensis* **157**, 9–142

Kenney, J. 2012 'Burnt mounds in north-west Wales: are these ubiquitous features really so dull?', in Britnell, W.J. and Silvester, R.J. (eds) *Reflections on the past:*

Essays in honour of Frances Lynch Bangor, Cambrian Archaeological Association, 254–79

Lacaille, A. D. 1954 'Palaeoliths from the Lower Reaches of the Bristol Avon', *Antiq. J.* **34**, 1–27

Lanting, J.N., Aerts-Bijma, A.T. and van der Plicht, J. 2001 'Dating of cremated bones', *Radiocarbon* **43**, 249–54

Last, J. (ed.) 2007a *Beyond the grave: New perspectives on barrows* Oxford, Oxbow Books

Last, J. 2007b 'Covering Old Ground: barrows as closures', in Last (ed.) 2007a, 156–75

Law, R. 2016 'The Collared Urn assemblage', in Evans, C. Tabor, J. and Vander Linden, M. (eds) *Twice-crossed river: Prehistoric and palaeoenvironmental investigations at Barleycroft Farm/Over, Cambridgeshire. The Archaeology of the Lower Ouse Valley, Volume III* Cambridge: McDonald Institute for Archaeological Research, 374–83

Longworth, I.H. 1984 *Collared Urns of the Bronze Age in Great Britain and Ireland* Cambridge, Cambridge University Press

Lynch, F. 1993 *Excavations in the Brenig Valley. A Mesolithic and Bronze Age landscape in North Wales,* Cambrian Archaeology Monograph **5** Bangor, Cambrian Archaeological Association

Lynch, F. and Musson, C. 2001 'A prehistoric and early medieval complex at Llandegai, near Bangor, North Wales', *Archaeol. Cambrensis* **150**, 17–142

Lynch, F., Aldhouse-Green, S. and Davies, J.L. 2000 *Prehistoric Wales* Stroud, Sutton Publishing

Lyman, R.L. 1994 *Vertebrate taphonomy: Cambridge manuals in archaeology* Cambridge, Cambridge University Press

Mann, R.W. and Murphy, S.P. 1990 *Regional atlas of bone disease: A guide to pathologic and normal variation in the human skeleton* Illinois, C.C. Thomas

Margary, I.D. 1973 *Roman roads in Britain* (3rd edn) London, John Baker

Marshall, E. C. and Murphy, K. 1991 'The excavation of two Bronze Age cairns with associated standing stones in Dyfed: Parc Maen and Aber Camddwr II', *Archaeol. Cambrensis* **140**, 28–76

Maynard, D. 2011 'The burnt mounds', in Cuttler, R., Davidson, A. and Hughes, G. *A corridor through time: The archaeology of the A55 Anglesey road scheme* Oxford, Oxbow Books, 122–30

Mays, S., Brickley, M. and Dodwell, N. 2004 *Human bones from archaeological sites. Guidelines for producing assessment documents and analytical reports* Swindon, English Heritage

McKinley, J. 1994a 'Bone fragment size in British cremation burials and its implications for pyre technology and ritual', *J. Archaeol. Sci.* **21**, 339–42

McKinley, J. 1994b 'The Anglo-Saxon cemetery at Spong Hill, North Elmham Part VIII the cremations', *E. Anglian Archaeol.* **69**

McKinley, J. 1997 'Bronze Age 'barrows' and funerary rites and rituals of cremation', *Proc. Prehist. Soc.* **63**, 129–45

McKinley, J. 1998 'Archaeological manifestations of cremation', *The Archaeologist* **33**, 18–20

McKinley, J. 2000 'The analysis of cremated bone', in Cox, M. and Mays, S. (eds) *Human osteology in archaeology and forensic science* London, Greenwich Medical Media, 403–21

McKinley, J. 2005 'Archaeology of Britain: Antiquity', in Davies, D.J. and Mates, L.H. (eds) *Encyclopedia of cremation* London, Ashgate, 9–12

McQuade, M., Molloy, B. and Moriarty, C. 2009 *In the shadow of the Galtees: Archaeological excavations along the N8 Cashel to Mitchelstown road scheme,* NRA Scheme Monograph **4** Dublin, National Roads Authority

Moffett, L., Robinson, M.A. and Straker, S. 1989 'Cereals, fruits and nuts: Charred plant remains from Neolithic sites in England and Wales and the Neolithic economy', in Milles, A. Williams, D. and Gardner, N. (eds) *The beginnings of agriculture,* Brit. Archaeol. Rep. Int. Ser. **496**; Symposia of the Association for Environmental Archaeology **8** Oxford, British Archaeological Reports, 243–61

Monk, M.A. and Kelleher, E. 2005 'An assessment of the archaeological evidence for Irish corn-drying kilns in the light of the results of archaeological experiments and archaeobotanical studies', *J. Irish Archaeol.* 14, 77–114

Monk, M.A. and Power, O. 2014 'Casting light from the fire of corn-drying kilns on the later Irish Iron Age', *Ireland Archaeology* **28**(3), 39–4

Mook, W.G. 1986 'Business meeting: recommendations/resolutions adopted by the twelfth international radiocarbon conference', *Radiocarbon* **28**, 799

Mook, W.G. and Waterbolk, H.T. 1985 *Radiocarbon dating* Strasbourg, European Science Foundation

Morris, E. L. 2015 'Pottery', in Richmond, A., Francis, K. and Morris, E.L. 'Two Bronze Age cremation groups at Coity Link Road, Bridgend', *Archaeol. Cambrensis* **164**, 26–30

Munsell Color 2000 *Munsell soil color charts* New Windsor (NY), Munsell Color

Murphy, K. 1990 'The excavation of a Bronze Age round barrow at Goodwin's Row, Glandy Cross, Llandissilio East, Dyfed', *Archaeology in Wales* **30**, 1–6

Murphy, K. and Murphy, F. 2013 'The excavation of two Bronze Age round barrows at Pant y Butler, Llangoedmor, Ceredigion, 2009–10', *Archaeol. Cambrensis* **162**, 33–60

Needham, S. 1996 'Chronology and periodization in the British bronze age', *Acta Archaeologia* **67**, 121–40

Needham, S.P. 2005 'Transforming Beaker Culture in north-west Europe: processes of fusion and fission', *Proc. Prehist. Soc.* **71**, 171–217

Needham, S., Parker Pearson, M., Tyler, A., Richards, M. and Jay, M. 2010 'A first 'Wessex 1' date from Wessex', *Antiquity* **84(324)**, 363–73

Neef, R., Cappers, R.T.J. and Bekker, R.M. 2012 Digital atlas of economic plants in archaeology, *Groningen Archaeological Studies* **17** Eelde, Barkhuis Publishing http://depa.eldoc.ub.rug.nl/ (accessed June–October 2015)

Pannett, A. 2012 'Pits, pots and plant remains: trends in Neolithic deposition', in Anderson-Whymark and Thomas (eds) 2012, 126–43

Peterson, R. 2007 'What were you thinking of? Round barrows and the dwelling perspective', in Last (ed.) 2007a, 127–39

Pollard, J. 2001 'The aesthetics of depositional practice', *World Archaeology* **33(2)**, 315–33

Rackham, J. 2013 'The palaeoenvironmental evidence', in Hart and Leonard 2013b, 17–34

Rackham, J. 2014 'Appendix C: the palaeoenvironmental evidence', in Barber and Hart 2014a, 23–35

Ramboll. 2011 *A477 St Clears to Red Roses road improvement environmental statement and reference design* Unpublished report

Ramboll. 2012 *A477 St Clears to Red Roses road improvement archaeology design* Unpublished report

Ramboll. 2013 *A477 St Clears to Red Roses improvement: Archaeological post-excavation research project: Instruction to tenderers* Unpublished report

RCHAMW (Royal Commission on the Ancient and Historical Monuments of Wales) 2014 'Marros sands, peat deposits; marros sands, submerged forest,' http://www.coflein.gov.uk/en/site/417719/details/MARROS+SANDS%2C+PEAT+EXPOSURE%3BMARROS+SANDS%2C+SUBMERGED+FOREST/ (accessed 1 September 2014)

Rebay-Salisbury, K. 2010 'Cremations; fragmented bodies in the Bronze and Iron Ages', in Rebay-Salisbury, K., Sørensen, M.L.S. and Hughes, J. (eds) 2010 *Body parts and bodies whole: Changing relations and meanings* Oxbow, Oxford, 64–71

Reimer, P.J., Bard, E., Bayliss, A., Beck, J.W., Blackwell, P.G., Bronk Ramsey, C., Buck, C.E., Cheng, H., Edwards, R.L., Friedrich, M., Grootes, P.M., Guilderson, T.P., Haflidason, H., Hajdas, I., Hatté, C., Heaton, T.J., Hoffmann, D.L., Hogg, A.G., Hughen, K.A., Kaiser, K.F., Kromer, B., Manning, S.W., Niu, M., Reimer, R.W., Richards, D. A., Scott, E.M., Southon, J.R., Staff, R.A., Turney, C. S.M. and van der Plicht, J. 2013 'IntCal13 and Marine13 radiocarbon age calibration curves 0–50,000 years cal BP', *Radiocarbon* **55**, 1869–87

Reynolds, P. J. and Langley. J.K. 1979 'Romano-British corn-drying oven: an experiment', *Archaeol. J.* **136**, 27–42

Richmond, A., Francis, K. and Morris, E.L 2015 'Two Bronze Age cremation groups at Coity Link Road, Bridgend', *Archaeol. Cambrensis* **164**, 25–35

Roberts, C. and Cox, M. 2003 *Health and disease in Britain* Gloucester, Sutton Publishing

Roberts, C. and Manchester, K, 2005 *The archaeology of disease* (3rd edn) New York, Cornell University Press

Robinson, M. 2000 'Further considerations of Neolithic charred cereals, fruits and nuts', in Fairbairn (ed.) 2000, 85–90

Savory, H.N. 1980 *Guide catalogue of the Bronze Age collections* Cardiff, National Museum of Wales

Schlee, D. 2009 'Excavations on the A40 Bypass at Robeston Wathen, Pembrokeshire Dyfed Archaeological Trust Report no. 2010/4', Appendix 1 in *Welsh Assembly Government A40 Pemblewin to Slebech Park Improvement Report*, Hyder Consulting, report for Welsh Assembly Government

Schlee, D. 2013 'The excavation of Fan round barrow, near Talsarn, Ceredigion, 2010–11', *Archaeol. Cambrensis* **162**, 67–104

Schmidt, C.W. and Symes S.A. (eds) 2008 *The analysis of burned human remains* London, Academic Press

Schoch, W., Heller, I., Schweingruber, F.H. and Kienast, F. 2004 'Wood anatomy of central European species', www.woodanatomy.ch (accessed June–October 2015)

Scott, E.M. 2003 'The third international radiocarbon intercomparison (TIRI) and the fourth international radiocarbon intercomparison (FIRI) 1990–2002: results, analyses, and conclusions', *Radiocarbon* **45**, 135–50

Scott, E.M., Cook, G.T., Naysmith, P., Bryant, C. and O'Donnell, D. 2007 'A report on phase 1 of the 5th international radiocarbon intercomparison (VIRI)', *Radiocarbon* **49**, 409–26

Scott, E.M., Cook, G.T. and Naysmith, P. 2010a 'A report on phase 2 of the fifth international radiocarbon intercomparison (VIRI)', *Radiocarbon* **52**, 846–58

Scott, E.M., Cook, G.T. and Naysmith, P. 2010b 'The fifth radiocarbon intercomparison (VIRI): an assessment of laboratory performance in stage 3', *Radiocarbon* **52**, 859–65

Sell, S.H. 1998 'Excavation of a Bronze Age settlement at the Atlantic Trading Estate, Barry, Glamorgan', *Studia Celtica* **32**, 1–26

Slota, P.J., Jull, A.J.T., Linick, T.W. and Toolin, L.J. 1987 'Preparation of small samples for ^{14}C accelerator targets by catalytic reduction of CO', *Radiocarbon* **29**, 303–6

Smith, G. 2008 'Lithics', in Kenney 2008, 23–5

Smith, W. 2002 *A review of archaeological wood analyses in Southern England,* Centre for Archaeology Report **75/2002** Swindon, English Heritage

Snoeck, C., Brock, F. and Schulting, R.J. 2014 'Carbon exchanges between bone apatite and fuels during cremation: impact on radiocarbon dates', *Radiocarbon* **56**, 591–602

Stace, C. 1997 *New flora of the British Isles* Cambridge, Cambridge University Press

Stastney, P. and Batchelor, R. 2014 'Appendix 15: Geoarchaeological and bioarchaeological assessment', in Barber *et al.* 2014, 176–84

Steier, P. and Rom, W. 2000 'The use of Bayesian statistics for 14C dates of chronologically ordered samples: a critical analysis', *Radiocarbon* **42**, 183–98

Stevens, C.J. and Fuller, D.Q. 2012 'Did Neolithic farming fail? The case for a Bronze Age agricultural revolution in the British Isles', *Antiquity* **86**, 707–22

Strahan, A., Cantrill, T.C., Dixon, E.E.L., Thomas H.H. and Jones, O.T. 1914 *The geology of the South Wales coalfield. Part XI: The country around Haverfordwest* London, HMSO

Stratascan. 2012 *A477 Red Roses to St Clears: ES informed geophysical surveys* Job Ref: J3042

Stuiver, M. and Polach, H.A. 1977 'Reporting of 14C data', *Radiocarbon* **19**, 355–63

Stuiver, M. and Reimer, P.J. 1986 'A computer program for radiocarbon age calculation', *Radiocarbon* **28**, 1022–30

Stuiver, M. and Reimer, P.J. 1993 'Extended 14C data base and revised CALIB 3.0 14C age calibration program', *Radiocarbon* **35**, 215–30

Thomas, J. 1999 *Understanding the Neolithic* London, Routledge

Thomas, J. 2012 'Introduction: beyond the mundane?' in Anderson-Whymark and Thomas (eds) 2012, 1–12

Thorpe, R.S., Williams-Thorpe, O., Jenkins, D.G. and Watson, J.S. with contributions by Ixer, R.A. and Thomas R.G. 1991 'The geological sources and transport of the bluestones of Stonehenge, Wiltshire, UK', *Proc. Prehist. Soc.* **57**, 103–57

Tomalin, D. 1988 'Armorican *vases à anses* and their occurrence in Southern Britain', *Proc. Prehist. Soc.* **54**, 204–22

Trotter, M. and Hixon, B.B. 1973 'Sequential changes in weight, density and percentage of ash weight of human skeletons from an early fetal period through old age', *Anatomical Record* **179**, 1–18

Tucker, M.E. 1982 *Sedimentary rocks in the field* Chichester, Wiley

Ubelaker, D.H. and Rife, J.L. 2007 'The practice of cremation in the Roman-era cemetery at Kenchreai,

Greece: The perspective from archaeology and forensic science', *Bioarchaeology of the Near East* **1**, 35–57

van der Veen, M. 1989 'Charred grain assemblages from Roman-period corn driers in Britain', *Archaeol. J.* **146**, 302–19

Vandeputte, K., Moens, L. and Dams, R. 1996 'Improved sealed-tube combustion of organic samples to CO_2 for stable isotope analysis, radiocarbon dating and percent carbon determinations', *Analytical Letters* **29**, 2761–73

Wainwright, G.J. 1967 *Coygan Camp: A Prehistoric, Romano-British and Dark Age settlement in Carmarthenshire* Cardiff, The Cambrian Archaeological Association

Wainwright, G.J. and Longworth, I.H. 1971 *Durrington Walls excavations 1966–1969* London, Society of Antiquaries

Walker, K.E. forthcoming *The Archaeology of the South Wales gas pipeline 2006–8*, Cotswold Archaeology Monograph **10** Cirencester, Cotswold Archaeology

Walsh, S. 2013 *Identity as process: An archaeological and osteological study of Early Bronze Age burials in Northern England* Unpublished PhD Thesis, University of Central Lancashire

Weiss, K.M. 1972 'On the systematic bias in skeletal sexing', *American Journal of Physical Anthropology* **37**, 239–50

Wheeler, E.A., Baas, P. and Gasson, P.E. 1989 'IAWA list of microscopic features for hardwood identification', *IAWA Bulletin ns.* **10**, 219–332

Whittle, A., Healy, F. and Bayliss, A. 2011 *Gathering time: Dating the Early Neolithic enclosures of southern Britain and Ireland* Oxford, Oxbow Books

Wilkin, N.C.A. 2014 *Food vessel pottery from Early Bronze Age funerary contexts in Northern England: A typological and contextual study* Unpublished PhD thesis, University of Birmingham http://etheses.bham.ac.uk/5192/ (accessed January 2016)

Wilkinson, K.N. and Batchelor, C.R. 2012 *A477 St Clears to Red Roses, Carmarthenshire: Geoarchaeological, bioarchaeological and chronometric assessment* Unpublished report **1213–3**, Winchester, ARCA

Wilkinson, K.N. and Watson, N. 2012 *A477 St Clears to Red Roses, Carmarthenshire: geoarchaeological borehole survey* Unpublished report **1112–17**, Winchester, ARCA

Wood, J. 2001 *Prehistoric cooking* Stroud, Tempus Publishing Ltd

Zohary, D., Hopf, M. and Weiss, E. 2013 *Domestication of plants in the Old World* Oxford, Oxford University Press

Index

Note: Page locators in italics represents tables and figures.